How
We
Learn

How We Learn

The Surprising Truth About When, Where, and Why It Happens

· ·

Benedict Carey

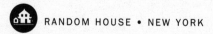 RANDOM HOUSE · NEW YORK

2015 Random House Trade Paperback Edition

Published in the United States by Random House,
an imprint and division of Penguin Random House LLC,
New York.

RANDOM HOUSE and the HOUSE colophon are registered
trademarks of Penguin Random House LLC.

Originally published in hardcover in the United States
by Random House, an imprint and division of
Penguin Random House LLC, in 2015.

Interior art credits:

Pg. 162, middle left: *Orange Zest*, original oil painting
by Judy Hawkins (www.judyhawkinspaintings.com).
Courtesy of the artist.

Pg. 162, bottom left: *Spring Creek Prairie 3*, 2013,
oil painting by Philip Juras. Courtesy of the artist.

Pg. 192: Henri Matisse, *Portrait of Madame Matisse
(The Green Line)*, 1905, 2014 Succession H. Matisse/
Artists Rights Society (ARS), New York.

Library of Congress Cataloging-in-Publication Data
Carey, Benedict.
How we learn: the surprising truth about when,
where, and why it happens/Benedict Carey.
pages   cm
ISBN 978-0-8129-8429-3
eBook ISBN 978-0-8129-9389-9
1. Learning, Psychology of.   2. Learning.   I. Title.
BF318.C366 2014
153.1'5—dc23
2013049850

Printed in the United States of America on acid-free paper

www.atrandom.com

9 8 7 6 5 4 3 2 1

Illustrations by Steve Clark and Zaremba

Book design by Mary A. Wirth

For my parents

Contents
· · · · · · · · · · · · · ·

Part Three: Problem Solving

Part Four: Tapping the Subconscious

Introduction

· · · · · · · · · · · · · ·

Broaden the Margins

I was a grind.

That was the word for it back in the day: The kid who sweated the details, who made flashcards. A striver, a grade-hog, a worker bee—*that* kid—and I can see him clearly now, almost forty years later, bent over a textbook, squinting in the glow of a cheap desk lamp.

I can see him early in the morning, too, up and studying at five o'clock: sophomore year, high school, his stomach on low boil because he can't quite master—what? The quadratic formula? The terms of the Louisiana Purchase? The Lend-Lease policy, the mean value theorem, Eliot's use of irony as a metaphor for . . . some damn thing?

Never mind.

It's long gone, the entire curriculum. All that remains is the dread. Time's running out, there's too much to learn, and some of it is probably beyond reach. But there's something else in there, too, a lower-frequency signal that takes a while to pick up, like a dripping faucet in a downstairs bathroom: doubt. The nagging sense of having strayed off the trail when the gifted students were arriving at the lodge without breaking a sweat. Like so many others, I grew up believing that learning was all self-discipline: a hard, lonely climb up the sheer rock face of knowledge to where the smart people lived. I was driven more by a fear of falling than by anything like curiosity or wonder.

That fear made for an odd species of student. To my siblings, I was Mr. Perfect, the serious older brother who got mostly As. To my classmates, I was the Invisible Man, too unsure of my grasp of the material to speak up. I don't blame my young self, my parents, or my teachers for this split personality. How could I? The only strategy any of us knew for deepening learning—drive yourself like a sled dog—works, to some extent; effort is the single most important factor in academic success.

Yet that was the strategy I was already using. I needed something more, something different—and I felt it had to exist.

The first hint that it did, for me, came in the form of other students, those two or three kids in algebra or history who had—what was it?—a cool head, an ability to do their best without that hunted-animal look. It was as if they'd been told it was okay not to understand everything right away; that it would come in time; that their doubt was itself a valuable instrument. But the real conversion experience for me came later, when applying for college. College was the mission all along, of course. And it failed; I failed. I sent out a dozen applications and got shut down. All those years laboring before the mast and, in the end, I had nothing to show for it but a handful of thin envelopes and one spot on a waiting list—to a college I attended for a year before dropping out.

What went wrong?

I had no idea. I aimed too high, I wasn't perfect enough, I choked on the SATs. No matter. I was too busy feeling rejected to think about it. No, worse than rejected. I felt like a chump. Like I'd been scammed by some bogus self-improvement cult, paid dues to a guru who split with the money. So, after dropping out, I made an attitude adjustment. I loosened my grip. I stopped sprinting. Broadened the margins, to paraphrase Thoreau. It wasn't so much a grand strategy—I was a teenager, I couldn't see more than three feet in front of my face—as a simple instinct to pick my head up and look around.

I begged my way into the University of Colorado, sending an application along with a pleading letter. It was a simpler time then; it's a state school; and I was accepted without much back-and-forth. In Boulder, I began to live more for the day. Hiked a lot, skied a little, consumed too much of everything. I slept in when I could, napped at all hours, and studied here and there, mixing in large doses of mostly legal activities for which large colleges are justifiably known. I'm not saying that I majored in gin and tonics; I never let go of my studies— just allowed them to become *part* of my life, rather than its central purpose. And somewhere in that tangle of good living and bad, I became a student. Not just any student, either, but one who wore the burden lightly, in math and physics, and was willing to risk failure in some very difficult courses.

The change wasn't sudden or dramatic. No bells rang out, no angels sang. It happened by degrees, like these things do. For years afterward, I thought about college like I suspect many people do: I'd performed pretty well despite my scattered existence, my bad habits. I never stopped to ask whether those habits were, in fact, bad.

* * *

In the early 2000s, I began to follow the science of learning and memory as a reporter, first for the *Los Angeles Times* and then for *The New York Times*. This subject—specifically, how the brain learns most efficiently—was not central to my beat. I spent most of my time on larger fields related to behavior, like psychiatry and brain biology. But I kept coming back to learning, because the story was such an improbable one. Here were legit scientists, investigating the effect of apparently trivial things on learning and memory. Background music. Study location, i.e., where you hit the books. Videogame breaks. Honestly, did those things matter at test time, when it came time to perform?

If so, why?

Each finding had an explanation, and each explanation seemed to say something about the brain that wasn't obvious. And the deeper I looked, the more odd results I found. Distractions can aid learning. Napping does, too. Quitting before a project is done: not all bad, as an almost done project lingers in memory far longer than one that is completed. Taking a test on a subject *before* you know anything about it improves subsequent learning. Something about these findings nagged at me. They're not quite believable at first, but they're worth trying—because they're small, easy, doable. There's no excuse for ignoring them. In the past few years, every time I have taken on some new project, for work or fun, every time I've thought about reviving a long-neglected skill, like classical guitar or speaking Spanish, the self-questioning starts:

"Isn't there a better way?"

"Shouldn't I be trying . . . ?"

And so I have. After experimenting with many of the techniques described in the studies, I began to feel a creeping familiarity, and it didn't take long to identify its source: college. My jumbled, ad-hoc approach to learning in Colorado did not precisely embody the latest principles of cognitive science—nothing in the real world is that clean. The rhythm felt similar, though, in the way the studies and techniques seeped into my daily life, into conversation, idle thoughts, even dreams.

That connection was personal, and it got me thinking about the science of learning as a whole, rather than as a list of self-help ideas. The ideas—the techniques—are each sound on their own, that much was clear. The harder part was putting them together. They must fit together somehow, and in time I saw that the only way they could was as oddball features of the underlying system itself—the living brain in action. To say it another way, the collective findings of modern learning science provide much more than a recipe for how to learn more efficiently. They describe a way of life. Once I understood that, I was able to look back on my college experience with new eyes. I'd lightened up on my studies, all right, but in doing so I'd also allowed topics to flow into my nonacademic life in a way I hadn't before. And it's when the brain lives with studied material that it reveals its strengths and weaknesses—its limitations and immense possibilities—as a learning machine.

The brain is not like a muscle, at least not in any straightforward sense. It is something else altogether, sensitive to mood, to timing, to circadian rhythms, as well as to location, environment. It registers far more than we're conscious of and often adds previously unnoticed details when revisiting a memory or learned fact. It works hard at night, during sleep, searching for hidden links and deeper significance in the day's events. It has a strong preference for meaning over randomness, and finds nonsense offensive. It doesn't take orders so well, either, as we all know—forgetting precious facts needed for an exam while somehow remembering entire scenes from *The Godfather* or the lineup of the 1986 Boston Red Sox.

If the brain is a learning machine, then it's an eccentric one. And it performs best when its quirks are exploited.

• • •

In the past few decades, researchers have uncovered and road-tested a host of techniques that deepen learning—techniques that remain largely unknown outside scientific circles. These approaches aren't get-smarter schemes that require computer software, gadgets, or medication. Nor are they based on any grand teaching philosophy, intended to lift the performance of entire classrooms (which no one has done, reliably). On the contrary, they are all small alterations, alterations in how we study or practice that we can apply individually, in our own lives, right now. The hardest part in doing so may be trusting that they work. That requires some suspension of disbelief because this research defies everything we've been told about how best to learn.

Consider the boilerplate advice to seek out a "quiet place" and make that a dedicated study area. This seems beyond obvious. It's easier to concentrate without noise, and settling in at the same desk is a signal to the brain that says, *it's time to work*. Yet we work more effectively, scientists have found, when we continually alter our study routines and abandon any "dedicated space" in favor of varied locations. Sticking to one learning ritual, in other words, slows us down.

Another common assumption is that the best way to master a particular skill—say, long division or playing a musical scale—is by devoting a block of time to repetitively practicing just that. Wrong again. Studies find that the brain picks up patterns more efficiently when presented with a mixed bag of related tasks than when it's force-fed just one, no matter the age of the student or the subject area, whether Italian phrases or chemical bonds. I can't help thinking again of my own strained, scattered existence in college, up all hours and down napping many afternoons, in blithe defiance of any kind of schedule. I'm not going to say that such free-form living always leads to mastery. But I will argue that integrating learning into the more random demands of life can improve recall in many circumstances—and that what looks like rank procrastination or distraction often is nothing of the kind.

The science of learning—to take just one implication—casts a different light on the growing alarm over distraction and our addiction to digital media. The fear is that plugged-in Emily and Josh, pulled in ten directions at once by texts, tweets, and Facebook messages, cannot concentrate well enough to consolidate studied information. Even worse, that all this scattered thinking will, over time, somehow weaken their brains' ability to learn in the future. This is a red herring. Distractions can of course interfere with some kinds of learning, in particular when absorption or continued attention is needed—when reading a story, say, or listening to a lecture—and if gossiping on social media steals from study time. Yet we now know that a brief distraction can help when we're stuck on a math problem or tied up in a creative knot and need to shake free.

In short, it is not that there is a right way and wrong way to learn. It's that there are different strategies, each uniquely suited to capturing a particular type of information. A good hunter tailors the trap to the prey.

• • •

I won't pretend, in these pages, that the science of learning has been worked out. It hasn't, and the field is producing a swarm of new ideas that continue to complicate the picture. Dyslexia improves pattern recognition. Bilingual kids are better learners. Math anxiety is a brain disorder. Games are the best learning tool. Music training enhances science aptitude. But much of this is background noise, a rustling of the leaves. The aim in this book is to trace the trunk of the tree, the basic theory and findings that have stood up to scrutiny—and upon which learning can be improved.

The book unfolds in four sections, and from the bottom up, so to speak. It will begin with an introduction to what scientists know about how brain cells form and hold on to new information. Having a handle on this basic biology will provide a strong physical analogy for the so-called cognitive basis of learning. Cognitive science is a step up the ladder from biology and, most important for us, it clarifies how remembering, forgetting, and learning are related. These two chapters form the theoretical foundation for all that follows.

The second section will detail techniques that strengthen our hold on facts, whether we're trying to remember Arabic characters, the elements of the periodic table, or the major players of the Velvet Revolution. *Retention* tools. The third section will focus on *comprehension* techniques, the kind we need to solve problems in math and science, as well as work our way through long, complex assignments, like term papers, work presentations, blueprints, and compositions. Appreciating how these approaches work, or at least how scientists think they do, will help us remember them and, more critically, decide whether they're of any practical use—today, in our daily lives. And finally, section four will explore two ways to co-opt the subconscious mind to amplify the techniques we've just described. I think of this as the "learning without thinking" part of the story, and it's a reassuring one to hear—and to tell.

The treasure at the end of this rainbow is not necessarily "brilliance." Brilliance is a fine aspiration, and Godspeed to those who have the genes, drive, luck, and connections to win that lottery. But shooting for a goal so vague puts a person at risk of worshiping an ideal—and missing the target. No, this book is about something that is, at once, more humble and more grand: How to integrate the exotica of new subjects into daily life, in a way that makes them seep under our skin. How to make learning more a part of living and less an isolated chore. We will mine the latest science to unearth the tools necessary to pull this off, and to do so without feeling buried or oppressed. And we will show that some of what we've been taught to think of as our worst enemies—laziness, ignorance, distraction—can also work in our favor.

Part One

Basic Theory

The Story Maker

The Biology of Memory

The science of learning is, at bottom, a study of the mental muscle doing the work—the living brain—and how it manages the streaming sights, sounds, and scents of daily life. That it does so at all is miracle enough. That it does so routinely is beyond extraordinary.

Think of the waves of information rushing in every waking moment, the hiss of the kettle, the flicker of movement in the hall, the twinge of back pain, the tang of smoke. Then add the demands of a typical layer of multitasking—say, preparing a meal while monitoring a preschooler, periodically returning work emails, and picking up the phone to catch up with a friend.

Insane.

The machine that can do all that at once is more than merely complex. It's a cauldron of activity. It's churning like a kicked beehive.

Consider several numbers. The average human brain contains 100 billion neurons, the cells that make up its gray matter. Most of these cells link to thousands of other neurons, forming a universe of intertwining networks that communicate in a ceaseless, silent electrical storm with a storage capacity, in digital terms, of a million gigabytes. That's enough to hold three million TV shows. This biological machine hums along even when it's "at rest," staring blankly at the bird feeder or some island daydream, using about 90 percent of the energy it burns while doing a crossword puzzle. Parts of the brain are highly active during sleep, too.

The brain is a dark, mostly featureless planet, and it helps to have a map. A simple one will do, to start. The sketch below shows several areas that are central to learning: the entorhinal cortex, which acts as a kind of filter for incoming information; the hippocampus, where memory formation begins; and the neocortex, where conscious memories are stored once they're flagged as keepers.

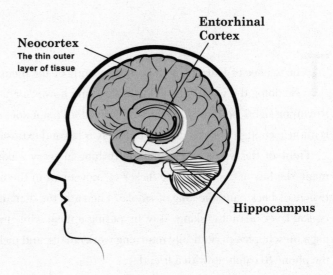

This diagram is more than a snapshot. It hints at how the brain operates. The brain has modules, specialized components that divide the labor. The entorhinal cortex does one thing, and the hippocampus does another. The right hemisphere performs different functions from the left one. There are dedicated sensory areas, too, processing what you see, hear, and feel. Each does its own job and together they generate a coherent whole, a continually updating record of past, present, and possible future.

In a way, the brain's modules are like specialists in a movie production crew. The cinematographer is framing shots, zooming in tight, dropping back, stockpiling footage. The sound engineer is recording, fiddling with volume, filtering background noise. There are editors and writers, a graphics person, a prop stylist, a composer working to supply tone, feeling—the emotional content—as well as someone keeping the books, tracking invoices, the facts and figures. And there's a director, deciding which pieces go where, braiding all these elements together to tell a story that holds up. Not just any story, of course, but the one that best explains the "material" pouring through the senses. The brain interprets scenes in the instants after they happen, inserting judgments, meaning, and context on the fly. It also reconstructs them later on—*what exactly did the boss mean by that comment?*—scrutinizing the original footage to see how and where it fits into the larger movie.

It's a story of a life—our own private documentary—and the film "crew" serves as an animating metaphor for what's happening behind the scenes. How a memory forms. How it's retrieved. Why it seems to fade, change, or grow more lucid over time. And how we might manipulate each step, to make the details richer, more vivid, clearer.

Remember, the director of this documentary is not some film school graduate, or a Hollywood prince with an entourage. It's you.

· · ·

Before wading into brain biology, I want to say a word about metaphors. They are imprecise, practically by definition. They obscure as much as they reveal. And they're often self-serving,* crafted to serve

*Self-serving is right.

some pet purpose—in the way that the "chemical imbalance" theory of depression supports the use of antidepressant medication. (No one knows what causes depression or why the drugs have the effects they do.)

Fair enough, all around. Our film crew metaphor is a loose one, to be sure—but then so is scientists' understanding of the biology of memory, to put it mildly. The best we can do is dramatize what matters most to learning, and the film crew does that just fine.

To see how, let's track down a specific memory in our own brain.

Let's make it an interesting one, too, not the capital of Ohio or a friend's phone number or the name of the actor who played Frodo. No, let's make it the first day of high school. Those tentative steps into the main hallway, the leering presence of the older kids, the gunmetal thump of slamming lockers. Everyone over age fourteen remembers some detail from that day, and usually an entire video clip.

That memory exists in the brain as a network of linked cells. Those cells activate—or "fire"—together, like a net of lights in a department store Christmas display. When the blue lights blink on, the image of a sleigh appears; when the reds come on, it's a snowflake. In much the same way, our neural networks produce patterns that the brain reads as images, thoughts, and feelings.

The cells that link to form these networks are called neurons. A neuron is essentially a biological switch. It receives signals from one side and—when it "flips" or fires—sends a signal out the other, to the neurons to which it's linked.

The neuron network that forms a specific memory is not a random collection. It includes many of the same cells that flared when a specific memory was first formed—when we first heard that gunmetal thump of lockers. It's as if these cells are bound in collective witness of that experience. The connections between the cells, called synapses, thicken with repeated use, facilitating faster transmission of signals.

Intuitively, this makes some sense; many remembered experiences feel like mental reenactments. But not until 2008 did scientists capture memory formation and retrieval directly, in individual human brain cells. In an experiment, doctors at the University of California, Los Angeles, threaded filament-like electrodes deep into the brains of thirteen people with epilepsy who were awaiting surgery.

This is routine practice. Epilepsy is not well understood; the tiny hurricanes of electrical activity that cause seizures seem to come out of the blue. These squalls often originate in the same neighborhood of the brain for any one individual, yet the location varies from person to person. Surgeons can remove these small epicenters of activity but first they have to find them, by witnessing and recording a seizure. That's what the electrodes are for, pinpointing location. And it takes time. Patients may lie in the hospital with electrode implants for days on end before a seizure strikes. The UCLA team took advantage of this waiting period to answer a fundamental question.

Each patient watched a series of five- to ten-second video clips of well-known shows like *Seinfeld* and *The Simpsons,* celebrities like Elvis, or familiar landmarks. After a short break, the researchers asked each person to freely recall as many of the videos as possible, calling them out as they came to mind. During the initial viewing of the videos, a computer had recorded the firing of about one hundred neurons. The firing pattern was different for each clip; some neurons fired furiously and others were quiet. When a patient later recalled one of the clips, say of Homer Simpson, the brain showed exactly the same pattern as it had originally, as if replaying the experience.

"It's astounding to see this in a single trial; the phenomenon is strong, and we knew we were listening in the right place," the senior author of the study, Itzhak Fried, a professor of neurosurgery at UCLA and Tel Aviv University, told me.

There the experiment ended, and it's not clear what happened to the memory of those brief clips over time. If a person had seen hundreds of *Simpsons* episodes, then this five-second clip of Homer might not stand out for long. But it could. If some element of participating in the experiment was especially striking—for example, the sight of a man in a white coat fiddling with wires coming out of your exposed brain as Homer belly-laughed—then that memory could leap to mind easily, for life.

My first day of high school was in September 1974. I can still see the face of the teacher I approached in the hallway when the bell rang for the first class. I was lost, the hallway was swarmed, my head racing with the idea that I might be late, might miss something. I can still see streams of dusty morning light in that hallway, the ugly teal walls, an older kid at his locker, stashing a pack of Winstons. I swerved beside the teacher and said, "Excuse me" in a voice that was louder than I wanted. He stopped, looked down at my schedule: a kind face, wire-rimmed glasses, wispy red hair.

"You can follow me," he said, with a half smile. "You're in my class."

Saved.

I have not thought about that for more than thirty-five years, and yet there it is. Not only does it come back but it does so in rich detail, and it keeps filling itself out the longer I inhabit the moment: here's the sensation of my backpack slipping off my shoulder as I held out my schedule; now the hesitation in my step, not wanting to walk with a teacher. I trailed a few steps behind.

This kind of time travel is what scientists call episodic, or autobiographical memory, for obvious reasons. It has some of the same sensual texture as the original experience, the same narrative structure. Not so with the capital of Ohio, or a friend's phone number: We don't remember exactly when or where we learned those things. Those are what researchers call *semantic* memories, embedded not in narrative scenes but in a web of associations. The capital of Ohio, Columbus, may bring to mind images from a visit there, the face of a friend who moved to Ohio, or the grade school riddle, "What's round on both sides and high in the middle?" This network is factual, not scenic. Yet it, too, "fills in" as the brain retrieves "Columbus" from memory.

In a universe full of wonders, this has to be on the short list: Some molecular bookmark keeps those neuron networks available for life and gives us nothing less than our history, our identity.

Scientists do not yet know how such a bookmark could work. It's nothing like a digital link on a computer screen. Neural networks are continually in flux, and the one that formed back in 1974 is far different from the one I have now. I've lost some detail and color, and I have undoubtedly done a little editing in retrospect, maybe a lot.

It's like writing about a terrifying summer camp adventure in eighth grade, the morning after it happened, and then writing about it again, six years later, in college. The second essay is much different. You have changed, so has your brain, and the biology of this change is shrouded in mystery and colored by personal experience. Still, the scene itself—the plot—is fundamentally intact, and researchers do have an idea of where that memory must live and why. It's strangely reassuring, too. If that first day of high school feels like it's right there on the top of your head, it's a nice coincidence of language. Because, in a sense, that's exactly where it is.

. . .

For much of the twentieth century scientists believed that memories were diffuse, distributed through the areas of the brain that support thinking, like pulp in an orange. Any two neurons look more or less the same, for one thing; and they either fire or they don't. No single brain area looked essential for memory formation.

Scientists had known since the nineteenth century that *some* skills, like language, are concentrated in specific brain regions. Yet those seemed to be exceptions. In the 1940s, the neuroscientist Karl Lashley showed that rats that learned to navigate a maze were largely unfazed when given surgical injuries in a variety of brain areas. If there was some single memory center, then at least one of those incisions should have caused severe deficits. Lashley concluded that virtually any area of the thinking brain was capable of supporting memory; if one area was injured, another could pick up the slack.

In the 1950s, however, this theory began to fall apart. Brain scientists began to discover, first, that developing nerve cells—baby neurons, so to speak—are coded to congregate in specific locations in the brain, as if preassigned a job. "You're a visual cell, go to the back of the brain." "You, over there, you're a motor neuron, go straight to the motor area." This discovery undermined the "interchangeable parts" hypothesis.

The knockout punch fell when an English psychologist named Brenda Milner met a Hartford, Connecticut, man named Henry Molaison. Molaison was a tinkerer and machine repairman who had trouble keeping a job because he suffered devastating seizures, as many as two or three a day, which came with little warning and often knocked him down, out cold. Life had become impossible to manage, a daily minefield. In 1953, at the age of twenty-seven, he arrived at the office of William Beecher Scoville, a neurosurgeon at Hartford Hospital, hoping for relief.

Molaison probably had a form of epilepsy, but he did not do well on antiseizure drugs, the only standard treatment available at the time. Scoville, a well-known and highly skilled surgeon, suspected that whatever their cause the seizures originated in the medial temporal lobes. Each of these lobes—there's one in each hemisphere, mirroring one another, like the core of a split apple—contains a structure called the hippocampus, which was implicated in many seizure disorders.

Scoville decided that the best option was to surgically remove from Molaison's brain two finger-shaped slivers of tissue, each including the hippocampus. It was a gamble; it was also an era when many doctors, Scoville prominent among them, considered brain surgery a promising treatment for a wide variety of mental disorders, including schizophrenia and severe depression. And sure enough, postop, Molaison had far fewer seizures.

He also lost his ability to form new memories.

Every time he had breakfast, every time he met a friend, every time he walked the dog in the park, it was as if he was doing so for the first time. He still had some memories from before the surgery, of his parents, his childhood home, of hikes in the woods as a kid. He had excellent short-term memory, the ability to keep a phone number or name in mind for thirty seconds or so by rehearsing it, and he could make small talk. He was as alert and sensitive as any other young man, despite his loss. Yet he could not hold a job and lived, more so than any mystic, in the moment.

In 1953, Scoville described his patient's struggles to a pair of doctors in Montreal, Wilder Penfield and Brenda Milner, a young researcher who worked with him. Milner soon began taking the night train down to Hartford every few months to spend time with Molaison and explore his memory. It was the start of a most unusual, decade-long partnership, with Milner continually introducing Molaison to novel experiments and he cooperating, nodding his head and fully understanding their purpose—for as long as his short-term memory could hold on. In those fleeting moments they were collaborators, Milner said, and that collaboration would quickly and forever alter the understanding of learning and memory.

In her first experiment, conducted in Scoville's office, Milner had Molaison try to remember the numbers 5, 8, and 4. She then left the office to have coffee and returned twenty minutes later, asking "What were the numbers?" He'd remembered them by mentally rehearsing while she was gone.

"Well, that's very good," Milner said. "And do you remember my name?"

"No, I'm sorry," he said. "My trouble is my memory."

"I'm Dr. Milner, and I come from Montreal."

"Oh, Montreal, Canada—I was in Canada once, I went to Toronto."

"Oh. Do you still remember the number?"

"Number?" Molaison said. "Was there a number?"

"He was a very gracious man, very patient, always willing to try the tasks I would give him," Milner, now a professor of cognitive neuroscience at the Montreal Neurological Institute and McGill University, told me. "And yet every time I walked in the room, it was like we'd never met."

In 1962, Milner presented a landmark study in which she and Molaison—now known as H.M. to protect his privacy—demonstrated that a part of his memory was fully intact. In a series of trials, she had him draw a five-point star on a piece of paper while he watched his drawing hand in a mirror. This is awkward, and Milner made it more so. She had him practice tracing the star between borders, as if working his way through a star-shaped maze. Every time H.M. tried this, it struck him as an entirely new experience. He had no memory of doing it before. Yet with practice he became proficient. "At one point after many of these trials, he said to me, 'Huh, this was easier than I thought it would be,'" Milner said.

The implications of Milner's research took some time to sink in. Molaison could not remember new names, faces, facts, or experiences. His brain could register the new information but, without a hippocampus, could not hold on to it. This structure and others nearby—which had been removed in the surgery—are clearly necessary to form such memories.

He could develop new physical skills, however, like tracing the star and later, in his old age, using a walker. This ability, called motor learning, is not dependent on the hippocampus. Milner's work showed that there were at least two systems in the brain to handle memory, one conscious and the other subconscious. We can track and write down what we learned today in history class, or in geometry, but not in soccer practice or gymnastics, not in anything like the same way. Those kinds of physical skills accumulate without our having to think much about them. We may be able to name the day of the week when we first rode a bike at age six, but we cannot point to the exact physical abilities that led up to that accomplishment. Those skills—the balance, the steering, the pedal motion—refined themselves and came together suddenly, without our having to track or "study" them.

The theory that memory was uniformly distributed, then, was wrong. The brain had specific areas that handled different types of memory formation.

Henry Molaison's story didn't end there. One of Milner's students, Suzanne Corkin, later carried on the work with him at the Massachusetts Institute of Technology. In the course of hundreds of studies spanning more than forty years, she showed that he had many presurgery memories, of the war, of FDR, of the layout of his childhood house. "Gist memories, we call them," Dr. Corkin told me. "He had the memories, but he couldn't place them in time exactly; he couldn't give you a narrative."

Studies done in others with injuries in the same areas of the brain showed a similar before/after pattern. Without a functioning hippocampus, people cannot form new, conscious memories. Virtually all of the names, facts, faces, and experiences they do remember predate their injury. Those memories, once formed, must therefore reside elsewhere, outside the hippocampus.

The only viable candidate, scientists knew, was the brain's thin outer layer, the neocortex. The neocortex is the seat of human consciousness, an intricate quilt of tissue in which each patch has a specialized purpose. Visual patches are in the back. Motor control areas are on the side, near the ears. One patch on the left side helps interpret language; another nearby handles spoken language, as well as written.

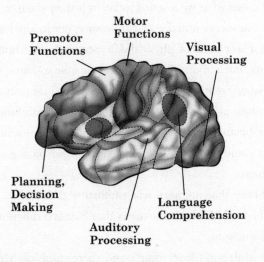

This layer—the "top" of the brain, as it were—is the only area with the tools capable of re-creating the rich sensory texture of an autobiographical memory, or the assortment of factual associations for the word "Ohio" or the number 12. The first-day-of-high-school network (or networks; there likely are many) must be contained there, largely if not entirely. My first-day memory is predominantly visual (the red hair, the glasses, the teal walls) and auditory (the hallway noise, the slamming lockers, the teacher's voice)—so the network has plenty of neurons in the visual and audio cortex. Yours may include the smell of the cafeteria, the deadweight feel of your backpack, with plenty of cells in those cortical patches.

To the extent that it's possible to locate a memory in the brain, that's where it resides: in neighborhoods along the neocortex primarily, not at any single address.

That the brain can find this thing and bring it to life so fast—instantaneously, for most of us, complete with emotion, and layers of detail—defies easy explanation. No one knows how that happens. And it's this instant access that creates what to me is the brain's grandest illusion: that memories are "filed away" like video scenes that can be opened with a neural click, and snapped closed again.

The truth is stranger—and far more useful.

· · ·

The risk of peering too closely inside the brain is that you can lose track of what's on the outside—i.e., the person. Not some generic human, either, but a real one. Someone who drinks milk straight from the carton, forgets friends' birthdays, and who can't find the house keys, never mind calculate the surface area of a pyramid.

Let's take a moment to review. The close-up of the brain has provided a glimpse of what cells do to form a memory. They fire together during an experience. Then they stabilize as a network through the hippocampus. Finally, they consolidate along the neocortex in a shifting array that preserves the basic plot points. Nonetheless, to grasp what people do to *retrieve* a memory—to remember—requires stepping back for a wide shot. We've zoomed in, à la Google Maps, to see cells at street level; it's time to zoom out and have a look at the larger organism: at people whose perceptions reveal the secrets of memory retrieval.

The people in question are, again, epilepsy patients (to whom brain science owes debts without end).

In some epilepsy cases, the flares of brain activity spread like a chemical fire, sweeping across wide stretches of the brain and causing the kind of full-body, blackout seizures that struck H.M. as a young man. Those seizures are so hard to live with, and often so resistant to drug treatment, that people consider brain surgery. No one has the same procedure H.M. underwent, of course, but there are other options. One of those is called split brain surgery. The surgeon severs the connections between the left and right hemispheres of the brain, so the storms of activity are confined to one side.

This quiets the seizures, all right. But at what cost? The brain's left and right halves cannot "talk" to each other at all; split brain surgery must cause serious damage, drastically altering someone's personality, or at least their perceptions. Yet it doesn't. The changes are so subtle, in fact, that the first studies of these so-called split brain patients in the 1950s found no differences in thinking or perception at all. No slip in IQ; no deficits in analytical thinking.

The changes had to be there—the brain was effectively *cut in half*—but it would take some very clever experiments to reveal them.

In the early 1960s, a trio of scientists at the California Institute of Technology finally did so, by devising a way to flash pictures to one hemisphere at a time. *Bingo*. When split brain patients saw a picture of a fork with only their right hemisphere, they couldn't say what it was. They couldn't name it. Due to the severed connection, their left hemisphere, where language is centered, received no information from the right side. And the right hemisphere—which "saw" the fork—had no language to name it.

And here was the kicker: The right hemisphere could direct the hand it controls to *draw* the fork.

The Caltech trio didn't stop there. In a series of experiments with these patients, the group showed that the right hemisphere could also identify objects by touch, correctly selecting a mug or a pair of scissors by feel after seeing the image of one.

The implications were clear. The left hemisphere was the intellectual, the wordsmith, and it could be severed from the right without any significant loss of IQ. The right side was the artist, the visual-spatial expert. The two worked together, like copilots.

This work percolated into the common language and fast, as shorthand for types of skills and types of people: "He's a right brain guy, she's more left brain." It felt right, too: Our aesthetic sensibility, open and sensual, must come from a different place than cool logic.

What does any of this have to do with memory?

It took another quarter century to find out. And it wouldn't happen until scientists posed a more fundamental question: Why don't we *feel* two-brained, if we have these two copilots?

"That was the question, ultimately," said Michael Gazzaniga, who coauthored the Caltech studies with Roger Sperry and Joseph Bogen in the 1960s. "Why, if we have these separate systems, is it that the brain has a sense of unity?"

That question hung over the field, unanswered, for decades. The deeper that scientists probed, the more confounding the mystery seemed to be. The left brain/right brain differences revealed a clear, and fascinating, division of labor. Yet scientists kept finding other, more intricate, divisions. The brain has thousands, perhaps millions, of specialized modules, each performing a special skill—one calculates a change in light, for instance, another parses a voice tone, a third detects changes in facial expression. The more experiments that scientists did, the more specializing they found, and all of these mini-programs run at the same time, often across *both* hemispheres. That is, the brain sustains a sense of unity not only in the presence of its left and right copilots. It does so amid a cacophony of competing voices coming from all quarters, the neural equivalent of open outcry at the Chicago Board of Trade.

How?

The split brain surgery would again provide an answer.

In the early 1980s, Dr. Gazzaniga performed more of his signature experiments with split brain patients—this time with an added twist. In one, for example, he flashed a patient two pictures: The man's left hemisphere saw a chicken foot, and his right saw a snow scene. (Remember, the left is where language skills are centered, and the right is holistic, sensual; it has no words for what it sees.) Dr. Gazzaniga then had the man choose related images for each picture from an array visible to both hemispheres, say, a fork, a shovel, a chicken, and a toothbrush. The man chose a chicken to go with the foot, and a shovel to go with the snow. So far, so good.

Then Dr. Gazzaniga asked him why he chose those items—and got a surprise. The man had a ready answer for one choice: The chicken goes with the foot. His left hemisphere had seen the foot. It had words to describe it and a good rationale for connecting it to the chicken.

Yet his left brain had *not* seen the picture of the snow, only the shovel. He had chosen the shovel on instinct but had no conscious explanation for doing so. Now, asked to explain the connection, he searched his left brain for the symbolic representation of the snow and found nothing. Looking down at the picture of the shovel, the man said, "And you need a shovel to clean out the chicken shed."

The left hemisphere was just throwing out an explanation based on what it could see: the shovel. "It was just making up any old BS," Gazzaniga told me, laughing at the memory of the experiment. "Making up a story."

In subsequent studies he and others showed that the pattern was consistent. The left hemisphere takes whatever information it gets and tells a tale to conscious awareness. It does this continually in daily life, and we've all caught it in the act—overhearing our name being whispered, for example, and filling in the blanks with assumptions about what people are gossiping about.

The brain's cacophony of voices feels coherent because some module or network is providing a running narration. "It only took me twenty-five years to ask the right question to figure it out," Gazzaniga said, "which was why? Why did you pick the shovel?"

All we know about this module is it resides somewhere in the left hemisphere. No one has any idea how it works, or how it strings together so much information so fast. It does have a name. Gazzaniga decided to call our left brain narrating system "the interpreter."

This is our director, in the film crew metaphor. The one who makes sense of each scene, seeking patterns and inserting judgments based on the material; the one who fits loose facts into a larger whole to understand a subject. Not only makes sense but *makes up a story,* as Gazzaniga put it—creating meaning, narrative, cause and effect.

It's more than an interpreter. It's a story maker.

This module is vital to forming a memory in the first place. It's busy answering the question "What just happened?" in the moment, and those judgments are encoded through the hippocampus. That's only part of the job, however. It also answers the questions "What happened yesterday?" "What did I make for dinner last night?" And, for global religions class, "What were the four founding truths of Buddhism, again?"

Here, too, it gathers the available evidence, only this time it gets the sensory or factual cues from inside the brain, not from outside. *Think.* To recall the Buddha's truths, start with just one, or a fragment of one. *Anguish.* The Buddha talked about anguish. He said anguish was . . . to be understood. That's right, that's truth number one. The second truth had to do with meditation, with not acting, with letting go. Let go of anguish? That's it; or close. Another truth brings to mind a nature trail, a monk padding along in robes—the path. Walking the path? Follow the path?

So it goes. Each time we run the tape back, a new detail seems to emerge: The smell of smoke in the kitchen; the phone call from a telemarketer. The feeling of calmness when reading "let go of anguish"—no, it was let go of the *sources* of anguish. Not walk the path, but *cultivate* the path. These details seem "new" in part because the brain absorbs a lot more information in the moment than we're consciously aware of, and those perceptions can surface during remembering. That is to say: The brain does not store facts, ideas, and experiences like a computer does, as a file that is clicked open, always displaying the identical image. It embeds them in networks of perceptions, facts, and thoughts, slightly different combinations of which bubble up each time. And that just retrieved memory does not overwrite the previous one but intertwines and overlaps with it. Nothing is completely lost, but the memory trace is altered and for good.

As scientists put it, using our memories changes our memories.

After all the discussion of neurons and cell networks; after Lashley's rats and H.M.; after the hippocampus, split brain patients, and the story maker, this seems elementary, even mundane.

It's not.

Chapter Two

The Power of Forgetting

A New Theory of Learning

Memory contests are misleading spectacles, especially in the final rounds.

At that point, there are only a handful of people left onstage and their faces reflect all varieties of exhaustion, terror, and concentration. The stakes are high, they've come a long way already, and any mistake can end it all. In a particularly tough to watch scene from the documentary *Spellbound*, about the Scripps National Spelling Bee, one twelve-year-old trips over the word "opsimath." He appears to be familiar with the word, he's digging deep, there's a moment when he seems to have it—but then he inserts an "o" where it doesn't belong.

Clang!

A bell rings—meaning: *wrong answer*—and the boy's eyes bulge in stunned disbelief. A gasp sweeps through the crowd, followed by clapping, consolation applause for effort. He slinks offstage, numb. Variations of this scene repeat, as other well-prepped contestants miss a word. They slump at the microphone, or blink without seeing, before being bathed in the same lukewarm applause. In contrast, those who move to the next round seem confident, locked in. The winner smiles when she hears her final word—"logorrhea"—and nails it.

These competitions tend to leave us with two impressions. One is that the contestants, and especially the winners, must be extra-human. How on earth are they doing that? Their brains must be not only bigger and faster but also *different* from the standard-issue version (i.e., ours). Maybe they even have "photographic" memories.

Not so. Yes, it's true that some people are born with genetic advantages, in memory capacity and processing speed (though no one has yet identified an "intelligence gene" or knows with any certainty how one would function). It's true, too, that these kinds of contests tend to draw from the higher end of the spectrum, from people who take a nerdy interest in stockpiling facts. Still, a brain is a brain is a brain, and the healthy ones all work the same way. With enough preparation and devotion, each is capable of seemingly wizardlike feats of memory. And photographic memories, as far as scientists can tell, don't exist, at least not in the way that we imagine.

The other impression is more insidious, because it reinforces a common, self-defeating assumption: To forget is to fail. This appears self-evident. The world is so full of absentmindedness, tuned-out teenagers, misplaced keys, and fear of creeping dementia that forgetting feels dysfunctional, or ominous. If learning is building up skills and knowledge, then forgetting is losing some of what was gained. It seems like the enemy of learning.

It's not. The truth is nearly the opposite.

Of course it can be a disaster to space out on a daughter's birthday, to forget which trail leads back to the cabin, or to draw a blank at test time. Yet there are large upsides to forgetting, too. One is that it is nature's most sophisticated spam filter. It's what allows the brain to focus, enabling sought-after facts to pop to mind.

One way to dramatize this would be to parade all those spelling prodigies back onstage again for another kind of competition, a fast-paced tournament of the obvious. Quick: Name the last book you read. The last movie you saw. The local drugstore. The secretary of state. The World Series champions. And then faster still: your Gmail password, your sister's middle name, the vice president of the United States.

In this hypothetical contest, each of those highly concentrated minds would be drawing a lot of blanks. Why? Not due to mere absentmindedness or preoccupation. No, these kids are alert and highly focused. So focused, in fact, that they're blocking out trivial information.

Think about it: To hold so many obscure words in mind and keep the spellings straight, the brain must apply a filter. To say it another way, the brain must suppress—forget—competing information, so that "apathetic" doesn't leak into "apothecary," or "penumbra" into "penultimate," and keep any distracting trivia from bubbling to the surface, whether song lyrics, book titles, or names of movie actors.

We engage in this kind of focused forgetting all the time, without giving it much thought. To lock in a new computer password, for example, we must block the old one from coming to mind; to absorb a new language, we must hold off the corresponding words in our native tongue. When thoroughly immersed in a topic or novel or computation, it's natural to blank on even common nouns—"could you pass me the whatyoucallit, the thing you eat with?"

Fork.

As the nineteenth-century American psychologist William James observed, "If we remembered everything, we should on most occasions be as ill off as if we remembered nothing."

The study of forgetting has, in the past few decades, forced a fundamental reconsideration of how learning works. In a way, it has also altered what the words "remember" and "forget" mean. "The relationship between learning and forgetting is not so simple and in certain important respects is quite the opposite of what people assume," Robert Bjork, a psychologist at the University of California, Los Angeles, told me. "We assume it's all bad, a failure of the system. But more often, forgetting is a friend to learning."

The "losers" in memory competitions, this research suggests, stumble not because they remember too little. They have studied tens, perhaps hundreds of thousands of words, and often they are familiar with the word they ultimately misspell. In many cases, they stumble because they remember too much. If recollecting is just that—a *re-collection* of perceptions, facts, and ideas scattered in intertwining neural networks in the dark storm of the brain—then forgetting acts to block the background noise, the static, so that the right signals stand out. The sharpness of the one depends on the strength of the other.

Another large upside of forgetting has nothing to do with its active filtering property. Normal forgetting—that passive decay we so often bemoan—is also helpful for subsequent learning. I think of this as the muscle-building property of forgetting: Some "breakdown" must occur for us to strengthen learning when we revisit the material. Without a little forgetting, you get no benefit from further study. It is what allows learning to build, like an exercised muscle.

This system is far from perfect. We have instantaneous and flawless recall of many isolated facts, it's true: Seoul is the capital of South Korea, 3 is the square root of 9, and J. K. Rowling is the author of the *Harry Potter* books. Yet no complex memory comes back exactly the same way twice, in part because the forgetting filter blocks some relevant details along with many irrelevant ones. Features that previously were blocked or forgotten often reemerge. This drift in memory is perhaps most obvious when it comes to the sort of childhood tales we all tell and embellish. The time we borrowed the family car at age fourteen; the time we got lost on the metro the first time we visited the city. After rolling out those yarns enough times, it can be tough to tell what's true and what's not.

The point is not that memory is nothing more than a pile of loose facts and a catalog of tall tales. It's that retrieving any memory alters its accessibility, and often its content.

There is an emerging theory that accounts for these and related ideas. It's called the New Theory of Disuse, to distinguish it from an older, outdated principle stating, simply, that memories evaporate entirely from the brain over time if they're not used. The new theory is far more than an updating, though. It's an overhaul, recasting forgetting as the best friend of learning, rather than its rival.

A better name for it, then, might be the Forget to Learn theory. That phrase captures its literal implications and its general spirit, its reassuring voice. One implication, for instance, is that forgetting a huge chunk of what we've just learned, especially when it's a brand-new topic, is not necessarily evidence of laziness, attention deficits, or a faulty character. On the contrary, it is a sign that the brain is working as it should.

No one knows why we should be such poor judges of forgetting or other mental skills that are so indispensable, so automatic, that they feel deeply familiar. Yet we are. And it helps to count the ways.

. . .

Let's go back to the beginning, then. Let's go back to the first learning laboratory of them all, to its sole occupant, and his most important contribution—the Forgetting Curve. The Forgetting Curve is exactly what it sounds like, a graph of memory loss over time. In particular, it charts the rate at which newly learned information fades from memory. It's a learning curve, turned upside-down:

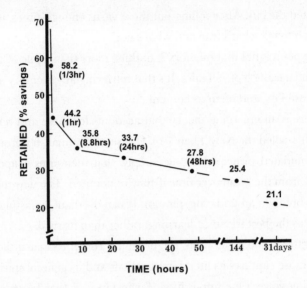

This curve, first published in the late 1880s, falls well short of breathtaking. It's what anyone might draw if asked to guess how memory changes with time. Yet its creator, Hermann Ebbinghaus, wasn't one for idle guesswork. He was exacting by nature, compulsive about evidence. He had to be, given his ambitions. In the late 1870s, as a young philosophy Ph.D., he zigzagged through Europe, thinking big. He longed to bridge philosophy and science, to apply rigorous measurement to some aspect of human nature or psychology. The only problem was, he didn't know where to start. He was poking around in a secondhand Paris bookstall one afternoon when he pulled from the shelf a volume called *Elements of Psychophysics* by Gustav Fechner. A scientist with a mystical bent, Fechner saw a unifying mathematical connection between the inner, mental world and the outer, natural one. He argued that every human experience, even one as ephemeral as memory, should be reducible to measurable units that could be plugged into an equation of some sort. Fechner's reputation as a scientist—he'd done elegant experiments on the sensation of touch—lent his more grandiose ideas some weight.

As he read, Ebbinghaus felt something inside him shift—a sensation he would describe, years later, to a student. He must have glimpsed his future as well, right then and there, because he later dedicated his greatest work, *Memory: A Contribution to Experimental Psychology,* to Fechner.

The memory equation. Did it even exist? If so, could it be written down?

Memories come in so many shapes and sizes. There are the hour-long and the lifelong; there are dates and numbers, recipes and recitals; not to mention stories, emotional perceptions, the look on a child's face when he's dropped at the bus stop on the first day of school, the knowing smile shared between two friends who think no one is looking: the tapestry of hijinks and heartbreaks that make up a life. Our *ability* to recall specific facts also varies widely. Some people are good with names and faces; others are much better at retrieving numbers, dates, formulas. How on earth do you measure such a shape-shifting ghost, much less study it?

A generation of scientists before Ebbinghaus had essentially stood down, taking a pass on the question. It was too much. The variables were overwhelming.

Yet where some saw a justified caution, Ebbinghaus saw a lack of nerve. "At the very worst we should prefer to see resignation arise from the failure of earnest investigations rather than from the persistent, helpless astonishment in the face of the difficulties," he wrote, in explaining his motives for pursuing the memory equation. He would take the dare if there was no one else. He reasoned from first principles. To study how the brain stores new information, he needed information that was, in fact, new. A list of nouns or names or numbers simply wouldn't do; people walk around with an enormous storehouse of associations for all of these things. Even abstract sketches have a Rorschach-like, evocative quality. Stare long enough at a cloud and it begins to look like a dog's head, which in turn activates hundreds of dog-related circuits in the brain. Our brain can impute meaning to almost anything.

How Ebbinghaus arrived at his solution remains a mystery. "Was it an invention in the commonly accepted sense of the term, that is to say, deliberate?" wrote the American psychologist David Shakow, much later, in a biographical essay. "Or was it largely a discovery? What part did the gurgle of an infant, a transient progression to infancy, the reading of *Jabberwocky*, the expletives of the Paris coachman for the London cabbie, play?"

What Ebbinghaus created was a catalog of nonsense sounds. These were single syllables, formed by sticking a vowel between two consonants. RUR, HAL, MEK, BES, SOK, DUS. By and large, they were meaningless.

Ebbinghaus had found his generic memory "units."

He created about 2,300 of them—a pool of all possible syllables, or at least as many as he could think of. He put together lists of the syllables, random groupings of between seven and thirty-six each. Then he began to memorize one list at a time, reading the syllables out loud, pacing himself with a metronome, keeping track of how many repetitions he needed to produce a perfect score.

By the time he landed a job as an instructor, at the University of Berlin in 1880, he'd logged more than eight hundred hours of practice with his nonsense sounds. He continued the work in his small office, pacing the floor, a compact, bushy-bearded man in Ben Franklin spectacles, spitting out the syllables at a rate of as many as 150 a minute. (In another era or another country, he might have been hauled off and fitted with a lunatic suit.) He tested himself at various intervals: Twenty minutes after studying. An hour. A day later, then a week. He varied the duration of his practice sessions, too, and found (surprise) that more practice sessions generally resulted in higher test scores and a slower rate of forgetting.

In 1885, he published his results in *Memory: A Contribution to Experimental Psychology*, describing a simple way to calculate the rate of forgetting after a study session. The equation wasn't much to look at, but it was the first rigorous principle in the emerging branch of psychology—and precisely what he'd set out to find a decade earlier in that Paris bookstall.

Ebbinghaus had his equation (others would plot it as a graph).

He hadn't changed the world. He did, however, launch the science of learning. "It is not too much to say that the recourse to nonsense syllables, as a means to the study of association, marks the most considerable advance in this chapter of psychology since the time of Aristotle," wrote English scientist Edward Titchener a generation later.

Ebbinghaus's Forgetting Curve captured the minds of many theorists and would not let go. In 1914, the influential American education researcher Edward Thorndike turned Ebbinghaus's curve into a "law" of learning. He called it the Law of Disuse, which asserted that learned information, without continued use, decays from memory entirely—i.e., use it or lose it.

The law felt right. It certainly seemed to square with experience, defining how most people thought of learning and to this day still do. Yet that definition hides more than it reveals.

· · ·

Here's an at-home exercise that is simple, painless, and full of literary nutrition. Take five minutes and study the verse below. Read it carefully and try to commit it to memory. It's from the poet Henry Wadsworth Longfellow's "The Wreck of the Hesperus."

> *At daybreak, on the bleak sea-beach,*
> *A fisherman stood aghast,*
> *To see the form of a maiden fair,*
> *Lashed close to a drifting mast.*

> *The salt sea was frozen on her breast,*
> *The salt tears in her eyes;*
> *And he saw her hair, like the brown sea-weed,*
> *On the billows fall and rise.*

Such was the wreck of the Hesperus,
In the midnight and the snow!
Christ save us all from a death like this,
On the reef of Norman's Woe!

Okay, now put the book aside and make a cup of coffee, take a walk, listen to the news. Distract yourself for about five minutes, the same amount of time you took to study it. Then, sit and write down as much of the poem as you can. Save the result (you'll need it later).

This is exactly the test that an English teacher and researcher named Philip Boswood Ballard began administering to school-children in the early 1900s in London's working-class East End. The children were thought to be poor learners, and Ballard was curious to find out why. Was it a deficit of initial learning? Or did something happen later that interfered with recall? To find out, he had them study various material, including ballads like Longfellow's, to see if he could pinpoint the source of their learning problems.

Only the children had no obvious learning deficits that Ballard could find. On the contrary.

Their scores five minutes after studying were nothing special. Some did well and others didn't. Ballard wasn't finished, however. He wanted to know what happened to the studied verse over time. Did memory somehow falter in the days after these children studied? To find out, he gave them another test, two days later. The students were not expecting to be retested and yet their scores improved by an average of 10 percent. Ballard tested them once more, again unannounced, days later.

"J.T. improved from 15 to 21 lines in three days," he wrote of one student. "Imagined she saw the lines in front of her." Of another, who improved from three to eleven lines in seven days, he remarked: "Pictured the words on the blackboard (the poetry in this case was learnt from the blackboard)." A third, who recalled nine lines on the first test and, days later, thirteen, told Ballard, "as I began to write it, I could picture it on the paper before me."

This improvement wasn't merely odd. It was a flat contradiction of Ebbinghaus.

Ballard doubted what he was seeing and ran hundreds of additional tests, with more than ten thousand subjects, over the next several years. The results were the same: Memory improved in the first few days without any further study, and only began to taper off after day four or so, on average.

Ballard reported his findings in 1913, in a paper that seems to have caused mostly confusion. Few scientists appreciated what he'd done, and even today he is little more than a footnote in psychology, a far more obscure figure than Ebbinghaus. Still, Ballard knew what he had. "We not only tend to forget what we have once remembered," he wrote, "but we also tend to remember what we have once forgotten."

Memory does not have just one tendency over time, toward decay. It has two.

The other—"reminiscence," Ballard called it—is a kind of growth, a bubbling up of facts or words that we don't recall having learned in the first place. Both tendencies occur in the days after we've tried to memorize a poem or a list of words.

What could possibly be going on?

One clue comes from Ebbinghaus. He had tested memory using only nonsense syllables. The brain has no place to "put" these letter trios. They're not related to one another or to anything else; they're not part of a structured language or pattern. The brain doesn't hold on to nonsense syllables for long, then, *because they are nonsense*. Ebbinghaus acknowledged as much himself, writing that his famous curve might not apply to anything more than what he had studied directly.

Forgetting, remember, is not only a passive process of decay but also an active one, of filtering. It works to block distracting information, to clear away useless clutter. Nonsense syllables are clutter; Longfellow's "The Wreck of the Hesperus" is not. The poem may or may not become useful in our daily life, but at least it is nested in a mesh of neural networks representing words and patterns we recognize. That could account for why there would be a difference in how well we remember nonsense syllables versus a poem, a short story, or other material that makes sense. Yet it does not explain the *increase* in clarity after two days without rehearsal, the "salt tears" and "hair like brown sea-weed" floating up from the neural deep. Those "slow" East Enders showed Ballard that remembering and forgetting are not related to each other in the way everyone assumed.

The Forgetting Curve was misleading and, at best, incomplete. It might even need to be replaced altogether.

• • •

In the decades after Ballard published his findings, there was a modest flare of interest in "spontaneous improvement." The effect should be easy to find, scientists reasoned, in all kinds of learning. Yet it wasn't. Researchers ran scores of experiments, and the results were all over the place. In one huge 1924 trial, for instance, people studied a word list, and took a test immediately afterward. They were then given a follow-up test, after varying delays: eight minutes, sixteen minutes, three days, a week. They did worse over time, on average, not better.

In a 1937 experiment, subjects who studied nonsense syllables showed some spontaneous improvement after an initial exam—but only for about five minutes, after which their scores plunged. A widely cited 1940 study found that people's recall of a set of words, a set of brief sentences, and a paragraph of prose all declined over a twenty-four-hour period. Even when researchers found improvement for one kind of material, like poetry, they'd find the opposite result for something else, like vocabulary lists. "Experimental psychologists began to tinker with Ballard's approach and, as if struggling in quicksand, became progressively mired in confusion and doubt," wrote Matthew Hugh Erdelyi, of Brooklyn College, in his history of the era, *The Recovery of Unconscious Memories*.

The mixed findings inevitably led to questions about Ballard's methods. Were the children he tested really recalling more over time, or was their improvement due to some flaw in the experimental design? It wasn't a rhetorical question. What if, for example, the children had rehearsed the poem on their own time, between tests? In that case, Ballard had nothing.

In an influential review of all published research up through 1943, one British learning theorist, C. E. Buxton, concluded that Ballard's spontaneous improvement effect was a "now-you-see-it-now-you-don't phenomenon"—in other words, a phantom. It wasn't long before many scientists followed Buxton's lead and begged off the hunt. There were far better things to do with the tools of psychology than chase phantoms, and certainly more culturally fashionable ones.

Freudian therapy was on the rise, and its ideas of recovered memories easily trumped Ballard's scraps of Longfellow for sex appeal. The two men's conceptions of recovery were virtually identical, except that Freud was talking about repressed emotional trauma. Excavating those memories and "working through" them could relieve chronic, disabling anxiety, he claimed. It could change lives. If those were phantoms, they were far more lifelike than a heap of recited poetry.

Besides, the real juice in learning science by the middle of the century was in reinforcement. It was the high summer of behaviorism. The American psychologist B. F. Skinner showed how rewards and punishments could alter behavior, and accelerate learning in many circumstances. Skinner tested various reward schedules against one another and got striking results: An automatic reward for a correct answer leads to little learning; occasional, periodic rewards are much more effective. Skinner's work, which was enormously influential among educators, focused on improving teaching, rather than on the peculiarities of memory.

Yet Ballard's findings didn't disappear completely. They continued to marinate in the minds of a small group of psychologists who couldn't shake the idea that something consequential might be slipping through the cracks. In the 1960s and 1970s, these curious few began to separate the poetry from the nonsense.

The Ballard effect was, and is, real. It was not due to an experimental design flaw; the children in his studies could not have rehearsed lines that they did not remember after the first test. You can't practice what you don't remember. The reason researchers had had so much trouble isolating Ballard's "reminiscence" was because the strength of this effect is highly dependent on the material being used. For nonsense syllables, and for most lists of vocabulary words or random sentences, it's zero: There's no spontaneous improvement on test scores after a day or two. By contrast, reminiscence is strong for imagery, for photographs, drawings, paintings—and poetry, with its word-pictures. And it takes time to happen. Ballard had identified the "bubbling up" of new verse in the first few days after study, when it's strongest. Other researchers had looked for it too early, minutes afterward, or too late, after a week or more.

Matthew Erdelyi was one of those who was instrumental in clarifying reminiscence, and he began by testing a junior colleague, Jeff Kleinbard, then at Stanford University. Erdelyi gave Kleinbard a group of forty pictures to study in a single sitting, on the pretext that he "should have the experience of being a subject" before conducting experiments of his own. In fact, he *was* a subject, and Erdelyi tested him repeatedly, without warning, over the following week. The results were so clear and reliable—Kleinbard remembered increasingly more on tests over the first two days—that the two of them set up larger studies. In one, they had a group of young adults try to memorize a series of sixty sketches. The participants saw the sketches one at a time, projected on a screen, five seconds apart: simple drawings of things like a boot, a chair, a television.

The group took a test right after and tried to recall all sixty, in seven minutes, writing down a word to describe each sketch recalled (the sketches had no accompanying words). The average score was 27. Ten hours later, however, their average was 32; a day later, 34; by four days, it was up to 38, where it plateaued. A comparison group, who studied sixty *words* presented on slides, improved from 27 to 30 in the first ten hours—and no more. Their scores slipped slightly over the next several days. Soon it was beyond dispute that memory, as Erdelyi put it in a recent paper, "is a heterogeneous, mottled system that both improves and declines over time."

Which left theorists with a larger riddle. Why does recall of pictures improve while recall of word lists does not?

Scientists had speculated about the answers all along. Maybe it was a matter of having more time to search memory (two tests versus one). Or perhaps the delay between tests relaxed the mind, eased fatigue. Yet it wasn't until the 1980s that psychologists had enough hard evidence to begin building a more complete model that accounts for the Ballard effect and other peculiarities of memory. The theory that emerged is less a grand blueprint for how the mind works than a set of principles based on research, a theory that encompasses Ebbinghaus and Ballard, as well as many other seemingly opposed ideas and characters. The scientists who have shepherded the theory along and characterized it most clearly are Robert Bjork of UCLA and his wife, Elizabeth Ligon Bjork, also at UCLA. The new theory of disuse ("Forget to Learn," as we're calling it) is largely their baby.

The first principle theory is this: Any memory has two strengths, a storage strength and a retrieval strength.

Storage strength is just that, a measure of how well learned something is. It builds up steadily with studying, and more sharply with use. The multiplication table is a good example. It's drilled into our heads in grade school, and we use it continually throughout life, in a wide variety of situations, from balancing the bank account to calculating tips to helping our fourth grader with homework. Its storage strength is enormous.

According to the Bjorks' theory, storage strength can increase but it never decreases.

This does not mean that everything we see, hear, or say is stored forever, until we die. More than 99 percent of experience is fleeting, here and gone. The brain holds on to only what's relevant, useful, or interesting—or may be so in the future. It does mean that everything we have *deliberately* committed to memory—the multiplication table, a childhood phone number, the combination to our first locker—is all there, and for good. This seems beyond belief at first, given the sheer volume of information we absorb and how mundane so much of it is. Remember from chapter 1, though, that biologically speaking there's space to burn: in digital terms, storage space for three million TV shows. That is more than enough to record every second of a long life, cradle to grave. Volume is not an issue.

As for the mundane, it's impossible to prove that it's *all* there, every meaningless detail. Still, every once in a while the brain sends up a whisper of dumbfounding trivia. It happens to everyone throughout life; I'll offer an example of my own. In researching this book, I spent some time in college libraries, the old-school kind, with basements and subbasements full of stacks of old books that create the vague sensation of being on an archaeological dig. It was the musty smell, I think, that on one afternoon took me back to a month-long period in 1982 when I worked at my college library. I was hunting down an old book in some deserted corner of the Columbia University library, feeling claustrophobic and lost—when a name popped into my head. Larry C_____. The name of the man at the library who was (I guess) my supervisor. I met him once. Lovely guy—only I had no idea I ever knew his name. Still, here I was, seeing him in my mind's eye walking away from that one meeting, and even seeing that his boat shoes were worn in the back the way some people's get, angling toward one another.

One meeting. The shoes. Perfectly meaningless. Yet I must have known the name, and I must have stored that impression of him walking off. Why on earth would I have kept that information? Because it was, at one point in my life, useful. And the Forget to Learn theory says: If I stored it, it's in there for good.

That is, no memory is ever "lost" in the sense that it's faded away, that it's gone. Rather, it is not currently accessible. Its *retrieval strength* is low, or near zero.

Retrieval strength, on the other hand, is a measure of how easily a nugget of information comes to mind. It, too, increases with studying, and with use. Without reinforcement, however, retrieval strength drops off quickly, and its capacity is relatively small (compared to storage). At any given time, we can pull up only a limited number of items in connection with any given cue or reminder.

For example, a *quack-quack* cell phone ring overheard on the bus might bring to mind the name of a friend who has the same ring, as well as several people who are owed calls. It may also trigger an older vision of the family dog belly-flopping into a lake to pursue a flotilla of ducks; or your first raincoat, bright yellow with a duckbill on the hood. Thousands of other quack associations, some meaningful at the time they formed, are entirely off the radar.

Compared to storage, retrieval strength is fickle. It can build quickly but also weaken quickly.

One way to think of storage and retrieval is to picture a huge party in which everyone you ever met is in attendance (at the age when you last saw them). Mom and Dad; your first grade teacher; the brand-new neighbors next door; the guy who taught driver's-ed in sophomore year: They're all here, mingling. Retrieval is a matter of how quickly a person's name comes to mind. Storage, by contrast, is a matter of how *familiar* the person is. Mom and Dad, there's no escaping them (retrieval high, storage high). The first grade teacher, her name isn't jumping to mind (retrieval low) but that's definitely her right there over by the door (storage high). The new neighbors, by contrast, just introduced themselves ("Justin and Maria"— retrieval high), but they're not familiar yet (storage low). Tomorrow morning, their names will be harder to recall. As for the driver's-ed guy, the name's not coming back, and he wouldn't be so easy to pick out of a lineup, either. The class was only two months long (retrieval low, storage low).

The act of finding and naming each person increases both strengths, remember. The first grade teacher—once she's reintroduced—is now highly retrievable. This is due to the passive side of forgetting, the fading of retrieval strength over time. The theory says that that drop facilitates deeper learning once the fact or memory is found again. Again, think of this aspect of the Forget to Learn theory in terms of building muscle. Doing pull-ups induces tissue breakdown in muscles that, after a day's rest, leads to *more* strength the next time you do the exercise.

That's not all. The harder we have to work to retrieve a memory, the greater the subsequent spike in retrieval and storage strength (learning). The Bjorks call this principle *desirable difficulty,* and its importance will become apparent in the coming pages. That driver's-ed teacher, once he's spotted, is now *way* more familiar than he was before, and you may remember things about him you forgot you knew: not just his name and nickname but his crooked smile, his favorite phrases.

The brain developed this system for a good reason, the Bjorks argue. In its nomadic hominid youth, the brain was continually re-freshing its mental map to adapt to changing weather, terrain, and predators. Retrieval strength evolved to update information quickly, keeping the most relevant details handy. It lives for the day. Storage strength, on the other hand, evolved so that old tricks could be re-learned, and fast, if needed. Seasons pass, but they repeat; so do weather and terrain. Storage strength plans for the future.

This combination of flighty retrieval and steady storage—the tor-toise and the hare—is no less important to modern-day survival. Kids who grow up in North American households, for example, learn to look people in the eye when speaking, especially a teacher or parent. Kids in Japanese homes learn the opposite: Keep your gaze down, especially when speaking to an authority figure. To move suc-cessfully from one culture to the other, people must block—or *forget*—their native customs to quickly absorb and practice the new ones. The native ways are hardly forgotten; their storage strength is high. But blocking them to transition to a new culture drives down their retrieval strength.

And being able to do this can be a matter of life or death. An Australian who moves to the United States, for instance, must learn to drive on the right side of the road instead of the left, upending almost every driving instinct he has. There's little room for error; one Melbourne daydream and he wakes up in a ditch. Here again, the memory system forgets all the old instincts to make room for the new ones. And that's not all. If twenty years later he gets homesick and moves back to Australia, he will have to switch to driving on the left again. Yet that change will come much more easily than the first one did. The old instincts are still there, and their storage strength is still high. The old dog quickly relearns old tricks.

"Compared to some kind of system in which out-of-date memo-ries were to be overwritten or erased," Bjork writes, "having such memories become inaccessible but remain in storage has important advantages. Because those memories are inaccessible, they don't interfere with current information and procedures. But because they remain in memory they can—at least under certain circumstances—be relearned."

Thus, forgetting is critical to the learning of new skills *and* to the preservation and reacquisition of old ones.

Now let's return to our friend Philip Ballard. The first test his students took not only measured how much of the "Hesperus" poem they remembered. It also increased the storage and retrieval strengths of the verse they did remember, making it more firmly anchored in memory and more easily accessible than it was before the test. Hit, unexpectedly, with the same test two days later, most of the lines they recalled on test number 1 came back clearly and quickly—and as a result, their brains had time to scrounge for more words, using the remembered verse as a skeleton guide, a partially completed jigsaw puzzle, a packet of cues to shake loose extra lines. This is a poem, after all, swollen with imagery and meaning, precisely the material that shows the strongest "reminiscence" effect of all.

Voilà! They do better.

Yes, the *Hesperus* will eventually sink if the brain stops thinking about it, and its retrieval strength will inch toward zero. But a third test, and a fourth, would anchor the poem in memory more richly still, as the brain—now being called on to use the poem regularly— would continue its search for patterns within the poem, perhaps pulling up another half line or two with each exam. Will it all come back, with enough testing, even if only half was remembered the first time? Not likely. You get something back, not everything.

Try it yourself, after a day or two. Write down as much of the "The Wreck of the Hesperus" as you can, without looking. Give yourself as much time as you took on the first test at the top of the chapter. Compare the results. If you're like most people, you did a little better on the second test.

Using memory changes memory—and for the better. Forgetting enables and deepens learning, by filtering out distracting information *and* by allowing some breakdown that, after reuse, drives retrieval and storage strength higher than they were originally. Those are the basic principles that emerge from brain biology and cognitive science, and they underlie—and will help us understand—the various learning techniques yet to come.

Part Two

. . . .

Retention

Chapter Three

Breaking Good Habits

The Effect of Context on Learning

Don't forget your brain vitamins.

In college, that's what passed for exam-taking advice, at least among those of us who frequented a hippified pill shop in downtown Boulder. There, on a shelf behind the counter, between vials of brown serum, lotus seeds, and hemp balm, were bottles of something called "Study Aid." The label on the back listed herbs, root products, fiber, and "natural extracts."

The not-so-secret ingredient was, most likely, speed.

One dose delivered a bump in confidence and motivation, along with a night of focused study time. That was the upside. The downside, after sequential doses, was a ragged withdrawal that dead-ended into a sudden, dreamless sleep—not ideal for operating heavy machinery, and a clear and present danger when sitting through a long exam. Close your eyes for a second and you were out, pencil clattering to the floor, liable to awake to the words, "Time's up, please hand in your work."

The don't-forget-your-vitamins advice meant, above all, stay conscious. When in doubt, take an extra dose to cross the finish line. Over time, though, I began to wonder if there was something more to it. When I studied on a vitamin, I worked with a kind of silly abandon, talking to myself, pacing. And when it came time to take the test, I wanted some of that manic energy back. I wanted to hear the internal conversation, to have the same physical connection with the material. I began to think—we all did—that taking "Study Aid" right before the test made that connection happen. It wasn't only keeping us upright; it made us feel mentally closer to what we'd studied, and as a result we thought we remembered more of it.

Did we actually know this to be true? No, of course not, we never tested it—we wouldn't have known how if we'd wanted to. Yet we felt like we had a lucky charm, a way to put our head "in the same place" during test-taking as during studying. Essential it was, too, especially during finals week, with two and sometimes three tests falling on the same day. That kind of pressure drives people deep into their worst habits, whether chocolate and cigarettes, brain vitamins and nail-biting, cases of diet cola, or much stronger stuff. When hunkered down in this psychological survival mode, it can be a profound comfort to believe that a favorite "study aid" also improves exam performance. And so we did.

"Brain chemistry," our theory went, "you want the same brain chemistry."

For a long time afterward, I looked back on that kind of theorizing as pure rationalization, the undergraduate mind at its self-justifying finest. We had so many crackpot theories then, about dating and getting rich and studying, that I'd discarded the whole list. Still, millions of students have developed some version of the brain chemistry idea, and I think its enduring attraction is rooted in something deeper than wishful thinking. The theory fits in nicely with what we've been told about good study habits from Day 1—be consistent.

Consistency has been a hallmark of education manuals since the

1900s, and the principle is built into our every assumption about good study habits. Develop a ritual, a daily schedule, a single place and time set aside for study and nothing else. Find a private corner of the house or the library, and a quiet niche of the day, early or late. These ideas go back at least to the Puritans and their ideal of study as devotion, but they have not changed a whit. "Choose an area that is quiet and free from distractions," begins a study guide from Baylor University, though it could be from any institution. It continues:

"Develop a study ritual to use each time you study."

"Use earplugs or a headset to block out noise."

"Say no to those who want to alter your study time."

Et cetera. It is all about consistency.

And so is the "Study Aid" brain chemistry theory, if you think about it. Using the same "vitamin"—or, okay, mind-altering substance—to prepare and, later, to perform may not be particularly Puritan. But it's nothing if not consistent.

It is also, within reason, correct.

Studying while seriously impaired is wasted time, in more ways than one, as millions of students have learned the hard way. Yet, generally speaking, we perform better on tests when in the same state of mind as when we studied—and, yes, that includes mild states of intoxication from alcohol or pot, as well as arousal from stimulants. Moods, preoccupations, and perceptions matter, too: how we feel while studying, where we are, what we see and hear. The scientific investigation into these influences—the inner mental context, so to speak, as well as the outer one—has revealed subtle dimensions of learning that we rarely, if ever, notice but can exploit to optimize our time. Along the way, paradoxically, this research has also demolished the consistency doctrine.

· · ·

The story begins twenty feet underwater, just off the coast of Oban, Scotland.

Oban, on the Sound of Mull and facing the islands known as the Southern Hebrides, is a premier diving destination. It's within easy range of the *Rondo,* an American steamer that sank here in 1934 and sits—jackknifed, nose-down—in 150 feet of water, a magnet for explorers in scuba gear. A half dozen other shipwrecks are also close— the Irish *Thesis,* lost in 1889; the Swedish *Hispania,* which went down in 1954—and the waters course with dogfish, octopus, cuttlefish, and the psychedelic sea slugs called nudibranchs.

It was here, in 1975, that a pair of psychologists from nearby Stirling University recruited a group of divers to participate in an unusual learning experiment.

The psychologists, D. R. Godden and A. D. Baddeley, wanted to test a hypothesis that many learning theorists favored: that people remember more of what they studied when they return to that same study environment. This is a variation on the detective novel line, "Now, Mrs. Higgins, let's return to the night of the murder. Tell me exactly what you saw and heard." Like the detective, psychologists hypothesized that features of the study location—the lighting, the wallpaper, the background music—provide the brain "cues" to shake free more information. The difference is that Mrs. Higgins is trying to revisit a dramatic scene, an autobiographical memory, and the researchers were applying the same idea—*reinstatement,* they called it—to facts, to what the Estonian psychologist Endel Tulving called "semantic memories."

The idea seems far-fetched. Who on earth remembers what was playing through the headphones when he or she learned the definition of an isosceles triangle, or an ionic bond, or the role of Viola in *Twelfth Night?* And when Godden and Baddeley dreamed up their experiment, the evidence for reinstatement was shabby at best. In one previous experiment, for example, participants tried to memorize word lists they heard through earphones while standing with their heads inside a box containing multicolored flashing lights (two dropped out due to nausea). In another, subjects studied nonsense syllables while strapped to a board, which tipped on an axis like a teeter-totter, as in some cruel school yard prank.

The reinstatement seemed to facilitate better memory but Godden and Baddeley weren't convinced. They wanted to test-drive reinstatement theory in an environment that was unusual but found in nature, not created by imaginative psychologists. So they had a group of eighteen scuba divers study a list of thirty-six words while submerged twenty feet underwater. The researchers split the divers into two groups. An hour later, one group took a test on the words on dry land, while the others strapped on their equipment and took the test back down under, using a waterproof mike to communicate with those on land doing the scoring. The results indeed depended strongly on test location. The divers who took the test underwater did better than those who took it on land, remembering about 30 percent more words. That's a lot, and the two psychologists concluded that, "recall is better if the environment of the original learning is reinstated."

Maybe the bubbles streaming past the diving mask acted as a cue, accentuating the vowels in the studied words. Maybe it was the rhythmic bellows of the breath in the mouthpiece, or the weight of the tank, plus the sight of swarming nudibranchs. Or the fact that those semantic memories became part of an episodic one (learning while diving). Perhaps all of the above. Reinstatement seemed to work, anyway—for underwater learning.

The Oban experiment lent comfort and encouragement to what would become a somewhat haphazard exploration of the influence of context on memory. The study materials in these experiments were almost always word lists, or word pairs, and the tests were usually on free recall. In one investigation, for example, people who studied a list of nonsense syllables on blue-gray cards remembered 20 percent more of them on a later test when the test cards were also blue-gray (as opposed to, say, red). In another, students who got exam questions from the same instructor who taught the material did 10 percent better than getting them from a neutral test proctor.

A psychologist named Steven M. Smith performed some of the most interesting experiments in this area, and it's worth looking at one of his in detail to see how scientists measure and think about so-called contextual cues. In 1985 Smith, at Texas A&M University, convened a group of fifty-four Psych 101 students—psychologists' standard guinea pigs—and had them study a list of forty words. He divided the students into three groups. One group studied in silence. Another had a jazz number, Milt Jackson's "People Make the World Go Around," playing in the background. The third had Mozart's Piano Concerto Number 24 in C Minor. The music was on when the subjects arrived in their assigned rooms, and they had no reason to believe it was relevant to the experiment. They spent ten minutes memorizing, and left.

The students returned to the study room two days later and, without warning, they were given a test to see how many words they could freely recall. This time, Smith changed the tune for many of them. He subdivided the three groups. Some who'd studied to jazz took the test with jazz again; others took it with the Mozart; and others in silence. Likewise for those who studied with Mozart or in silence: They tested either in the same condition, or one of the other two. Nothing else changed.

Nothing, that is, except their scores.

Smith found that those who studied with Milt Jackson playing and took the test with the same music recalled twenty-one words on average—twice as many as those who studied with Jackson and took the test to Mozart, or in silence. Similarly, those who studied with Mozart recalled nearly twice as many words with Mozart playing than in silence or with the jazz in the background.

The punch line: Of those who studied and tested in the same condition, the silence-silence group did the worst. They recalled, on average, about half the words that the jazz-jazz or classical-classical groups did (eleven versus twenty). This is bizarre, and it raised an unexpected question: Could quiet somehow be *inhibiting* memory?

The answer was no. If it had, then those who'd studied with jazz would have done worse taking the test in silence than with Mozart (vice versa, for those who'd studied with classical). They hadn't.

What to make of this, then? The higher test scores square with reinstatement theory: The background music weaves itself subconsciously into the fabric of stored memory. Cue up the same music, and more of those words are likely to resurface. The lower scores in the quiet room (after quiet study) are harder to explain. Smith argued that they may be due to an *absence* of cues to reinstate. The students "do not encode the absence of sound any more than they might encode the absence of any type of stimulus, such as pain or food," he wrote. As a result the study environment is impoverished, compared to one with music in the background.

By themselves, experiments like Smith's and the others don't tell us how to study, of course. We can't cue up our own personal soundtrack for an exam, and we certainly can't retrofit the exam room with the same furniture, wallpaper, and ambience as where we studied. Even if we could, it's not clear which cues are important or how strong they really are. Still, this research establishes a couple of points that are valuable in developing a study strategy. The first is that our assumptions about learning are suspect, if not wrong. Having *something* going on in the study environment, like music, is better than nothing (so much for sanctity of the quiet study room).

The second point is that the experience of studying has more dimensions than we notice, some of which can have an impact on retention. The contextual cues scientists describe—music, light, background colors—are annoyingly ephemeral, it's true. They're subconscious, usually untraceable. Nonetheless, it is possible to recognize them at work in our own lives. Think of an instance in which you *do* remember exactly where and when you learned something. I'm not talking about hearing you made the high school all-star team or got chosen prom queen, either. I mean a factual, academic, *seman-*

tic memory, like who assassinated Archduke Franz Ferdinand, or how Socrates died and why.

For me, it's a late night in 1982, when I was studying for a test in the university's math building. The buildings were open all night back then, and you could walk in and take a classroom for yourself, spread out, use the blackboard, and no roommates bursting in with beer or other temptations. I did it all the time, and sometimes the only other person in the place was an old guy roaming the halls, disheveled but kindly, a former physics teacher. He would wander into my classroom occasionally and say something like, "Do you know why quartz is used in watches?" I would say no, and he would explain. He was legit, he knew his stuff, and one night he strolled in and asked whether I knew how to derive the Pythagorean theorem using geometric figures. I did not. The Pythagorean theorem, the most famous equation in math, states that adding the square of the two short sides of a right triangle equals the square of the longest side. It existed in my head as $a^2 + b^2 = c^2$, and I have no idea where I was when I learned that.

On that night, however, I learned a simple way to derive it— a beautiful thing it is, too—and I still can see what the guy was wearing (blue slacks, up to his chest), hear his voice (barely, he mumbled), and recall precisely where on the board he drew the figure (lower left corner):

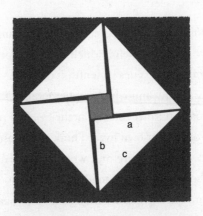

The proof is done by calculating the area of the large square (c squared) and making it equal to the sum of the figures inside: four triangles (area: ½ a x c times 4) plus the area of the little box ((a—b) squared). Try it. Simplify the right side of that equation and watch what you get. I remember it any time I sit alone in some classroom or conference room under dimmed fluorescent lights, like if I've arrived first for a meeting. Those cues bring back the memory of that night and the proof itself (although it takes some futzing to get the triangles in place).

Those are contextual cues, when they're conscious and visible. The reason I can recall them is that they're also part of a scene, an autobiographical memory. The science tells us that, at least when it comes to retention of new facts, the subconscious ones are valuable, too. Not always—when we're submerged in analytical work, they're negligible—and not necessarily all of them. Only sometimes. So what, though? When it comes to learning, we'll take any edge we can get.

I recall something else about that night, too. Normally, when visited by the Ghost of Physics Past, I was not entirely patient. I had work to do. I could do without the lecture about the properties of quartz. That night, though, I'd finished most of my studying and was in an open, expansive mood. I was happy to sit and listen and even hear about how "physics students today, they don't learn any of this . . . ."

That mood was part of my "environment," too, wasn't it? It had to be—I remember it. I wouldn't have sat still for the lesson otherwise. If psychologists' theory about reinstating sights and sounds was correct, then they'd have to show that it applied to internal mental states as well—to jealousy, anxiety, grumpiness, confidence—the entire mix-tape of emotions running through our heads.

The question was, how?

· · ·

No one who's gone through a bad breakup while trying to be a student will doubt the impact of mood on learning. Moods color everything we do, and when they're extreme they can determine what we remember. The clearest demonstration comes from psychiatry, and the study of bipolar disorder. People with this condition are the extreme athletes of the emotional realm. Their moods cycle between weeks or months of buoyant, manic activity and periods of dark, paralyzing depression, and they know too well that those cycles determine what they remember and what they don't. "There is a particular kind of pain, elation, loneliness, and terror involved in this kind of madness," wrote the psychologist Kay Redfield Jamison, who has a diagnosis of bipolar. "When you're high it's tremendous. The ideas and feelings are fast and frequent like shooting stars, and you follow them until you find better and brighter ones. . . . But, somewhere, this changes. The fast ideas are far too fast, and there are far too many; overwhelming confusion replaces clarity. Memory goes."

Indeed, researchers showed in a 1974 study that people with bipolar disorder have state-dependent memory: They remember best what happened during manic phases when they're again manic. And vice versa: When depressed, they recall events and concepts they'd learned when they were down. As the study's authors put it, "associations or episodic events . . . can be regenerated more completely in a similar mood state than they can in a different mood state."

Yet bipolar is an extraordinary condition, and learning scientists could hardly rely on it to measure the effects of emotion on the rest of us. For most people, moods come and go, coloring our experience rather than defining it. Their impact on memory, if significant at all, would be far weaker than for those with bipolar. And to measure this impact in a rigorous way would mean inducing the same mood in groups of people, reliably and continuously. That's a tall order, so learning scientists began to focus not on moods per se but on the influence of differing "internal mental states." Altered states.

This was the 1970s, after all, when hundreds of thousands of young people were experimenting with consciousness-altering drugs, primarily LSD and marijuana. These recreational users, many of them college students, weren't interested in the effect of the drugs on their grades—they were enjoying themselves. Yet there were all sorts of rumors about the possible benefits of such substances on learning. Hallucinogens were said to be "mind-expanding," capable of opening up new ways of thinking about the world. Pot allowed the brain to see connections it hadn't before (often too many, resulting in late night sessions full of perfect nonsense). Clearly, altered states intensified experience; might they intensify memory?

The rigorous research into our inner study environment would begin with drugs—the recreational kind. And its primary sponsor was the U.S. government, which, beginning in the early 1970s, funded a string of experiments that might be called the Studying Under the Influence series. By then, a scattering of research reports had already appeared, suggesting that some drugs, like barbiturates and alcohol, could produce so-called state-dependent learning in modest amounts—the "Study Aid" effect. The government-backed researchers wanted to clarify the picture.

These experiments tended to follow a similar blueprint: Get people high and have them study something; then give them a test hours later—either after getting high again or after ingesting a placebo. We'll take a close look at one of these studies, to show what serious scientists and serious stoners can do when they put their heads together. In 1975, a research team led by James Eric Eich of the National Institute of Mental Health set out to test the effect of pot on retention (word lists again), as well as learn something about *how* the drug alters what the brain does with newly studied information. The researchers recruited thirty college students and recent graduates, brought them into their lab, and gave each a joint. Half of the group got a real one and half got a "placebo marijuana cigarette," which looked and smelled real but delivered no THC, the active drug. "The subjects took deep inhalations, maintained them for 15 seconds, and repeated this process every 60 seconds," the authors wrote. "The entire cigarette was smoked, with the aid of a holder, usually in about eight minutes." These were not novices. On average, the participants smoked pot about five times a week. Within twenty minutes, those who smoked the full-strength joint were moderately high, based on their own ratings and physical measures, like pulse rate. Those who smoked the placebo did not show the same physiological changes.

At this point, all thirty studied.

They were handed sheets of paper and given a minute and a half to try to commit to memory forty-eight words. The words appeared grouped by category—for example, "A type of vehicle—streetcar, bus, helicopter, train," or "A musical instrument—cello, organ, trumpet, banjo." The categories were part of the experimental manipulation. We all look for patterns when trying to memorize a long list of items, bunching together those that look or sound the same, or are somehow related. The scientists wanted to see whether smoking pot influenced these "higher-order" cues we use to retrieve information later on, so they provided the categories. When the ninety seconds were up, the papers were taken away.

Four hours later, when the effects of the drug had worn off, the participants returned to the lab and had another smoke. Some who'd been given a real joint the first time got a placebo this time around, and vice versa. Others smoked the same type both times. Twenty minutes later, without further study, they took a test.

Some got a free recall test, writing down as many of the words as they could remember in six minutes. Others took a "cued recall" test, in which they saw the list of categories ("A type of vehicle") and filled in as many of the words in that category as they could. And sure enough—on the free recall—those who'd smoked a real joint on both occasions remembered 40 percent more than those who got a real one to study and a placebo for the test. The reverse was also true to a lesser extent: Those who initially studied on the placebo joint did better after smoking another placebo, compared to a real joint. The participants' memories functioned best when their brain was in the same state during study as during testing, high or not high.

Why? The cued-recall test (the one with the categories) helped provide an answer. The scores on this test were uniformly high, no matter what the students smoked or when. This finding suggests that the brain stores roughly the same *number* of words when moderately high as when not—the words are in there, either way. Yet it must organize them in a different way for later retrieval. That "retrieval key" comes back most clearly when the brain is in the same state, stoned or sober. The key becomes superfluous, however, when the categories are printed right there on the page. There's no need for it, because an external one is handy. As the authors wrote, "The accessibility of retrieval cues which have been encoded in drug associated state—such as that produced by a moderate dose of marijuana—appears to depend, in part, on restoration of that state at the time of desired recall."

The joint-placebo study also gives us an idea how strong these internal, drug-induced memory cues are. Not so strong. Give someone a real hint—like a category name—and it easily trumps the internal cues. The same thing turned out to be true for alcohol and other drugs that these researchers and others eventually studied: Internal and external cues can be good reminders, but they pale next to strong hints.

The personality of the learning brain that emerges from all this work on external and internal cues is of a shifty-eyed dinner companion. It is tracking the main conversation (the homework assignment, the music notation, the hard facts) and occasionally becoming engaged in it. At the same time, it's also periodically having a quick look around, taking in the room, sketching in sights and sounds and smells, as well as noting its internal reactions, its feelings and sensations. These features—the background music, a flickering candle, a pang of hunger—help our companion recall points made during the conversation later on, especially when the topic is a new one. Still, a strong hint is better.

I think about this, again, in terms of the geometric proof of the Pythagorean theorem. Summoning up that late night scene in the math building three decades ago, I can begin to reconstruct the proof, but as I said it takes some futzing to get the triangles in place. However, if someone sketches out just part of the drawing, it all comes back immediately. The strong hint provided by a partial drawing trumps the weaker ones provided by reinstating my learning environment.

In a world that provided strong hints when needed, this system would be ideal. Just as it would be wonderful if, whenever we had to perform on some test, we could easily re-create the precise environment in which we studied, piping in the same music that was playing, dialing up the same afternoon light, the same mental state—all of the internal and external features that were present when the brain stored the material in the first place.

I'll say this for those "Study Aids": I could control where, when, and how much, and I believe that the vitamins allowed me to heap more information into my fragile mind at the times when I most needed to. Stimulants and other substances become a psychological crutch for so many for the same reason that researchers used them in studies—they're a quick and reliable way to reproduce a particular mental state.

But there's a better way. There's a way to exploit the effects of internal and external cues without having to bet on any single environment or rely on a drug to power through.

• • •

Take a look at the table below and see if you detect any patterns, any system to group the numbers and letters in memory:

6	6	8	0
5	4	3	2
1	6	8	4
7	9	3	5
4	2	3	7
3	8	9	1
1	0	0	2
3	4	5	1
2	7	6	8
1	9	2	6
2	9	6	7
5	5	2	0
x	0	1	x

Give up? You should. There aren't any good storage patterns, because the man who put it together invented it that way. He designed it to be as challenging as possible to remember, a random collection.

In the mid-1920s, Alexander Luria, a neuropsychologist at the University of Moscow, was studying memory when he met a newspaper reporter named Solomon Shereshevsky. Shereshevsky had been working at a city paper and behaving in ways that made his editor suspicious. Every morning, the staff gathered to go through a long list of the coming day's activities—the events, people, and potential stories the editor wanted tracked. The reporters all took careful notes, except for Shereshevsky, who didn't even bring a notebook. The boss, convinced the reporter was slacking, confronted him on it.

I don't need to take notes, Shereshevsky replied, I just remember. He proceeded to detail that morning's long list of assignments, without error. Not only that day's but the previous day's meeting, and the one before that. He just remembered things, he said. This performance struck the editor as so extraordinary that he recommended that he go see Luria.

And so began a famous collaboration. For the next four decades, Luria tested and retested Shereshevsky—"S.," as he called him in print to protect his identity—eventually producing a panoramic exploration of one of the largest, most precise memories the world has known. S.'s feats of memory seemed beyond explaining. He could study an entire matrix of random numbers for fifteen minutes and recall the entire thing a week—a month, even a decade—later.

He could do the same for lists of words, for poems, for short reading selections, in his native Russian and in languages that were completely foreign to him, like Italian. Luria's extensive interviews with S. about his memory, detailed in his book *The Mind of a Mnemonist*, revealed that S. had a condition called synesthesia, in which perceptions are mixed and unusually vivid. Sounds have shapes, colors; letters have taste, fragrance. "Even numbers remind me of images," S. told Luria. "Take the number one. This is a proud, well-built man. Two is a high-spirited woman, three a gloomy person . . . as for the number 87, what I see is a fat woman and a man twirling his mustache." He attached an unusual number of cues to each thing he memorized, including internally generated images *and* details of the learning environment, like the sound of Luria's voice.

Shereshevsky's recall of words, numbers, and voices was so complete, in fact, that often one performance encroached on another performance, especially when they occurred in the same place, with no difference in context. He had to work to block related material. "Writing something down means I'll know I won't have to remember it," he told Luria. "So I started doing this with small matters like phone numbers, last names, errands of one sort or another. But I got nowhere, for in my mind I continued to see what I've written." He lacked a normal forgetting filter, and it often frustrated him.

Luria had Shereshevsky study one of his number-letter matrices on May 10, 1939. S. examined it for three minutes. After a short break, he could recite it without error, row by row, column by column, or along the diagonals. Several months later, Luria tested him again—without warning—on the same table. "The only difference in the two performances was that for the latter one he needed more time to 'revive' the entire situation in which the experiment had originally been carried out," Luria wrote. "To 'see' the room in which we had been sitting; to 'hear' my voice; to 'reproduce' an image of himself looking at the board." S. reinhabited the May 10 study session to bring back the matrix.

Shereshevsky was a prodigy, and his methods are largely off-limits to the rest of us. We can't revive our study surroundings in nearly so much detail, and even if we could, there's no chance that the entire table would scroll back up in pristine clarity. Our minds don't work in the same way. Yet S.'s use of multiple perceptions—audio, visual, sensual—hints at how we can capitalize on context. We can easily multiply the number of perceptions connected to a given memory— most simply, by varying *where* we study.

How much could a simple change in venue aid recall?

In the mid-1970s, a trio of psychologists performed an experiment to answer that question. Steven Smith, Robert Bjork, and another psychologist, Arthur Glenberg, wondered what would happen if people studied the same material twice, only in two different places. They presented a group of students with a list of forty four-letter words, like "ball" and "fork." Half the students studied the words in two ten-minute sessions, a few hours apart, either in the same small, cluttered, basement room or in a neat windowed room looking out on a courtyard. The other half studied the words in two settings: once in that small, windowless room and again in the neat windowed one overlooking the courtyard. Two groups. The same words. In the same order. The same amount of time. One group in the same environment both times, the other in two distinct ones.

"I considered myself, the experimenter, part of the environment, too," Smith told me. "In the windowless, basement room I looked like I usually did, long wild hair, flannel shirt, construction boots. In the modern conference room, I had my hair slicked back, I wore a tie, I had on the suit my dad wore to my bar mitzvah.

Some of the students who studied in both places thought I was a different guy."

After the second session the students rated each word on whether it evoked positive or negative associations. This was a ruse, to give them the impression that they were done with those words, that there was no reason to think about or practice them. In fact, they weren't done. In the third phase of the experiment, three hours later, researchers had the students write down as many of the words as they could in ten minutes. This test occurred in a third, "neutral" room, a regular classroom. There was no reinstatement, as in previous context studies. The third room was one that the participants *hadn't been in before* and was nothing like the other two where they had studied.

The difference in scores was striking. The one-room group recalled an average of sixteen of the forty studied words. The two-rooms group recalled twenty-four. A simple change in venue improved retrieval strength (memory) by 40 percent. Or, as the authors put it, the experiment "showed strong recall improvements with variation of environmental context."

No one knows for sure why changing rooms could be better for recall than staying put. One possibility is that the brain encodes one subset of the words in one room, and a slightly different set in the other. Those two subsets overlap, and two subsets are better than one. Or it may be that rehearsing in two rooms doubles the number of contextual cues linked to any single word, fact, or idea being studied. In one room, the beige walls, fluorescent lighting, and clutter of stacked books color the memory of the word "fork"; in the other, "fork" is intertwined with the natural light pouring through the window, the sight of an old oak in the courtyard, the hum of an air conditioner. The material is embedded in two sensory layers, and that could give the brain at least one more opportunity to "revive" what it can of the study conditions and retrieve the words, or concepts. If Door Number 1 doesn't work, it can try Door Number 2. We do this sort of perspective shifting all the time when, say, trying to remember the name of an actor. We pull up scenes from his most recent movie: There's his face, but no name. We recall his face in the newspaper, his cameo on a TV show, maybe even a time we saw him onstage. We use multiple mental lenses to tease out the name and, in general, more detail.

Smith has since gone digital. He uses short video clips to create backgrounds, rather than herding students from room to room. In a typical experiment, he divides participants into two groups. One studies, say, twenty words in Swahili over five practice sessions of ten minutes each. The words appear on a movie screen, one at a time, transposed over a single, soundless background clip in all five sessions (of a train station, for example). This is the "same environment" condition. The other group studies the identical words, also over five ten-minute sessions, only those words appear over a different video background during each practice period (rainstorm, train station, desert scene, traffic jam, living room). A visual simulation, no more. Yet on tests taken two days later, the varied background group came out ahead, remembering an average of sixteen of the Swahili words, compared to nine or ten for the one-background group.

I have to admit I'm a sucker for this stuff. I love studies like these, because I can't sit still for more than twenty minutes to study, if that. I want to believe that this kind of restlessness can deepen learning, and I often wish that the evidence for context variation was a little more . . . airtight.

The research has a meandering feel to it, to be honest. Scientists are still debating which cues matter most, when, and how strong they really are. Because context effects are subtle, they're hard to reproduce in experiments. The definition of "context," for that matter, is a moving target. If it includes moods, movement, and background music, it could by extension mean *any* change in the way we engage our vocabulary lists, history chapters, or Spanish homework. Think about it. Writing notes by hand is one kind of activity; typing them using a keyboard is another. The same goes for studying while standing up versus sitting down, versus running on a treadmill. Daniel Willingham, a leading authority on the application of learning techniques in classrooms, advises his own students, when they're reviewing for an exam, not to work straight from their notes. "I tell them to put the notes aside and create an entirely new outline, reorganizing the material," he told me. "It forces you to think about the material again, and in a different way."

Isn't *how* we do something part of the "environment," too?

It is. Yet the larger message of context research is that, in the end, it doesn't much matter which aspects of the environment you vary, so long as you vary what you can. The philosopher John Locke once described the case of a man who had learned to dance by practicing according to a strict ritual, always in the same room, which contained an old trunk. Unfortunately, wrote Locke, "the idea of this remarkable piece of household stuff had so mixed itself with the turns and steps of all his dances, that though in that chamber he could dance excellently well, yet it was only when that trunk was there; he could not perform well in any other place unless that or some other trunk had its due position in the room."

This research says, take the trunk out of the room. Since we cannot predict the context in which we'll have to perform, we're better off varying the circumstances in which we prepare. We need to handle life's pop quizzes, its spontaneous pickup games and jam sessions, and the traditional advice to establish a strict practice routine is no way to do so. On the contrary: Try another room altogether. Another time of day. Take the guitar outside, into the park, into the woods. Change cafés. Switch practice courts. Put on blues instead of classical. Each alteration of the routine further enriches the skills being rehearsed, making them sharper and more accessible for a longer period of time. This kind of experimenting itself reinforces learning, and makes what you know increasingly independent of your surroundings.

Chapter Four

Spacing Out

The Advantage of Breaking Up Study Time

The oldest learning technique in memory science is also one of the most powerful, reliable, and easy to use. Psychologists have known about it for more than a hundred years and proven that it works to deepen the learning of subject areas or skills that call for rote memorization, like foreign vocabulary, scientific terms and concepts, equations, or musical scales. Yet mainstream education has largely ignored it. Few schools teach it as part of the regular curriculum. Few students even know about it, except as the sort of motherly advice that's safe to ignore:

> "Honey, don't you think it would be better to study for a little bit tonight and a little bit tomorrow, rather than trying to learn everything at once?"

The technique is called distributed learning or, more commonly, the spacing effect. People learn at least as much, and retain it much longer, when they distribute—or "space"—their study time than when they concentrate it. Mom's right, it is better to do a little today and a little tomorrow rather than everything at once. Not just better, a *lot* better. Distributed learning, in certain situations, can double the amount we remember later on.

This isn't to say that cramming is useless. The all-nighter is time-tested, with a long track record of improving exam scores the next day. In terms of reliability, though, this nocturnal sprint is a little like overstuffing a cheap suitcase: the contents hold for a while, then everything falls out. Researchers who study learning say the result from habitual cramming can be dramatic from one semester to the next. The students who do it "arrive for the second term, and they don't remember anything from the first term," Henry Roediger III, a psychologist at Washington University in St. Louis, told me. "It's like they never took the class."

The spacing effect is especially useful for memorizing new material. Try it yourself with two lists of, say, fifteen phone numbers or Russian vocabulary words. Study one list for ten minutes today and ten minutes tomorrow, and the other for twenty minutes tomorrow. Wait a week and test yourself to see how many of the total from both lists you can remember. Now go back to the two lists: The difference in what you recalled from each should be significant, and there's no obvious explanation for it. I like to think of the spacing effect in terms of lawn care in Los Angeles. L.A. is a city with a coastal desert climate and cultural commitment to the pristine lawn. I learned while living there for seven years that, to maintain one of those, it's far more effective to water for thirty minutes three times a week than for an hour and a half once a week. Flooding the lawn makes it look slightly more lush the next day, but that emerald gloss fades, sure enough. A healthy dose every couple days and you can look your neighbors in the eye, while using the same amount of water—or even less. Same goes for distributed learning. You're not spending any more time. You're not working any harder. But you remember more for longer.

A principle this powerful should have had a quick, clean ride from the lab into classrooms. What student wouldn't want to enhance learning without putting in any extra time or effort?

It hasn't happened, and for good reasons. One is that, as parents know too well, it's enough of a chore to get students to sit down for single study sessions, never mind multiple ones. The other is that for much of the last hundred years psychologists have—exasperatingly, inexplicably—confined the study of spacing to short lab experiments. It is as if doctors discovered a cure for diabetes and spent fifty years characterizing its molecular structure before giving it to a patient. Only in the last several years have researchers mapped out the best intervals to use when spacing study time. Is it more efficient to study a little bit today and a little bit tomorrow, or to do so every other day, or once a week? What if it's Tuesday, and the history final is on Friday? What if the exam is a month away? Do the spacing intervals change depending on the exam date?

I see the history of distributed learning as an object lesson in how to interpret research, especially the kind that's discussed in this book. The culture of science is to build on previous experimental evidence—to test, replicate, and extend it if possible. That tradition is invaluable, because it gives scientists a shared language, a common set of tools, so that Dr. Smith in Glasgow knows what Dr. Jones in Indianapolis is talking about when she describes the results of a "paired associates" test in a research paper. Without that lingua franca, no field could build a foundation of agreed-upon findings. Researchers would be following their own intuitions, inventing their own tests and tools, creating a swarm of results that might, or might not, be related to one another.

That tradition can be binding, however, and it kept the spacing effect under wraps, confined for decades to discussion in arcane journals. Breaking that confinement took, to varying degrees, the social upheaval caused by the Vietnam War, the work of a dogged Polish teenager, and the frustration of a senior researcher who said, essentially, *How can I use this in my own life?* That's a question we all should ask of any science purporting to improve learning, and it helped transform the spacing effect from a lab curiosity to something we can actually exploit.

. . .

We've already met Hermann Ebbinghaus, the man who gave learning science its first language. That language was nonsense syllables, and Ebbinghaus spent much of his adult life inventing them, reshuffling them, arranging them into short lists, long lists, studying those lists for fifteen minutes, a half hour, longer, then turning around and testing himself, carefully checking each test against the original list and study duration. He kept intricate records, logged everything into equations, doubled back and checked those equations, and then reloaded and tried different schedules of memorization—including spaced study. He found that he could learn a list of twelve syllables, repeating them flawlessly, if he performed sixty-eight repetitions on one day and seven more on the next. Yet he could do just as well with only *thirty-eight* repetitions total if they were spaced out over three days. "With any considerable number of repetitions," he wrote, "a suitable distribution of them over a space of time is decidedly more advantageous than the massing of them at a single time." It was the field's founder, then, who discovered the power of spacing.

The scientist who picked up the ball next would set the tone for a generation of research that barely moved forward an inch. Adolf Jost, an Austrian psychologist known mostly for advocating eugenics, did his own studies of spacing—also with nonsense syllables—and in 1897 formulated what became known as Jost's Law: "If two associations are of equal strength but of different age, a new repetition has a greater value for the older one." Translation: Studying a new concept right after you learn it doesn't deepen the memory much, if at all; studying it an hour later, or a day later, does. Jost basically repeated one of Ebbinghaus's experiments, found the very same thing, and got a law out of it, with his name attached. He managed to sound like he was extending the research without really doing so.

Other psychologists followed suit, first testing more nonsense syllables and gradually graduating to lists of words or word pairs. In a way, the science went backward in the first half of the twentieth century. The psychologists who followed Jost launched scores of experiments with small numbers of people studying "grouped" or "spaced" items over intervals of minutes or even seconds, getting so lost in minutiae that by 1960 the research had succeeded mostly in showing that the spacing effect "worked" during very short time periods. If you're told—three times, in succession—that James Monroe was the fifth president of the United States, you remember it for a while; if you're told it three times, at ten-minute intervals, you remember it for longer.

And it's nice to know if you're preparing for a trivia contest against your ten-year-old brother. But this focus on short intervals left a large question unanswered: Can spaced practice help people build and maintain a base of knowledge that's useful in school and in life?

In the 1970s a growing number of psychologists began asking just that, sensing that a big idea was being squandered. Some were questioning the field's entire research tradition, including its faith in the methods of Ebbinghaus. "This all began happening during the Vietnam War protests, when students and young people were questioning authority across the board," Harry P. Bahrick, a psychologist at Ohio Wesleyan University, told me. "That was what set these questions into motion, and people started speaking up. We spent all these years genuflecting to the giants in the field, and what did we have to show for it? Teachers and students don't care about how many words you do or don't remember in some ten-minute test taken in a lab. They want to know how spacing affects how well you learn French or German, how well you pick up math and science concepts. We couldn't tell them. We had to do something completely different."

Bahrick wasn't interested in extending lab findings. He wanted to blow the doors open and let in some air. He wanted to shake off the influence of Ebbinghaus, Jost, and the old guard and test long intervals, of weeks, months, years: the time periods relevant to lifetime learning. How does distributed learning contribute to building mastery of, say, auto mechanics, or music skills? Does it help at all, or are the benefits negligible? To answer that convincingly, he would have to test acquisition of the kind of knowledge that people couldn't get casually, at work, by reading the paper, or from friends. He chose foreign language. For the experiment he had in mind, his test subjects couldn't be just anyone, either. He had to find people who would stick with the experiment for years; who would not quit or fall out of touch; who would not misrepresent their effort; and who, ideally, could supervise their own studying.

He settled on his wife and kids. The Bahricks are a family of psychologists. His wife, Phyllis, a therapist, and his daughters, Lorraine and Audrey, both academic researchers, would be ideal subjects. "I'm not sure it's something they wanted to do, but I think they wanted to please me," Bahrick, who included himself as participant number four, told me. "And over the years it became a fun family project. We always had something to talk about, and we talked about it a lot."

The ground rules were as follows. Phyllis, Audrey, and Lorraine would study French vocabulary words, and Harry would study German. He compiled lists of three hundred unfamiliar words per person, and each Bahrick split his or her list into six groups of fifty and studied each of those groups according to a different schedule. For one list, it was once every two weeks; for another, it was once every month; for a third, it was once every two months. They used flashcards, with French or German on one side and English on the other, and drilled themselves in each session until they remembered the meaning of all the words on that list. It was a chore much of the time. It was tedious. No one was being paid for all that study time.

But it was also a start. The first truly long-term test of the spacing effect—the "Four Bahrick Study," as they called it—was under way.

. . .

The best foreign language program in the world is what I call the James Method. To implement this program, simply follow the example of the American writers Henry and William James and grow up the child of wealthy, cultured parents who see to it that throughout your childhood you travel widely in Europe and the Americas and receive language tutoring along the way. The Jameses were determined that their sons have what Henry Sr. called a "sensuous education." The most famous of the siblings, the novelist Henry, studied with tutors in Paris, Bologna, Geneva, and Bonn; he spent extended time in each place and returned periodically throughout his life. As a result, he became proficient in French, Italian, and German.

The James Method integrates foreign language and first-rate instruction into childhood development. That's not quite the same as growing up in a multilingual home, but it's a pretty close facsimile. Children absorb a new language quickly when forced to speak and understand it—when living with it—and that is what the James children did to some extent. They had to memorize non-English verbs and nouns like the rest of us but did so at a time when the language modules in their brain were still developing.

A nice gig if you can get it.

If not—if you spent your childhood closer to Geneva, Ohio, or Paris, Texas, and want to learn Farsi—you're at a spectacular disadvantage. You've got some not-so-sensual memorizing to do, and a lot of it, in relative isolation. There is no other way, no trick or secret code.

Consider learning English as a foreign language, a challenge that millions of people around the world face if they want a certain type of job, in the sciences certainly, but also in government, in sectors of the digital economy, in tourism and trade. An educated English speaker knows twenty to thirty thousand words, along with hundreds of idioms and expressions. Stockpiling half that many words is a tall order when you're starting from scratch. By one estimate, it takes roughly two hours of practice a day for five or so years to do so. And storing those words is only one part of the job. Remember, from the Forget to Learn theory, storage and retrieval are two different things. Just because you've studied (stored) the word "epitome" doesn't mean it's retrievable when you read or hear it. To build fluency—to keep this ever-expanding dictionary readily accessible, usable in the moment—it takes more than the time needed to store them.

How much more?

In 1982, about the time that Bahrick embarked on his family study, a nineteen-year-old Polish college student named Piotr Wozniak calculated an answer to that question based on his own experience: too much. At the rate he was going, Wozniak determined that he would have to study English four hours a day for years to become proficient enough to read scientific papers and converse with other scientists. He simply didn't have the time, not while carrying a load of computer science and biology courses. He'd have to find a more efficient system, if one existed, and the only experimental subject he had was himself. He began by building a database of about three thousand words and 1,400 scientific facts in English that he was trying to absorb. He divided the total into three equal groups and started to study according to different schedules. He tried intervals of two days, four days, a week, two weeks, and so on. He kept detailed records to determine when newly learned words or facts began to defy recall.

He began to see a pattern. He found that, after a single study session, he could recall a new word for a couple days. But if restudied on the next day, the word was retrievable for about a week. After a third review session, a week after the second, the word was retrievable for nearly a month. He continued to refine the ideal intervals for keeping his English sharp, and programmed a computer to track his progress.

"These optimum intervals are calculated on the basis of two contradictory criteria," he wrote at the time. "Intervals should be as long as possible to obtain the minimum frequency of repetitions, and to make the best use of the so-called spacing effect . . . Intervals should be short enough to ensure that the knowledge is still remembered."

Before long, Wozniak was living and learning according to the rhythms of his system, applying it to all his subjects. The English experiment became an algorithm, then a personal mission, and finally, in 1987, he turned it into a software package called Super-Memo. SuperMemo teaches according to Wozniak's calculations. It provides digital flashcards and a daily calendar for study, keeping track of when words were first studied and representing them according to the spacing effect. Each previously studied word pops up onscreen just before that word is about to drop out of reach of retrieval. It's easy to use and—after Wozniak made it available as freeware in the 1990s—the program took off, especially among young people trying to learn English in places like China and Poland (it's now a commercial website and an app).

In effect, Wozniak had reinvented Ebbinghaus for the digital age. His algorithm answered a crucial question about the timing of intervals. To build and retain foreign vocabulary, scientific definitions, or other factual information, it's best to review the material one or two days after initial study; then a week later; then about a month later. After that, the intervals are longer.

By 1992, researchers saw that what began as a lab curiosity in fact had enormous potential in education. One group had shown that teaching third graders addition once a day for ten days was far more effective than twice a day for five days. Another had shown that middle school students learned biology definitions like cell, mitosis, and chromosome far better in spaced sessions than in a single class. And ever-expanding intervals—as per SuperMemo—indeed appeared to be the most effective way to build a knowledge base, making the spacing effect "one of the most remarkable phenomenon to emerge from laboratory research on learning," one reviewer, psychologist Frank N. Dempster, of the University of Nevada, Las Vegas, wrote.

The next year, in 1993, the Four Bahrick Study appeared in the journal *Psychological Science*. If Wozniak helped establish the minimum intervals required to keep newly learned facts accessible, the Bahricks provided insight into the *maximum* intervals for lifetime learning. After five years, the family scored highest on the list they'd reviewed according to the most widely spaced, longest-running schedule: once every two months, for twenty-six sessions. They got 76 percent of those words on a final test, compared to 56 percent on a test of words studied once every two weeks for twenty-six sessions.

In the beginning of the study, the two-month wait meant they forgot a lot of words, compared to when they waited two weeks. That gap narrowed quickly; remember, they practiced until they knew *all* the words on their list during each study session. By the end, the two-month interval improved performance by 50 percent. "Who knew?" Bahrick said. "I had no idea. I thought, in two months, I might forget everything."

Why spaced study sessions have such a large impact on learning is still a matter of debate. Several factors are likely at work, depending on the interval. With very short intervals—seconds or minutes, as in the early studies—it may be that the brain becomes progressively less interested in a fact when it's repeated multiple times in rapid succession. It has just heard, and stored, the fact that James Monroe was the fifth president. If the same fact is repeated again, and then a third time, the brain pays progressively less attention.

For intermediate intervals of days or weeks, other factors might come into play. Recall the Forget to Learn theory, which holds that forgetting aids learning in two ways: actively, by filtering out competing facts, and passively, in that some forgetting allows subsequent practice to deepen learning, like an exercised muscle.

The example we used in chapter 2 was meeting the new neighbors for the first time ("Justin and Maria, what great names"). You remember the names right after hearing them, as retrieval strength is high. Yet storage strength is low, and by tomorrow morning the names will be on the tip of your tongue. Until you hear, from over the hedges—"Justin! Maria!"—and you got 'em, at least for the next several days. That is to say: Hearing the names again triggers a mental act, retrieval—*Oh that's right, Justin as in Timberlake and Maria as in Sharapova*—which boosts subsequent retrieval strength higher than it previously was. A day has passed between workouts, allowing strength to increase.

Spaced study—in many circumstances, including the neighbor example—also adds contextual cues, of the kind discussed in Chapter 3. You initially learned the names at the party, surrounded by friends and chatter, a glass of wine in hand. The second time, you heard them yelled out, over the hedges. The names are now embedded in two contexts, not just one. The same thing happens when reviewing a list of words or facts the second time (although context will likely be negligible, of course, if you're studying in the same place both days).

The effects described above are largely subconscious, running under the radar. We don't notice them. With longer intervals of a month or more, and especially with three or more sessions, we begin to notice some of the advantages that spacing allows, because they're obvious. For the Bahricks, the longer intervals helped them identify words they were most likely to have trouble remembering. "With longer spaces, you're forgetting more, but you find out what your weaknesses are and you correct for them," Bahrick told me. "You find out which mediators—which cues, which associations, or hints you used for each word—are working and which aren't. And if they're not working, you come up with new ones."

When I first start studying difficult material that comes with a new set of vocabulary (new software, the details of health insurance, the genetics of psychiatric disorders), I can study for an hour and return the next day and remember a few terms. Practically nothing.

The words and ideas are so strange at first that my brain has no way to categorize them, no place to put them. So be it. I now treat that first encounter as a casual walk-through, a meet-and-greet, and put in just twenty minutes. I know that in round two (twenty minutes) I'll get more traction, not to mention round three (also twenty minutes). I haven't used any more time, but I remember more.

By the 1990s, after its long incubation period in the lab, the spacing effect had grown legs and filled out—and in the process showed that it had real muscle. Results from classroom studies continued to roll in: Spaced review improves test scores for multiplication tables, for scientific definitions, for vocabulary. The truth is, nothing in learning science comes close in terms of immediate, significant, and reliable improvements to learning. Still, "spacing out" had no operating manual. The same questions about timing remained: What is the optimal study interval *given the test date*? What's the timing equation? Does one exist?

· · ·

The people who have worked hardest to turn the spacing effect into a practical strategy for everyday learning have one thing in common: They're teachers, as well as researchers. If students are cramming and not retaining anything, it's not all their fault. A good class should make the material stick, and spaced review (in class) is one way to do that. Teachers already do some reviewing, of course, but usually according to instinct or as part of standard curriculum, not guided by memory science. "I get sick of people taking my psych intro class and coming back next year and not remembering anything," Melody Wiseheart, a psychologist at York University in Toronto, told me. "It's a waste of time and money; people pay a lot for college. As a teacher, too, you want to teach so that people learn and remember: That's your job. You certainly want to know when it's best to review key concepts—what's the best time, given the spacing effect, to revisit material? What is the optimal schedule for students preparing for a test?"

In 2008, a research team led by Wiseheart and Harold Pashler, a psychologist at the University of California, San Diego, conducted a large study that provided the first good answer to those questions. The team enrolled 1,354 people of all ages, drawn from a pool of volunteers in the United States and abroad who had signed up to be "remote" research subjects, working online. Wiseheart and Pashler's group had them study thirty-two obscure facts: "What European nation consumes the most spicy Mexican food?": Norway. "Who invented snow golf?": Rudyard Kipling. "What day of the week did Columbus set sail for the New World in 1492?": Friday. "What's the name of the dog on the Cracker Jack box?": Bingo. Each participant studied the facts twice, on two separate occasions. For some, the two sessions were only ten minutes apart. For others, the interval was a day. For still another group, it was a month. The longest interval was six months. The researchers also varied the timing of the final exam. In total, there were twenty-six different study-test schedules for the researchers to compare.

The researchers compared all twenty-six different study schedules, and calculated the best intervals *given different test dates*. "To put it simply, if you want to know the optimal distribution of your study time, you need to decide how long you wish to remember something," Wiseheart and Pashler's group wrote. The optimal interval ranges can be read off a simple chart:

Time to Test	First Study Interval
1 Week	1-2 Days
1 Month	1 Week
3 Months	2 Weeks
6 Months	3 Weeks
1 Year	1 Month

Have a close look. These numbers aren't exact; there's wiggle room on either side. But they're close. If the test is in a week, and you want to split your study time in two, then do a session today and tomorrow, or today and the day after tomorrow. If you want to add a third, study the day before the test (just under a week later). If the test is a month away, then the best option is today, a week from today (for two sessions); for a third, wait three more weeks or so, until a day before the test. The further away the exam—that is, the more the time you have to prepare—the larger the optimal interval between sessions one and two. That optimal first interval declines as a *proportion* of the time-to-test, the Internet study found. If the test is in a week, the best interval is a day or two (20 to 40 percent). If it's in six months, the best interval is three to five weeks (10 to 20 percent). Wait any longer between study sessions, and performance goes down fairly quickly. For most students, in college, high school, or middle school, Wiseheart told me, "It basically means you're working with intervals of one day, two days, or one week. That should take care of most situations."

Let's take an example. Say there's a German exam in three months or so at the end of the semester. Most of us will spend at least two months of that time learning what it is we *need* to know for the exam, leaving at most a few weeks to review, if that (graduate students excepted). Let's say fifteen days, that's our window. For convenience, let's give ourselves nine hours total study time for that exam. The optimal schedule is the following: Three hours on Day 1. Three hours on Day 8. Three hours on Day 14, give or take a day. In each study session, we're reviewing the same material. On Day 15, according to the spacing effect, we'll do at least as well on the exam, compared to nine hours of cramming. The payoff is that we will retain that vocabulary for *much* longer, many months in this example. We'll do far better on any subsequent tests, like at the beginning of the following semester. And we'll do far better than cramming if the exam is delayed a few days. We've learned at least as much, in the same amount of time—and it sticks.

Again, cramming works fine in a pinch. It just doesn't last. Spacing does.

Yes, this kind of approach takes planning; nothing is entirely free. Still, spaced-out study is as close to a freebie as anything in learning science, and very much worth trying. Pick the subject area wisely. Remember, spacing is primarily a retention technique. Foreign languages. Science vocabulary. Names, places, dates, geography, memorizing speeches. Having more facts on board could very well help with comprehension, too, and several researchers are investigating just that, for math as well as other sciences. For now, though, this is a memorization strategy. The sensually educated William James, who became the philosopher-dean of early American psychology, was continually doling out advice about how to teach, learn, and remember (he didn't generally emphasize the tutors and fully subsidized travel he was lucky enough to have had). Here he is, though, in his 1901 book *Talks to Teachers on Psychology: And to Students on Some of Life's Ideals*, throwing out a whiff of the spacing effect: "Cramming seeks to stamp things in by intense application before the ordeal. But a thing thus learned can form few associations. On the other hand, the same thing recurring *on different days* in different contexts, read, recited, referred to again and again, related to other things and reviewed, gets well wrought into mental structure."

After more than a hundred years of research, we can finally say which days those are.

Chapter Five

The Hidden Value of Ignorance

The Many Dimensions of Testing

At some point in our lives, we all meet the Student Who Tests Well Without Trying. "I have no idea what happened," says she, holding up her 99 percent score. "I hardly even studied." It's a type you can never entirely escape, even in adulthood, as parents of school-age children quickly discover. "I don't know what it is, but Daniel just scores off the charts on these standardized tests," says Mom—dumbfounded!—at school pickup. "He certainly doesn't get it from me." No matter how much we prepare, no matter how early we rise, there's always someone who does better with less, who magically comes alive at game time.

I'm not here to explain that kid. I don't know of any study that looks at test taking as a discrete, stand-alone skill, or any evidence that it is an inborn gift, like perfect pitch. I don't need research to tell me that this type exists; I've seen it too often with my own eyes. I'm also old enough to know that being jealous isn't any way to close the gap between us and them. Neither is working harder. (Trust me, I've already tried that.)

No, the only way to develop any real test taking mojo is to understand more deeply what, exactly, testing *is*. The truth is not so self-evident, and it has more dimensions than you might guess.

The first thing to say about testing is this: Disasters happen. To everyone. Who hasn't opened a test booklet and encountered a list of questions that seem related to a different course altogether? I have a favorite story about this, a story I always go back to in the wake of any collapse. The teenage Winston Churchill spent weeks preparing for the entrance exam into Harrow, the prestigious English boys school. He wanted badly to get in. On the big day, in March of 1888, he opened the exam and found, instead of history and geography, an unexpected emphasis on Latin and Greek. His mind went blank, he wrote later, and he was unable to answer a single question. "I wrote my name at the top of the page. I wrote down the number of the question, '1.' After much reflection I put a bracket round it, thus, '(1).' But thereafter I could not think of anything connected with it that was either relevant or true. Incidentally there arrived from nowhere in particular a blot and several smudges. I gazed for two whole hours at this sad spectacle; and then merciful ushers collected up my piece of foolscap and carried it up to the Headmaster's table."

And that's *Winston Churchill*.

The next thing to say is less obvious, though it's rooted in a far more common type of blown test. We open the booklet and see familiar questions on material we've studied, stuff we've highlighted with yellow marker: names, ideas, formulas we could recite with ease only yesterday. No trick questions, no pink elephants, and still we lay an egg. Why? How? I did so myself on one of the worst possible days: a trigonometry final I needed to ace to get into an Advanced Placement course, junior year. I spent weeks preparing. Walking into the exam that day, I remember feeling pretty good. When the booklets were handed out, I scanned the questions and took an easy breath. The test had a few of the concepts I'd studied, as well as familiar kinds of questions, which I'd practiced dozens of times.

I can do this, I thought.

Yet I scored somewhere in the low 50s, in the very navel of aver-age. (These days, a score like that would prompt many parents to call a psychiatrist.) Who did I blame? Myself. I knew the material but didn't hear the music. I was a "bad test taker." I was kicking myself—but for all the wrong reasons.

The problem wasn't that I hadn't worked hard enough, or that I lacked the test taking "gene." No, my mistake was misjudging the depth of what I knew. I was duped by what psychologists call fluency, the belief that because facts or formulas or arguments are easy to remember *right now,* they'll remain that way tomorrow or the next day. The fluency illusion is so strong that, once we feel we've nailed some topic or assignment, we assume that further study won't help. We forget that we forget. Any number of study "aids" can create fluency illusions, including (yes) highlighting, making a study guide, and even chapter outlines provided by a teacher or a textbook. Flu-ency misperceptions are automatic. They form subconsciously and make us poor judges of what we need to restudy, or practice again. "We know that if you study something twice, in spaced sessions, it's harder to process the material the second time, and so people think it's counterproductive," as Nate Kornell, a psychologist at Williams College, told me. "But the opposite is true: You learn more, even though it feels harder. Fluency is playing a trick on judgment."

So it is that we end up attributing our poor test results to "test anxiety" or—too often—stupidity.

Let's recall the Bjorks' "desirable difficulty" principle: The harder your brain has to work to dig out a memory, the greater the increase in learning (retrieval and storage strength). Fluency, then, is the flip-side of that equation. The *easier* it is to call a fact to mind, the smaller the increase in learning. Repeating facts right after you've studied them gives you nothing, no added memory benefit.

The fluency illusion is the primary culprit in below-average test performances. Not anxiety. Not stupidity. Not unfairness or bad luck.

Fluency.

The best way to overcome this illusion and improve our testing skills is, conveniently, an effective study technique in its own right. The technique is not exactly a recent invention; people have been employing it since the dawn of formal education, probably longer. Here's the philosopher Francis Bacon, spelling it out in 1620: "If you read a piece of text through twenty times, you will not learn it by heart so easily as if you read it ten times while attempting to recite it from time to time and consulting the text when your memory fails." And here's the irrepressible William James, in 1890, musing about the same concept: "A curious peculiarity of our memory is that things are impressed better by active than by passive repetition. I mean that in learning—by heart, for example—when we almost know the piece, it pays better to wait and recollect by an effort from within, than to look at the book again. If we recover the words in the former way, we shall probably know them the next time; if in the latter way, we shall very likely need the book once more."

The technique is testing itself. Yes, I am aware of how circular this logic appears: better testing through testing. Don't be fooled. There's more to self-examination than you know. A test is not only a measurement tool, it alters what we remember and *changes* how we subsequently organize that knowledge in our minds. And it does so in ways that greatly improve later performance.

• • •

One of the first authoritative social registries in the New World was *Who's Who in America,* and the premiere volume, published in 1899, consisted of more than 8,500 entries—short bios of politicians, business leaders, clergymen, railroad lawyers, and sundry "distinguished Americans." The bios were detailed, compact, and historically rich. It takes all of thirty seconds, for example, to learn that Alexander Graham Bell received his patent for the telephone in 1876, just days after his twenty-ninth birthday, when he was a professor of vocal physiology at Boston University. And that his father, Alexander Melville Bell (the next entry), was an inventor, too, an expert in elocution who developed Visible Speech, a set of symbols used to help deaf people learn to speak. And that *his* father—Alexander Bell, no middle name, of Edinburgh—pioneered the treatment of speech impediments. Who knew? The two younger Bells, though both were born in Edinburgh, eventually settled in Washington, D.C. The father lived at 1525 35th Street, and the son at 1331 Connecticut Avenue. That's right, the addresses are here, too. (Henry James: Rye, Isle of Wight.)

In 1917, a young psychologist at Columbia University had an idea: He would use these condensed life entries to help answer a question. Arthur Gates was interested in, among other things, how the act of recitation interacts with memory. For centuries, students who received a classical education spent untold hours learning to recite from memory epic poems, historic monologues, and passages from scripture—a skill that's virtually lost today. Gates wanted to know whether there was an ideal ratio between reading (memorizing) and reciting (rehearsal). If you want to learn Psalm 23 (*The Lord is my shepherd, I shall not want . . .*) by heart—in, say, a half hour—how many of those minutes should you spend studying the verse on the page, and how many should you spend trying to recite from memory? What ratio anchors that material in memory most firmly? That would have been a crucial percentage to have, especially back when recitation was so central to education. The truth is, it's just as handy today, not only for actors working to memorize Henry V's St. Crispin's Day speech but for anyone preparing a presentation, learning a song, or studying poetry.

To find out if such a ratio existed, Gates enlisted five classes from a local school, ranging from third to eighth grade, for an experiment. He assigned each student a number of *Who's Who* entries to memorize and recite (the older students got five entries, the youngest ones three). He gave them each nine minutes to study along with specific

instructions on how to use that time: One group would spend a minute and forty-eight seconds memorizing, and seven minutes, twelve
seconds rehearsing (reciting); another would split its time in half,
equal parts memorizing and rehearsing; a third, eight minutes of its
time memorizing, and only a minute rehearsing. And so on.

Three hours later, it was showtime. Gates asked each student to
recite what he or she could remember of their assigned entries:

"Edgar Mayhew Bacon, author . . . born, uh, June 5, 1855,
Nassau, the Bahamas, and uh, went to private schools in
Tarrytown, N.Y.; worked in a bookstore in Albany, and then
I think became an artist . . . and then wrote, 'The New Ja-
maica'? . . . and 'Sleepy Hollow' maybe?"

One, after another, after another. Edith Wharton. Samuel Clem-
ens. Jane Addams. The brothers James. More than a hundred students, reciting.

And in the end, Gates had his ratio.

"In general," he concluded, "the best results are obtained by introducing recitation after devoting about 40 percent of the time to
reading. Introducing recitation too early or too late leads to poorer
results," Gates wrote. In the older grades, the percentage was even
smaller, closer to a third. "The superiority of optimal reading and
retention over reading alone is about 30 percent."

The quickest way to download that St. Crispin's Day speech, in
other words, is to spend the first third of your time memorizing it,
and the remaining two thirds reciting from memory.

Was this a landmark finding? Well, yes, actually. In hindsight, it
was the first rigorous demonstration of a learning technique that
scientists now consider one of the most powerful of all. Yet at the
time no one saw it. This was one study, in one group of schoolchildren. Gates didn't speculate on the broader implications of his results, either, at least not in the paper he published in the *Archives of*

Psychology, "Recitation as a Factor in Memorizing," and the study generated little scientific discussion or follow-up.

The reasons for this, I think, are plain enough. Through the first half of the twentieth century, psychology was relatively young and growing by fits and starts, whipsawed by its famous theorists. Freud's ideas still cast a long shadow and attracted hundreds of research projects. Ivan Pavlov's experiments helped launch decades of research on conditioned learning—stimulus-response experiments, many of them in animals. Research into education was in an exploratory phase, with psychologists looking into reading, into learning disabilities, phonics, even the effect of students' emotional life on grades. And it's important to say that psychology—like any science— proceeds in part by retrospective clue gathering. A scientist has an idea, a theory, or a goal, and looks backward to see if there's work to build on, if there's anyone who's had the same idea or reported results that are supportive of it. Science may be built on the shoulders of giants, but for a working researcher it's often necessary to ransack the literature to find out who those giants are. Creating a rationale for a research project can be an exercise in historical data mining—in finding shoulders to build on.

Gates's contribution is visible only in retrospect, but it was inevitable that its significance would be noticed. Improving education was, then as now, a subject of intense interest. And so, in the late 1930s, more than twenty years later, another researcher found in Gates's study a rationale for his own. Herbert F. Spitzer was a doctoral student at the State University of Iowa, who in 1938 was trawling for a dissertation project. He wasn't interested in recitation per se, and he didn't belong to the small club of academic psychologists who were focused on studying the intricacies of memory. He was intent on improving teaching methods, and one of the biggest questions hanging over teachers, from the very beginning of the profession, was *when* testing is most effective. Is it best to give one big exam at the end of a course? Or do periodic tests given earlier in the term make more sense?

We can only guess at Spitzer's thinking, because he did not spell it out in his writings. We know he'd read Gates's study, because he cites it in his own. We know, too, that he saw Gates's study for what it was. In particular, he recognized Gates's recitation as a form of self-examination. Studying a prose passage for five or ten minutes, then turning the page over to recite what you can without looking, isn't only practice. It's a test, and Gates had shown that that self-exam had a profound effect on final performance.

That is to say: Testing *is* studying, of a different and powerful kind.

Spitzer understood that, and then asked the next big question. If taking a test—whether recitation, rehearsal, self-exam, pop quiz, or sit-down exam—improves learning, then when is the best time to take it?

To try to find out, he mounted an enormous experiment, enlisting sixth graders at ninety-one different elementary schools in nine Iowa cities—3,605 students in all. He had them study an age-appropriate six-hundred-word article, similar to what they might get for homework. Some were assigned an article on peanuts, and others one on bamboo. They studied the passage once. Spitzer then divided the students into eight groups and had each group take several tests on the passages over the next two months. The tests for each group were all the same, multiple-choice, twenty-five questions, each with five possible answers. For example, for those who studied bamboo:

What usually happens to a bamboo plant after the flowering period?

a. It dies
b. It begins a new growth

    c. It sends up new plants from the roots

    d. It begins to branch out

    e. It begins to grow a rough bark

In essence, Spitzer conducted what was, and probably still is, the largest pop quiz experiment in history. The students had no idea that the quizzes were coming, or when. And each group got hit with quizzes at different times. Group 1 got one right after studying, then another a day later, and a third three weeks later. Group 6 didn't take their first quiz until three weeks after reading the passage. Again, the time the students had to study was identical. So were the questions on the quizzes.

Yet the groups' scores varied widely, and a pattern emerged.

The groups that took pop quizzes soon after reading the passage— once or twice within the first week—did the best on a final exam given at the end of two months, getting about 50 percent of the questions correct. (Remember, they'd studied their peanut or bamboo article only once.) By contrast, the groups who took their first pop quiz two weeks or more *after* studying scored much lower, below 30 percent on the final. Spitzer showed not only that testing is a powerful study technique, he showed it's one that should be deployed sooner rather than later.

"Immediate recall in the form of a test is an effective method of aiding the retention of learning and should, therefore, be employed more frequently," he concluded. "Achievement tests or examinations are learning devices and should not be considered only as tools for measuring achievement of pupils."

For lab researchers focused on improving retention, this finding should have rung a bell, and loudly. Recall, for a moment, Ballard's "reminiscence" from chapter 2. The schoolchildren in his "Wreck of the Hesperus" experiment studied the poem only once but continued to improve on subsequent tests given days later, remembering more and more of the poem as time passed. Those intervals between studying (memorizing) the poem and taking the tests—a day later, two days, a week—are exactly the ones that Spitzer found most helpful for retention. Between them, Gates and Spitzer had demonstrated that Ballard's young students improved not by some miracle but because each test was an additional study session. Even then, after Spitzer published his findings in *The Journal of Educational Psychology,* the bell didn't sound.

"We can only speculate as to why," wrote Henry Roediger III and Jeffrey Karpicke, also then at Washington University, in a landmark 2006 review of the testing effect, as they called it. One possible reason, they argued, is that psychologists were still primarily focused on the dynamics of forgetting: "For the purpose of measuring forgetting, repeated testing was deemed a confound, to be avoided." It "contaminated" forgetting, in the words of one of Spitzer's contemporaries.

Indeed it did, and does. And, as it happens, that contamination induces improvements in thinking and performance that no one predicted at the time. More than thirty years passed before someone picked up the ball again, finally seeing the possibilities of what Gates and Spitzer had found.

That piece of foolscap Winston Churchill turned in, with the smudges and blots? It was far from a failure, scientists now know—even if he scored a flat zero.

. . .

Let's take a breather from this academic parsing of ideas and do a simple experiment, shall we? Something light, something that gets this point across without feeling like homework. I've chosen two short passages from one author for your reading pleasure—and pleasure it should be, because they're from, in my estimation, one of the most savage humorists who ever strode the earth, however unsteadily. Brian O'Nolan, late of Dublin, was a longtime civil servant, crank, and pub-crawler who between 1930 and 1960 wrote novels, plays, and a much beloved satirical column for *The Irish Times*. Now, your assignment: Read the two selections below, four or five times. Spend five minutes on each, then put them aside and carry on with your chores and shirking of same. Both come from a chapter called "Bores" in O'Nolan's book *The Best of Myles:*

Passage 1: The Man Who Can Pack

This monster watches you try to stuff the contents of two wardrobes into an attaché case. You succeed, of course, but have forgotten to put in your golf clubs. You curse grimly but your "friend" is delighted. He knew this would happen. He approaches, offers consolation and advises you to go downstairs and take things easy while he "puts things right." Some days later, when you unpack your things in Glengariff, you find that he has not only got your golf clubs in but has included your bedroom carpet, the kit of the Gas Company man who has been working in your room, two ornamental vases and a card-table. Everything in view, in fact, except your razor. You have to wire 7 pounds to Cork to get a new leather bag (made of cardboard) to get all this junk home.

Passage 2: The Man Who Soles His Own Shoes

Quite innocently you complain about the quality of present-day footwear. You wryly exhibit a broken sole. "Must take them in tomorrow," you say vaguely. The monster is flabbergasted at this passive attitude, has already forced you into an armchair, pulled your shoes off and vanished with them into the scullery. He is back in an incredibly short space of time and restored your property to you announcing that the shoes are now "as good as new." You notice his own for the first time and instantly understand why his feet are deformed. You hobble home, apparently on stilts. Nailed to each shoe is an inch-thick slab of "leather" made from Shellac, saw-dust and cement.

Got all that? It's not *The Faerie Queene*, but it'll suffice for our purposes. Later in the day—an hour from now, if you're going with the program—restudy Passage 1. Sit down for five minutes and reread it a few more times, as if preparing to recite it from memory (which you are). When the five minutes are up, take a break, have a snack, and come back to Passage 2. This time, instead of restudying, test yourself on it. Without looking, write down as much of it as you can remember. If it's ten words, great. Three sentences? Even better. Then put it away without looking at it again.

The next day, test yourself on both passages. Give yourself, say, five minutes on each to recall as much as you can.

So: Which was better?

Eyeball the results, counting the words and phrases you remembered. Without being there to look over your shoulder and grade your work, I'm going to hazard a guess that you did markedly better on the second passage.

That is essentially the experimental protocol that a pair of psychologists—Karpicke, now at Purdue, and Roediger—have used in a series of studies over the past decade or so. They've used it repeatedly, with students of all ages, and across a broad spectrum of material—prose passages, word pairs, scientific subjects, medical topics. We'll review one of their experiments, briefly, just to be clear about the impact of self-examination. In a 2006 study, Karpicke and Roediger recruited 120 undergraduates and had them study two science-related passages, one on the sun and the other on sea otters. They studied one of the two passages twice, in separate seven-minute sessions. They studied the other one once, for seven minutes, and in the next seven-minute session were instructed to write down as much of the passage as they could recall without looking. (That was the "test," like we just did above with the O'Nolan passages.) Each student, then, had studied one passage two times—either the sea otters, or the sun—and the other just once, followed by a free recall test on it.

Karpicke and Roediger split the students into three groups, one of which took a test five minutes after the study sessions, one that got a test two days later, and one that tested a week later. The results are easily read off the following graph:

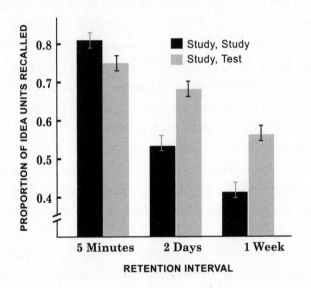

There are two key things to take away from this experiment. First, Karpicke and Roediger kept preparation time equal; the students got the same amount of time to try to learn both passages. Second, the "testing" prep *buried* the "study" prep when it really mattered, on the one-week test. In short, testing does not = studying, after all. In fact, testing > studying, and by a country mile, on delayed tests.

"Did we find something no one had ever found before? No, not really," Roediger told me. Other psychologists, most notably Chizuko Izawa, had shown similar effects in the 1960s and '70s at Stanford University. "People had noticed testing effects and gotten excited about them. But we did it with different material than before—the prose passages, in this case—and I think that's what caught people's attention. We showed that this could be applied to real classrooms, and showed how strong it could be. That's when the research started to take off."

Roediger, who's contributed an enormous body of work to learning science, both in experiments and theory, also happens to be one of the field's working historians. In a review paper published in 2006, he and Karpicke analyzed a century's worth of experiments, on all types of retention strategies (like spacing, repeated study, and context), and showed that the testing effect has been there all along, a strong, consistent "contaminant," slowing down forgetting. To measure any type of learning, after all, you have to administer a test. Yet if you're using the test only for measurement, like some physical education push-up contest, you fail to see it as an added workout—itself making contestants' memory muscles stronger.

The word "testing" is loaded, in ways that have nothing to do with learning science. Educators and experts have debated the value of standardized testing for decades, and reforms instituted by President George W. Bush in 2001—increasing the use of such exams—only inflamed the argument. Many teachers complain of having to "teach to the test," limiting their ability to fully explore subjects with their students. Others attack such tests as incomplete measures of learning, blind to all varieties of creative thinking. This debate, though unrelated to work like Karpicke and Roediger's, has effectively prevented their findings and those of others from being applied in classrooms as part of standard curricula. "When teachers hear the word 'testing,' because of all the negative connotations, all this baggage, they say, 'We don't need more tests, we need *less*,'" Robert Bjork, the UCLA psychologist, told me.

In part to soften this resistance, researchers have begun to call testing "retrieval practice." That phrase is a good one for theoretical reasons, too. If self-examination is more effective than straight studying (once we're familiar with the material), there must be reasons for it. One follows directly from the Bjorks' desirable difficulty principle.

When the brain is retrieving studied text, names, formulas, skills, or anything else, it's doing something different, and *harder,* than when it sees the information again, or restudies. That extra effort deepens the resulting storage and retrieval strength. We know the facts or skills better because we retrieved them ourselves, we didn't merely review them.

Roediger goes further still. When we successfully retrieve a fact, he argues, we then *re*-store it in memory in a different way than we did before. Not only has storage level spiked; the memory itself has new and different connections. It's now linked to other related facts that we've also retrieved. The network of cells holding the memory has itself been altered. Using our memory changes our memory in ways we don't anticipate.

And that's where the research into testing takes an odd turn indeed.

•   •   •

What if you somehow got hold of the final exam for a course on Day 1, before you'd even studied a thing? Imagine it just appeared in your inbox, sent mistakenly by the teacher. Would having that test matter? Would it help you prepare for taking the final at the end of the course?

Of course it would. You'd read the questions carefully. You'd know what to pay attention to and what to study in your notes. Your ears would perk up anytime the teacher mentioned something relevant to a specific question. If you were thorough, you'd have memorized the correct answer to every item before the course ended. On the day of that final, you'd be the first to finish, sauntering out with an A+ in your pocket.

And you'd be cheating.

But what if, instead, you took a test on Day 1 that was comprehensive but *not* a replica of the final exam? You'd bomb the thing, to be sure. You might not be able to understand a single question. And yet that experience, given what we've just learned about testing, might alter how you subsequently tune into the course itself during the rest of the term.

This is the idea behind *pretesting*, the latest permutation of the testing effect. In a series of experiments, psychologists like Roediger, Karpicke, the Bjorks, and Kornell have found that, in some circumstances, unsuccessful retrieval attempts—i.e., wrong answers—aren't merely random failures. Rather, the attempts themselves alter how we think about, and store, the information contained in the questions. On some kinds of tests, particularly multiple-choice, we learn from answering incorrectly—especially when given the correct answer soon afterward.

That is, *guessing wrongly* increases a person's likelihood of nailing that question, or a related one, on a later test.

That's a sketchy-sounding proposition on its face, it's true. Bombing tests on stuff you don't know sounds more like a recipe for discouragement and failure than an effective learning strategy. The best way to appreciate this is to try it yourself. That means taking another test. It'll be a short one, on something you don't know well—in my case, let's make it the capital cities of African nations. Choose any twelve and have a friend make up a simple multiple-choice quiz, with five possible answers for each nation. Give yourself ten seconds on each question; after each one, have your friend tell you the correct answer.

Ready? Put the smartphone down, close the computer, and give it a shot. Here are a few samples:

BOTSWANA:

- Gaborone
- Dar es Salaam

- Hargeisa
- Oran
- Zaria

(Friend: "Gaborone")

GHANA:

- Huambo
- Benin
- Accra
- Maputo
- Kumasi

(Friend: "Accra")

LESOTHO:

- Lusaka
- Juba
- Maseru
- Cotonou
- N'Djamena

(Friend: "Maseru")

And so on. You've just taken a test on which you've guessed, if you're anything like me, mostly wrong. Has taking that test improved your knowledge of those twelve capitals? Of course it has. Your friend *gave you the answers* after each question. Nothing surprising there.

We're not quite done, though. That was Phase 1 of our experiment, pretesting. Phase 2 will be what we think of as traditional studying. For that, you will need to choose another twelve unfamiliar nations, with the correct answer listed alongside, and then sit down and try to memorize them. Nigeria–Abuja. Eritrea–Asmara. Gambia–Banjul. Take the same amount of time—two minutes—as you took on the multiple-choice test. That's it. You're done for the day.

You have now effectively studied the capital cities of twenty-four African nations. You studied the first half by taking a multiple-choice pretest. You studied the other half the old-fashioned way, by straight memorization. We're going to compare your knowledge of the first twelve to your knowledge of the second twelve.

Tomorrow, take a multiple-choice test on all twenty-four of those nations, also with five possible choices under each nation. When you're done, compare the results. If you're like most people, you scored 10 to 20 percent higher on the countries in that first group, the ones where you guessed before hearing the correct answer. In the jargon of the field, your "unsuccessful retrieval attempts potentiated learning, increasing successful retrieval attempts on subsequent tests."

In plain English: The act of guessing engaged your mind in a different and more demanding way than straight memorization did, deepening the imprint of the correct answers. In even plainer English, the pretest drove home the information in a way that studying-as-usual did not.

Why? No one knows for sure. One possible explanation is that pretesting is another manifestation of desirable difficulty. You work a little harder by guessing first than by studying directly. A second possibility is that the wrong guesses eliminate the fluency illusion, the false impression that you knew the capital of Eritrea because you just saw or studied it. A third is that, in simply memorizing, you saw only the correct answer and weren't thrown off by the other four alternatives—the way you would be on a test. "Let's say you're studying capitals and you see that Australia's is Canberra," Robert Bjork told me. "Okay, that seems easy enough. But when the exam question appears, you see all sorts of other possibilities—Sydney, Melbourne, Adelaide—and suddenly you're not so sure. If you're studying just the correct answer, you don't appreciate all the other possible answers that could come to mind or appear on the test."

Taking a practice test provides us something else as well—a glimpse of the teacher's hand. "Even when you get wrong answers, it seems to improve subsequent study," Robert Bjork added, "because the test adjusts our thinking in some way to the kind of material we need to know."

That's a good thing, and not just for us. It's in the teacher's interest, too. You can teach facts and concepts all you want, but what's most important in the end is how students think about that material—how they organize it, mentally, and use it to make judgments about what's important and what's less so. To Elizabeth Bjork, that seemed the best explanation for why a pretest would promote more effective subsequent studying—it primes students to notice important concepts later on. To find out, she decided to run a pretesting trial in one of her own classes.

Bjork decided to start small, in her Psychology 100B class at UCLA, on research methods. She wouldn't give a comprehensive pre*final* on the first day of class. "It was a pilot study, really, and I decided to give the pretests for three individual lectures," she said. "The students would take each pretest a day or two before each of those lectures; we wanted to see whether they remembered the material better later."

She and Nicholas Soderstrom, a postdoctoral fellow, designed the three short pretests to have forty questions each, all multiple-choice. They also put together a cumulative exam to be given *after* the three lectures. The crucial question they wanted to answer was: Do students comprehend and retain pretested material better and longer than they do material that's not on a pretest but *is* in the lectures? To answer that, Bjork and Soderstrom did something clever on the final exam. They filled it with two kinds of questions: those that were related to the pretest questions and those that were not. "If pretesting helps, then students should do better on related questions during a later exam than on material we covered in the lectures but was not pretested," Bjork said. This is analogous to the African nation test we devised above. The first twelve capitals were "pretested"; the second twelve were not—they were studied in the usual way. By comparing our scores on the first twelve to the second twelve, on a comprehensive test of all twenty-four, we could judge whether pretesting made any difference.

Bjork and Soderstrom would compare students' scores on pretest-related questions to their scores on *non*-pretested ones on the cumulative final. The related questions were phrased differently but often had some of the same possible answers. For example, here's a pair of related questions, one from the pretest and the next from the cumulative exam:

Which of the following is true of scientific explanations?

a. They are less likely to be verified by empirical observation than other types of explanations.

b. They are accepted because they come from a trusted source or authority figure.

c. They are accepted only provisionally.

d. In the face of evidence that is inconsistent with a scientific explanation, the evidence will be questioned.

e. All of the above are true about scientific explanations.

Which of the following is true of explanations based on belief?

a. They are more likely to be verified by empirical observation than other types of explanations.

b. They are accepted because they come from a trusted source or authority figure.

    c. They are assumed to be true absolutely.

    d. In the face of evidence that is inconsistent with an expla-
       nation based on belief, the belief will be questioned.

    e. b and c above

The students tanked each pretest. Then they attended the relevant lecture a day or two later—in effect, getting the correct answers
to the questions they'd just tried to answer. Pretesting is most helpful
when people get prompt feedback (just as we did on our African capitals test).

Did those bombed tests make any difference in what the students
remembered later? The cumulative exam, covering all three pretested lectures, would tell. Bjork and Soderstrom gave that exam two
weeks after the last of the three lectures was presented, and it used
the same format as the others: forty multiple-choice questions, each
with five possible answers. Again, some of those exam questions
were related to pretest ones and others were not. The result? Success.
Bjork's Psych 100B class scored about 10 percent higher on the *related*
questions than on the unrelated ones. Not a slam dunk, 10 percent—
but not bad for a first attempt. "The best way you could say it for
now," she told me, "is that on the basis of preliminary data, giving
students a pretest on topics to be covered in a lecture improves their
ability to answer related questions about those topics on a later final
exam." Even when students bomb a test, she said, they get an opportunity to see the vocabulary used in the coming lectures and get a
sense of what kinds of questions and distinctions between concepts
are important.

Pretesting is not an entirely new concept. We have all taken practice tests at one time or another as a way of building familiarity—
and to questionable effect. Kids have been taking practice SATs for
years, just as adults have taken practices MCATs and GMATs and
LSATs. Yet the SAT and tests like it are general-knowledge exams,

and the practice runs are primarily about reducing anxiety and giving us a feel for format and timing. The research that the Bjorks, Roediger, Kornell, Karpicke and others have done is different. Their testing effect—pre- or post-study—applies to learning the kind of concepts, terms, and vocabulary that form a *specialized* knowledge base, say of introductory chemistry, biblical analysis, or music theory.

In school, testing is still testing. That's not going to change, not fundamentally. What is changing is our appreciation of what a test is. First, thanks to Gates, the Columbia researcher who studied recitation, it appeared to be at least equivalent to additional study: Answering does not only measure what you remember, it increases overall retention. Then, testing proved itself to be *superior* to additional study, in a broad variety of academic topics, and the same is likely true of things like music and dance, practicing from memory. Now we're beginning to understand that some kinds of tests improve later learning—even if we do poorly on them.

Is it possible that one day teachers and professors will give "prefinals" on the first day of class? Hard to say. A prefinal for an intro class in Arabic or Chinese might be a wash, just because the notations and symbols and alphabet are entirely alien. My guess is that prefinals are likely to be much more useful in humanities courses and the social sciences, because in those courses our minds have some scaffolding of language to work with, before making a guess. "At this point, we don't know what the ideal applications of pretesting are," Robert Bjork told me. "It's still a very new area."

Besides, in this book we're in the business of discovering what we can do for ourselves, in our own time. Here's what I would say, based on my conversations with the Bjorks, Roediger, and others pushing the limits of retrieval practice: Testing—recitation, self-examination, pretesting, call it what you like—is an enormously powerful technique capable of much more than simply measuring knowledge. It vanquishes the fluency trap that causes so many of us to think that we're poor test takers. It amplifies the value of our study time. And it gives us—in the case of pretesting—a detailed, specific preview of how we should begin to think about approaching a topic.

Testing has brought fear and self-loathing into so many hearts that changing its definition doesn't come easily. There's too much bad blood. Yet one way to do so is to think of the examination as merely one application of testing—one of many. Those applications remind me of what the great Argentine writer Jorge Luis Borges once said about his craft: "Writing long books is a laborious and impoverishing act of foolishness: expanding in five hundred pages an idea that could be perfectly explained in a few minutes. A better procedure is to pretend that those books already exist and to offer a summary, a commentary."

Pretend that the book already exists. Pretend you already know. Pretend you already can play something by Sabicas, that you already inhaled the St. Crispin's Day speech, that you have philosophy logic nailed to the door. Pretend you already are an expert and give a summary, a commentary—pretend and *perform*. That is the soul of self-examination: pretending you're an expert, just to see what you've got. This goes well beyond taking a quick peek at the "summary questions" at the end of the history chapter before reading, though that's a step in the right direction. Self-examination can be done at home. When working on guitar, I learn a few bars of a piece, slowly, painstakingly—then try to play it from memory several times in a row. When reading through a difficult scientific paper, I put it down after a couple times through and try to explain to someone what it says. If there's no one there to listen (or pretend to listen), I say it out loud to myself, trying as hard as I can to quote from the paper its main points. Many teachers have said that you don't really know a topic until you have to *teach* it, until you have to make it clear to someone else. Exactly right. One very effective way to think of self-examination is to say, "Okay, I've studied this stuff; now it's time to tell my brother, or spouse, or teenage daughter what it all means." If necessary, I write it down from memory. As coherently, succinctly, and clearly as I can.

Remember: These apparently simple attempts to communicate what you've learned, to yourself or others, are not merely a form of self-testing, in the conventional sense, but *studying*—the high-octane kind, 20 to 30 percent more powerful than if you continued sitting on your butt, staring at that outline. Better yet, those exercises will dispel the fluency illusion. They'll expose what you don't know, where you're confused, what you've forgotten—and fast.

That's ignorance of the best kind.

· ·

Problem Solving

Chapter Six

The Upside of Distraction

The Role of Incubation in Problem Solving

School hits us with at least as many psychological tests as academic ones. Hallway rejection. Playground fights. Hurtful gossip, bad grades, cafeteria food. Yet at the top of that trauma list, for many of us, is the stand-up presentation: being onstage in front of the class, delivering a memorized speech about black holes or the French Resistance or Piltdown Man, and wishing that life had a fast-forward button. I'm not proud to admit it, but I'm a charter member of that group. As a kid, I'd open my mouth to begin a presentation and the words would come out in a whisper.

I thought I'd moved beyond that long ago—until early one winter morning in 2011. I showed up at a middle school on the outskirts of New York City, expecting to give an informal talk to a class of twenty or thirty seventh graders about a mystery novel I'd written for kids, in which the clues are pre-algebra problems. When I arrived, however, I was ushered onto the stage of a large auditorium, a school staffer asking whether I needed any audiovisual equipment, computer connections, or PowerPoint. Uh, no. I sure didn't. The truth was, I didn't have a presentation at all. I had a couple of books under my arm and was prepared to answer a few questions about writing, nothing more. The auditorium was filling fast, with teachers herding their classes into rows. Apparently, this was a school-wide event.

I struggled to suppress panic. It crossed my mind to apologize and exit stage left, explaining that I simply wasn't ready, there'd been some kind of mistake. But it was too late. The crowd was settling in and suddenly the school librarian was onstage, one hand raised, asking for quiet. She introduced me and stepped aside. It was showtime . . . and I was eleven years old again. My mind went blank. I looked out into a sea of young faces, expectant, curious, impatient. In the back rows I could see kids already squirming.

I needed time. Or a magic trick.

I had neither, so I decided to start with a puzzle. The one that came to mind is ancient, probably dating to the Arab mathematicians of the seventh century. More recently, scientists have used it to study creative problem solving, the ability to discover answers that aren't intuitive or obvious. It's easy to explain and accessible for anyone, certainly for middle school students. I noticed a blackboard toward the back of the stage, and I rolled it up into the light. I picked up a piece of chalk and drew six vertical pencils about six inches apart, like a row of fence posts:

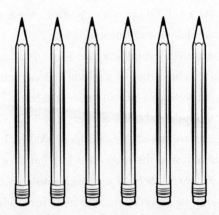

"This is a very famous puzzle, and I promise: Any of you here can solve it," I said. "Using these pencils, I want you to create four equilateral triangles, with one pencil forming the side of each triangle." I reminded them what an equilateral triangle is, one with three equal sides:

"So: six pencils. Four triangles. Easy, right? Go."

The fidgeting stopped. Suddenly, all eyes were on the blackboard. I could practically hear those mental circuits humming.

This is what psychologists call an insight problem, or more colloquially, an aha! problem. Why? Because your first idea for a solution usually doesn't work . . . so you try a few variations . . . and get nowhere . . . and then you stare at the ceiling for a minute . . . and then you switch tacks, try something else . . . feel blocked again . . . try a totally different approach . . . and then . . . aha!—you see it. An insight problem, by definition, is one that requires a person to shift his or her perspective and view the problem in a novel way. The problems are like riddles, and there are long-running debates over whether our ability to crack them is related to IQ or creative and analytical skills. A knack for puzzles doesn't necessarily make someone a good math, chemistry, or English student. The debate aside, I look at it this way: It sure doesn't hurt. We need creative ways of thinking to crack any real problem, whether it's in writing, math, or management. If the vault door doesn't open after we've tried all our usual combinations, then we've got to come up with some others—or look for another way in.

I explained some of this in the auditorium that morning, as the kids stared at the board and whispered to one another. After five minutes or so, a few students ventured up to the blackboard to sketch out their ideas. None worked. The drawings were of triangles with smaller triangles crisscrossing inside, and the sides weren't equal. Solid efforts all around, but nothing that opened the vault door.

At that point, the fidgeting started again, especially in the back rows. I continued with more of my shtick about math being like a mystery. That you need to make sure you've used all available information. That you should always chase down what seem like your stupidest ideas. That, if possible, you should try breaking the problem into smaller pieces. Still, I felt like I was starting to sound to them like the teachers in those old *Charlie Brown* movies (WAH-WAH WAH WAAH WAH), and the mental hum in the room began to dissipate. I needed another trick. I thought of another well-known insight problem and wrote it on the board beneath the chalk pencils:

SEQUENC_

"Okay, let's take a break and try another one," I told them. "Your only instruction for this one is to complete the sequence using any letter other than E."

I consider this a more approachable puzzle than the triangle one, because there's no scent of math in it. (Anything with geometric shapes or numbers instantly puts off an entire constituency of students who think they're "not a math person"—or have been told as much.) The SEQUENC_ puzzle is one we all feel we can solve. I hoped not only to keep them engaged but also to draw them in deeper—put them in the right frame of mind to tackle the Pencil

Problem. I could feel the difference in the crowd right away, too. There was a competitive vibe in the air, as if each kid in that audience sensed that this one was within his or her grasp and wanted to be the first to nail it. The teachers began to encourage them as well.

Concentrate, they said.

Think outside the box.

Quiet, you guys in the back.

Pay attention.

After a few more minutes, a girl near the front raised her hand and offered an answer in a voice that was barely audible, as if she was afraid to be wrong. She had it right, though. I had her come up to the board and fill in the answer—generating a chorus of *Oh man!* and *You're kidding me, that's it?* Such are insight problems, I told them. You have to let go of your first ideas, reexamine every detail you're given, and try to think more expansively.

By this time I was in the fourth quarter of my presentation and still the Pencil Problem mocked them from the board. I had a couple hints up my sleeve, waiting for deployment, but I wanted to let a few more minutes pass before giving anything away. That's when a boy in the back—the "Pay attention" district—raised his hand. "What about the number four and a triangle?" he said, holding up a diagram on a piece of paper that I couldn't make out from where I was standing. I invited him up, sensing he had something. He walked onto the stage, drew a simple figure on the board, then looked at me and shrugged. It was a strange moment. The crowd was pulling for him, I could tell, but his solution was not the generally accepted one. Not even close. But it worked.

So it is with the investigation into creative problem solving. The research itself is out of place in the lab-centric world of psychology, and its conclusions look off-base, not in line with the usual advice we hear, to concentrate, block distractions, and *think*. But they work.

· · ·

What *is* insight, anyway? When is the solution to a problem most likely to jump to mind, and why? What is happening in the mind when that flash of X-ray vision reveals an answer?

For much of our history, those questions have been fodder for poets, philosophers, and clerics. To Plato, thinking was a dynamic interaction between observation and argument, which produced "forms," or ideas, that are closer to reality than the ever-changing things we see, hear, and perceive. To this, Aristotle added the language of logic, a system for moving from one proposition to another—the jay is a bird, and birds have feathers; thus, the jay must have feathers—to discover the essential definitions of things and how they relate. He supplied the vocabulary for what we now call deduction (top-down reasoning, from first principles) and induction (bottom-up, making generalizations based on careful observations), the very foundation of scientific inquiry. In the seventeenth century, Descartes argued that creative problem solving required a retreat inward, to an intellectual realm beyond the senses, where truths could surface like mermaids from the deep.

This kind of stuff is a feast for late night dorm room discussions, or intellectual jousting among doctoral students. It's philosophy, focused on general principles and logical rules, on discovering "truth" and "essential properties." It's also perfectly useless for the student struggling with calculus, or the engineer trying to fix a software problem.

These are more immediate, everyday mental knots, and it was an English intellectual and educator who took the first steps toward answering the most relevant question: What actually happens when the mind is stuck on a problem—and then comes unstuck? What are the stages of solving a difficult problem, and when and how does the critical insight emerge?

Graham Wallas was known primarily for his theories about social advancement, and for cofounding the London School of Economics. In 1926, at the end of his career, he published *The Art of Thought,* a rambling meditation on learning and education that's part memoir, part manifesto. In it, he tells personal stories, drops names, reprints favorite poems. He takes shots at rival intellectuals. He also conducts a wide-ranging analysis of what scientists, poets, novelists, and other creative thinkers, throughout history, had written about how their own insights came about.

Wallas was not content to reprint those self-observations and speculate about them. He was determined to extract a formula of sorts: a *specific series of steps* that each of these thinkers took to reach a solution, a framework that anyone could use. Psychologists at the time had no language to describe these steps, no proper definitions to work with, and thus no way to study this most fundamental human ability. To Wallas, this was appalling. His goal was to invent a common language.

The raw material Wallas cites is fascinating to read. For example, he quotes the French mathematician Henri Poincaré, who had written extensively about his experience trying to work out the properties of a class of forms called Fuchsian functions. "Often when one works at a hard question, nothing good is accomplished at the first attack," Poincaré had observed. "Then one takes a rest, longer or shorter, and sits down anew to the work. During the first half hour, as before, nothing is found, and then all of a sudden the decisive idea presents itself to the mind." Wallas also quotes the German physicist Hermann von Helmholtz, who described how new ideas would bubble up after he'd worked hard on a problem and hit a wall: "Happy ideas come unexpectedly, without effort, like an inspiration," he wrote. "So far as I am concerned, they have never come to me when my mind was fatigued, or when I was at my working table . . . they came particularly readily during the slow ascent of wooded hills on a sunny day." The Belgian psychologist Julien Varendonck traced his insights to daydreaming after a period of work, sensing that "there is something going on in my foreconsciousness which must be in direct relation to my subject. I ought to stop reading for a little while and let it come to the surface."

None of these quotes is especially informative or illuminating by itself. Read too many of them, one after another, without the benefit of expertise in the fields or the precise calculations the person is working out, and they begin to sound a little like postgame comments from professional athletes: *I was in the zone, man; I felt like I was seeing everything in slow motion.*

Wallas saw, however, that the descriptions had an underlying structure. The thinkers had stalled on a particular problem and walked away. They could not see an opening. They had run out of ideas. The crucial insights came after the person had abandoned the work and was deliberately *not* thinking about it. Each insight experience, as it were, seemed to include a series of mental steps, which Wallas called "stages of control."

The first is *preparation:* the hours or days—or longer—that a person spends wrestling with whatever logical or creative knot he or she faces. Poincaré, for example, spent fifteen days trying to prove that Fuchsian functions could not exist, an extensive period of time given his expertise and how long he'd played with the ideas before sitting down to construct his proof. "Every day I seated myself at my work table, stayed an hour or two, tried a great number of combinations and reached no result," he wrote. Preparation includes not only understanding the specific problem that needs solving and the clues or instructions at hand; it means working to a point where you've exhausted all your ideas. You're not stalled, in other words. You're stuck—ending preparation.

The second stage is *incubation,* which begins when you put aside a problem. For Helmholtz, incubation began when he abandoned his work for the morning and continued as he took his walk in the woods, deliberately *not* thinking about work. For others, Wallas found, it occurred overnight, or during a meal, or when out with friends.

Some mental machinations were clearly occurring during this downtime, Wallas knew, and they were crucially important. Wallas was a psychologist, not a mind reader, but he ventured a guess about what was happening: "Some kind of internal mental process," he wrote, "is operating that associates new information with past information. A type of internal reorganization of the information seems to be going on without the individual being directly aware of it." That is to say, the mind works on the problem *off-line*, moving around the pieces it has in hand and adding one or two it has in reserve but didn't think to use at first. One way to think of this is in terms of a weekend handiwork project. There you are, for example, replacing an old, broken door handle and casing with a new one. It looks like an easy job, but there's a problem: The casing sits off-center, the bolt and latch don't line up right. You don't want to cut new holes, that'll ruin the door; you futz and futz and see it's not going to happen. You give up and break for lunch, and suddenly think . . . wait, why not use the *old* casing, put the new hardware in that? You threw the old casing away and suddenly remembered you still had it—in the garbage.

That's the general idea, at least, and in Wallas's conception, incubation has several components. One is that it's subconscious. We're not aware it's happening. Another is that the elements of the problem (the Pencil Problem, for example, presented at the school) are being assembled, taken apart, and reassembled. At some point "past information," perhaps knowledge about the properties of triangles we hadn't initially recalled, is braided in.

The third stage of control is called *illumination*. This is the aha! moment, the moment when the clouds part and the solution appears all at once. We all know that feeling, and it's a good one. Here's Poincaré again, on the Fuchsian functions problem giving up its secrets:

"One evening, contrary to my custom, I drank black coffee and could not sleep. Ideas rose in crowds; I felt them collide until pairs interlocked, so to speak, making a stable combination. By the next morning . . . I had only to write out the results."

The fourth and final stage in the paradigm is *verification,* checking to make sure those results, indeed, work.

Wallas's principal contribution was his definition of incubation. He did not see this as a passive step, as a matter of the brain resting and returning "fresh." He conceived of incubation as a less intense, subconscious continuation of the work. The brain is playing with concepts and ideas, pushing some to the side, fitting others together, as if absentmindedly working on a jigsaw puzzle. We don't see the result of that work until we sit down again and notice an entire corner of the jigsaw puzzle is now complete—revealing a piece of the picture that then tells us how to work with the remaining pieces. In a sense, the letting go allows people to get out of their own way, giving the subconscious a chance to toil on its own, without the conscious brain telling it where to go or what to do.

Wallas didn't say how long incubation should last. Nor did he specify what kinds of downtime activity—walks, naps, bar-hopping, pleasure reading, cooking—were best. He didn't try to explain, in scientific terms, what might be happening in our brains during incubation, either. The goal wasn't to lay out a research agenda, but to establish a vocabulary, to "discover how far the knowledge accumulated by modern psychology can be made useful for the improvement of the thought-processes of a working thinker." He expressed a modest hope that his book could induce others "to explore the problem with greater success than my own."

He had no idea.

. . .

The subsequent study of creative problem solving was not your typical white-coated lab enterprise. In the early days, in fact, it was more like shop class. To study how people solve problems, and to do so rigorously, psychologists needed to devise truly novel problems. This wasn't easy. Most of us grow up on a steady diet of riddles, jokes, wordplay, and math problems. We have a deep reservoir of previous experience to draw on. To test problem solving in the purest sense, then, scientists needed something completely different— ideally, not "academic" at all. So they settled on puzzles that demanded the manipulation not of symbols but of common household objects. As a result their labs looked less like labs than your grandfather's garage.

One of the more inventive of these shop class labs belonged to the University of Michigan psychologist Norman Maier, who was determined to describe the mental machinations that directly precede seeing a solution. In a 1931 experiment, Maier recruited sixty-one participants and brought them into a large room one at a time. Inside, each participant found tables, chairs, and an assortment of tools, including several clamps, a pair of pliers, a metal pole, and an extension cord. Two ropes hung from the ceiling to the floor, one in the middle of the room and the other about fifteen feet away next to a wall. "Your problem is to tie the ends of those two ropes together," they were told. The participants quickly discovered that it wasn't possible to grab one rope and simply walk over and grab the other; it didn't reach far enough. Maier then explained that they were free to use any object in the room, in any manner they chose, to tie the two together.

The puzzle had four solutions, some more obvious than others.

The first was to tie one rope to a chair and then walk the other rope over. Maier put this in the "easy" category. He considered two others slightly more difficult: Tie the extension cord to one of the ropes to make it long enough to reach, or use the pole to pull one rope to the other. The fourth solution was to swing the rope in the middle of the room like a pendulum and catch it as it neared the wall. Maier considered this the most advanced solution, because in order to make it happen you had to tie something heavy (like the pliers) to the rope so it would swing far enough.

After ten minutes, 40 percent of the students had landed on all four solutions without any help. But it was the remaining 60 percent that Maier was interested in: those who got at least one of the possibilities but not the hardest one, the weighted pendulum. At the ten-minute mark, they were stumped. They told Maier they'd run out of ideas, so he gave them a few minutes' break. In Wallas's terminology, these students were *incubating*, and Maier wanted to figure out what exactly was happening during this crucial period of time. Did the fourth solution appear as a completed whole? Or did it reveal itself in stages, growing out of a previous idea?

To find out, Maier decided to nudge the stumped students in the direction of the pendulum solution himself. After the break, he stood up and walked toward the window, deliberately brushing against the rope in the center of the room, causing it to swing ever-so-slightly, taking care to do so in full sight of the participants. Within two minutes, almost all of the participants were creating a pendulum.

When the experiment was over, Maier asked them how they arrived at the fourth answer. A few said that they'd had a vague notion to move the rope somehow, and the hint simply completed the thought. The solution appeared to them in stages, that is, and Maier's nudge made it click. Nothing new in that, we've all been there. Think of the game show *Wheel of Fortune*, where each letter fills in a blank of a common phrase. We feel ourselves nearing a solution, letter by letter, and know exactly which letter lights the lamp.

The rest of the group's answers, however, provided the real payoff. Most said that the solution appeared in a flash, and that they didn't get any hints at all—even though they clearly had. "I just realized the cord would swing if I fastened a weight to it," one said. The solution came from a previous physics class, said another. Were these participants just covering their embarrassment? Not likely, Maier argued. "The perception of the solution of a problem is like the perceiving of a hidden figure in a puzzle-picture," he wrote. "The hint was not experienced because the sudden experience of the solution dominated consciousness." Put another way, the glare of insight was so bright, it obscured the factors that led to it.

Maier's experiment is remembered because he'd shown that incubation is often—perhaps entirely—subconscious. The brain is scanning the environment, outside of conscious awareness, looking for clues. It was Maier who provided that clue in this experiment, of course, and it was a good one. The implication, however, was that the incubating brain is sensitive to any information in the environment that might be relevant to a solution: the motion of a pendulum clock, a swing set visible through the window, the swaying motion of the person's own arm.

Life is not always so generous with hints, clearly, so Maier hadn't completely explained incubation. People routinely generate creative solutions when no clues are available at all: with their eyes closed, in basement study rooms, in tucked-away cubicles. Successful incubation, then, must rely on other factors as well. Which ones? You can't ask people what they are, because the action is all offstage, and there's no easy way to pull back the curtain.

But what if you—you, the scientist—could block people from seeing a creative solution, in a way that was so subtle it went unnoticed. And what if you could also discreetly *remove* that obstacle, increasing the odds that the person saw the answer? Would that reveal anything about this hidden incubation? Is it even possible?

A young German psychologist named Karl Duncker thought so. Duncker was interested in how people became "unblocked" when trying to crack a problem requiring creative thinking, too, and he'd read Maier's study. In that paper, remember, Maier had concluded, "The perception of the solution of a problem is *like the perceiving of a hidden figure in a puzzle-picture.*" Duncker was familiar with picture puzzles. While Maier was conducting his experiments, Duncker was studying in Berlin under Max Wertheimer, one of the founders of the Gestalt school of psychology. Gestalt—"shape," or "form" in German—theory held that people perceive objects, ideas, and patterns whole, before summing their component parts. For example, to construct a visual image of the world—i.e., to see—the brain does a lot more than piece together the patches of light streaming through the eyes. It applies a series of assumptions: Objects are cohesive; surfaces are uniformly colored; spots that move together are part of the same object. These assumptions develop early in childhood and allow us to track an object—a baseball, say—when it disappears momentarily in the glare of the sun, or to recognize a scattering of moving spots behind a thicket of bushes as our lost dog. The brain "fills in" the form behind the bushes, which in turn affects how we perceive the spots.

Gestalt psychologists theorized that the brain does similar things with certain types of puzzles. That is, it sees them as a whole—it constructs an "internal representation"—based on built-in assumptions. When I first saw the Pencil Problem, for instance, I pictured an equilateral triangle on a flat plane, as if drawn on a piece of paper, and immediately began arranging the remaining pencils around that. My whole life, I'd worked geometry problems on paper; why should this be any different? I made an assumption—that the pencils lie in the same plane—and that "representation" determined not only how I thought about possible solutions, it also determined how I interpreted the given *instructions*. Many riddles exploit just this kind of automatic bias.*

Duncker suspected that Gestalt-like biases—those "mental representations"—could block people from seeing solutions. His innovation was to create puzzles with built-in—and removable—

---

*Here's a famous one that used to crease the eyebrows of my grandparents' generation: A doctor in Boston has a brother who is a doctor in Chicago, but the doctor in Chicago doesn't have a brother at all. How is that possible? Most people back then just assumed that any doctor must be a man, and thus came up with tangled family relations based on that mental representation. The answer, of course, is that the doctor in Boston is a woman.

"curtains," using everyday objects like boxes, boards, books, and pliers. The best known of these was the so-called candle problem. In a series of experiments, Duncker had subjects enter a room— alone—that contained chairs and a table. On this table were a hammer, a pair of pliers, and other tools, along with paper clips, pieces of paper, tape, string, and small boxes filled with odds and ends. One contained thumbtacks; another contained small candles, like you'd see on a birthday cake; others had buttons, or matches. The assignment: fasten three of the candles to the door, at eye height, so they could be lighted, using anything from the table. Each participant was given ten minutes to complete the assignment.

Most tried a few things, like pinning the candles to the door with the tacks, or fastening them with tape, before stalling out. But Duncker found that the success rate shot way up if he made one small adjustment: taking the tacks, matches, and other items *out* of the boxes. When the boxes were sitting on the table, empty, subjects saw that they could fasten those to the door with tacks, creating miniplatforms on which to mount the candles. Duncker hadn't changed the instructions or the available materials one bit. Yet by emptying the boxes, he'd altered their mental representation. They were no longer merely *containers*, incidental to the problem at hand; they were seen as available for use. In Duncker's terminology, when the boxes were full, they were "functionally fixed." It was as if people didn't see them at all.

This idea of fixedness infects our perceptions of many problems we encounter. We spend five minutes rifling through drawers searching for a pair of scissors to open a package when the keys in our pocket could do the job just as well. Mystery novelists are virtuosos at creating fixed ideas about characters, subtly prompting us to rule out the real killer until that last act (Agatha Christie's *The Murder of Roger Ackroyd* is a particularly devious specimen of this). Fixedness is what makes the SEQUENC_ puzzle a puzzle at all: We make an automatic assumption—that the "_" symbol represents an empty space, a *platform* for a letter—and it's hard to shake that assumption precisely because we're not even aware that we've made it.

Duncker ran comparison trials with all sorts of puzzles similar to the candle problem and concluded, "Under our experimental conditions, the object which is not fixed is almost twice as easily found as the object which is fixed." The same principle applies, to some extent, in Maier's pendulum experiment. Yes, the people trying to solve that problem first had to think of swinging the rope. Then, however, they had to devise a way to swing the rope far enough, by attaching the pliers. The pliers are pliers, a tool for squeezing things—until they become a weight for the pendulum. Until they become unfixed.

Between them, Maier and Duncker had discovered two mental operations that aid incubation, picking up clues from the environment, and breaking fixed assumptions, whether about the use of pliers, or the gender of a doctor. Here's the rub: They had demonstrated those properties by helping their stumped subjects along with hints. Most of us don't have a psychologist on call, ready to provide deskside incubation assistance whenever we're stuck. We've got to make it happen on our own. The question is, how?

• • •

You're shipwrecked. You swim and swim until finally you wash up on a desert island, a spit of sand no more than a mile around. As you stagger to your feet and scan the coastline, you realize: You've read about this place. It's the Isle of Pukool, famous for its strange caste system. Members of the highest caste never tell the truth; members of the lowest always do; and those in the middle are sometimes honest and sometimes not. Outwardly, the castes are indistinguishable. Your only chance of survival is to reach the hundred-foot Tower of Insight, a holy site of refuge where you can see for miles and send out a distress signal. You follow a winding footpath and arrive at the one intersection on the island, where three Pukoolians are lounging in the heat. You have two questions to ask (Pukool custom, you know) to find your way to that tower.

What do you ask?

I like this puzzle for several reasons. It captures the spirit of insight in a visceral way, for one. At first glance, it seems hairy—it echoes a famous problem in math logic, involving two guards and a man-eating lion*—yet absolutely no math expertise is required. If anything, math expertise is likely to get in the way. A five-year-old can solve it. Better still, we can use it as a way to think about the most recent research on incubation and problem solving, which has branched out like a climbing vine since its duct-tape-and-thumbtack days.

To review, Wallas's definition of incubation is a break that begins at the moment we hit an impasse and stop working on a problem directly, and ends with a breakthrough, the aha! insight. Maier and Duncker shone a light on what occurs mentally during incubation, what nudges people toward solutions. The question that then began to hang over the field in the last half of the twentieth century was *how*. Under what circumstances is incubation most likely to produce that aha! moment in real life? Wallas, Maier, and Duncker had incorporated breaks into their theories, but none specified how long of a break was ideal, or which *kind* of break was best. Should we hike in the woods, like Helmholtz? Go jogging for forty-five minutes? Stare into space? Some people prefer a nap, others a videogame. And there are students—I wish I were one of them—who will break from the knotty calculation they're stuck on and turn to their history reading, a different species of break altogether. The religious reformer

---

*You find yourself in a stadium, in front of a crowd, a pawn in a cruel life-or-death game. The stadium has two closed doors, a guard standing in front of each one. All you know is that behind one door is a hungry lion, and behind the other is a path out of the stadium—escape. One guard always tells the truth, and the other always lies, but you don't know which is which. You have one question you can ask of either guard to save your life. What's the question?

Martin Luther is said to have had some of his deepest insights on the toilet, as did the prolific French essayist Michel de Montaigne. Should we be parking ourselves there when trying to incubate?

To try to answer these kinds of questions, psychologists have used old-fashioned trial and error. In more than one hundred experiments over the past fifty years, they have tested scores of combinations of puzzles, incubation durations, and types of study breaks. For instance, are people able to solve more anagrams when they take a five-minute break to play a videogame, or when they take a twenty-minute break to read? Daydreaming for a few minutes might be better than both, one study found; so might a Ping-Pong match. The most productive type of break might change entirely with other kinds of puzzles—riddles, rebus diagrams, spatial problems—and then change again when hints are given. This shifting, multidimensional experience is what scientists are trying to characterize in labs. One well-known experiment will illustrate how they do so.

This experiment, conducted by two psychologists at Texas A&M University named Steven Smith (whom we've met before) and Steven Blankenship, used a simple word puzzle called a Remote Associates Test, or RAT. The subjects were given three words—"trip," "house," and "goal," for example—and the challenge was to find a fourth that completed a compound word with each. (*Field* was the solution to this one: "field trip," "field house," and "field goal.") Smith and Blankenship chose these puzzles in part because they could easily manipulate the level of difficulty by providing good hints, like "sports" for the example above (two of them are sports-related, and all you need is to find one and try it for the others) or bad hints, in the form of wrong answers, like "road," which works with "trip" and "house" but not "goal." The first kind of hint is akin to Maier's swinging rope. The second is like Duncker's filled boxes, creating a level of fixedness that is hard to overcome.

This experiment used the second kind, the bad clue. Smith and Blankenship wanted to know whether a short incubation break affects people differently when they're given bad hints—when they're "fixed," if you'll excuse the expression—versus when they're not. They recruited thirty-nine students and gave them twenty RAT puzzles each. The students were split into two groups. Half were given puzzles that had misleading words in italics next to the main clues (DARK *light*... SHOT *gun*... SUN *moon*), and the other half worked on the same puzzles, but without words next to the clues (DARK ... SHOT ... SUN). Both groups had ten minutes to solve as many puzzles as they could, and neither group did very well. Those who worked on the fixed ones solved two, on average, compared to five for the unfixed group.

The psychologists then gave their participants another ten minutes to work on the puzzles they hadn't solved the first time through. This time around, each group was subdivided: half took the retest immediately, and the other half got a five-minute break, during which they read a science fiction story. So: Two groups, one fixed and one not. Two conditions within each group, incubation and no incubation.

The result? The incubation break worked—but only for those who got the bad clues. They cracked about twice as many of their unsolved puzzles as the unfixed group who got a break.

The authors attributed the finding to what they called "selective forgetting." A fixating (misleading) word temporarily blocks other possible answers, they argued, but "as more time elapses, after the initial failed attempts, the retrieval block may wear off." It's as if the students' brains were temporarily frozen by the bad hints and the five-minute break allowed for some thawing out. This occurs all the time in normal daily life, most obviously when we get unclear directions—"the pharmacy is right at the end of Fowler Road, you can't miss it"—and we arrive at the given spot, backtracking, circling, rechecking the street names: no pharmacy. We're sure we're missing it somehow. Finally, we sit down on a bench, stare at the birds for a few minutes, and it hits us: *Oh, wait: maybe he meant the* other *end of*

Fowler Road. Or, the pharmacy moved. Or he has no idea what he's talking about. The initial assumption—the pharmacy must be around here, somewhere—no longer has a stranglehold on our mind. Other options have floated in. Romantic entanglements are another classic example: We become infatuated, we think we're in love, but time loosens the grip of the fixation. We come to see exasperating flaws. Maybe she's not the one, after all. What was I thinking?

In previous chapters, we've seen how forgetting can aid learning actively, as a filter, and passively, allowing subsequent study to ramp up memory. Here it is again, helping in another way, with creative problem solving.

As Smith and Blankenship were quick to note, selective forgetting is only one possible explanation for incubation, *in these specific circumstances* (RATs, fixed words, five-minute reading break). And theirs was just one experiment. Others have produced slightly different results: Longer breaks are better than shorter ones; playing a videogame is as good as reading; writing may help incubation for certain kinds of problems, such as spatial ones like the Pencil Problem. In each case—in each specific study—scientists have floated various theories about what's happening in the buildup to that aha! moment. Maybe it's selective forgetting. Maybe it's a reimagining of the problem. Maybe it's simple free-associating, the mind having had time to wander in search of ideas. No one knows for sure which process is the most crucial one, and it's likely that no one ever will. Our best guess? They all kick in at some level.

What does that mean for us, then? How do we develop a study strategy, if scores of experiments are saying various, often contradictory, things?

To try to make sense of the cacophony, let's return to the Isle of Pukool. How to find our Tower of Insight? The three Pukoolians are pointing in different directions, after all. It's hard to know who's being honest and who's not.

What to do?

Easy. *Look up.* The tower is one hundred feet tall, and the island is flat, and the size of a city park. No complex math logic required: The tower is visible for miles. Try this on a group of friends when they're in the mood. You'll notice that some people see the answer right away, and others never come close. I didn't come close. I spent hours concocting absurd, overly complex questions like, "Which way would those two fellow islanders say that you would say . . . ?" I wrote out the various possible answers on paper, using a math notation I'd forgotten I knew. When I finally heard the solution, it seemed somehow unfair, a cheap trick. On the contrary. Taking a step back and *looking around*—seeing if we've used all the available information; attempting to shake our initial assumptions and start from scratch; doing a mental inventory—is a fitting metaphor for what we have to do to make sense of the recent work on incubation. Looking at each study individually is like engaging the Pukoolians one-on-one, or staring so closely at a stereogram that the third dimension never emerges. You can't see the forest for the trees.

Thankfully, scientists have a method of stepping back to see the bigger picture, one they use when trying to make sense of a large number of varied results. The idea is to "pool" all the findings, positive and negative, and determine what the bulk of the evidence is saying. It's called meta-analysis, and it sometimes tells a clearer story than any single study, no matter how well done. In 2009, a pair of psychologists at Lancaster University in the United Kingdom did precisely this for insight-related research, ransacking the available literature—even hunting down unpublished manuscripts—and producing a high-quality, conservative meta-analysis. Ut Na Sio and Thomas C. Ormerod included thirty-seven of the most rigorous studies and concluded that the incubation effect is real, all right, but that it does not work the same in all circumstances.

Sio and Ormerod divided incubation breaks into three categories.

One was relaxing, like lying on the couch listening to music. Another was mildly active, like surfing the Internet. The third was highly engaging, like writing a short essay or digging into other homework. For math or spatial problems, like the Pencil Problem, people benefit from any of these three; it doesn't seem to matter which you choose. For linguistic problems like RAT puzzles or anagrams, on the other hand, breaks consisting of mild activity—videogames, solitaire, TV—seem to work best.

Sio and Ormerod found that longer incubation periods were better than short ones, although "long" in this world means about twenty minutes and "short" closer to five minutes—a narrow range determined by nothing more than the arbitrary choices of researchers. They also emphasized that people don't benefit from an incubation break *unless they have reached an impasse.* Their definition of "impasse" is not precise, but most of us know the difference between a speed bump and a brick wall. Here's what matters: Knock off and play a videogame too soon and you get nothing.

It's unlikely that scientists will ever give us specific incubation times for specific kinds of problems. That's going to vary depending on who we are and the way we work, individually. No matter. We can figure out how incubation works for ourselves by trying out different lengths of time and activities. We already take breaks from problem solving anyway, most of us, flopping down in front of the TV for a while or jumping on Facebook or calling a friend—we take breaks and feel guilty about it. The science of insight says not only that our guilt is misplaced. It says that many of those breaks *help* when we're stuck.

When I'm stuck, I sometimes walk around the block, or blast some music through the headphones, or wander the halls looking for someone to complain to. It depends on how much time I have. As a rule, though, I find the third option works best. I lose myself in the kvetching, I get a dose of energy, I return twenty minutes or so later, and I find that the intellectual knot, whatever it was, is a little looser.

The weight of this research turns the creeping hysteria over the dangers of social media and distracting electronic gadgets on its head. The fear that digital products are undermining our ability to think is misplaced. To the extent that such diversions steal our attention from learning that requires continuous focus—like a lecture, for instance, or a music lesson—of course they get in our way. The same is true if we spend half our study time on Facebook, or watching TV. The exact opposite is true, however, when we (or our kids) are stuck on a problem requiring insight and are motivated to solve it. In this case, distraction is not a hindrance: It's a valuable weapon.

As for the kid in the auditorium on the morning of my presentation, I can't know for sure what it was that helped him solve the Pencil Problem. He clearly studied the thing when I drew those six pencils side by side on the chalkboard—they all did. He didn't get it right away; he was stuck. And he had several types of incubation opportunities. He was in the back with his friends, the most restless part of the auditorium, where kids were constantly distracting one another. He got the imposed break created by the SEQUENC_ puzzle, which held the audience's attention for a few minutes. He also had the twenty minutes or so that passed after several students had drawn their first (and fixed) ideas, attempting to put all the triangles onto a flat plane. That is, he had all three types of the breaks that Sio and Ormerod described: relaxation, mild activity, and highly engaging activity. This was a spatial puzzle; any one of those could have thrown the switch, and having three is better than having just one, or two.

Let's reset the problem, then: Given six identical pencils, create four equilateral triangles, with one pencil forming the side of each triangle. If you haven't solved it already, try again now that you've been at least somewhat occupied by reading this chapter.

Got the answer yet? I'm not going to give it away, I've provided too many hints already. But I will show you what the eleven-year-old scratched on the board:

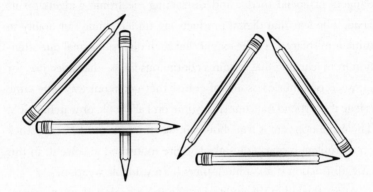

Take that, Archimedes! That's a stroke of mad kid-genius you won't see in any study or textbook, nor in early discussions of the puzzle, going back more than a hundred years. He incubated that one all on his own.

Chapter Seven

Quitting Before You're Ahead

The Accumulating Gifts of Percolation

think of incubation, at least as scientists have described it, as a drug. Not just any drug, either, but one that's fast-acting, like nicotine, and remains in the system for a short period of time. Studies of incubation, remember, have thus far looked almost exclusively at short breaks, of five to twenty minutes. Those quick hits are of primary interest when investigating how people solve problems that, at their core, have a single solution that is not readily apparent. Geometric proofs, for example. Philosophical logic. Chemical structures. The Pencil Problem. Taking an "incubation pill" here and there, when stuck, is powerful learning medicine, at least when dealing with problems that have right and wrong answers.

It is hardly a cure-all, though. Learning is not reducible to a series of discrete puzzles or riddles, after all; it's not a track meet where we only have to run sprints. We have to complete decathlons, too—all those assignments that require not just one solution or skill but many, strung together over time. Term papers. Business plans. Construction blueprints. Software platforms. Musical compositions, short stories, poems. Working through such projects is not like puzzle solving, where *the* solution suddenly strikes. No, completing these is more like navigating a labyrinth, with only occasional glimpses of which way to turn. And doing it well means stretching incubation out—sometimes way, way out.

To solve messier, protracted problems, we need more than a fast-acting dose, a short break here and there. We need an *extended-release* pill. Many of us already take longer breaks, after all—an hour, a day, a week, more—when working through some tangled project or other. We step away repeatedly, not only when we're tired but often because we're stuck. Part of this is likely instinctive. We're hoping that the break helps clear away the mental fog so that we can see a path out of the thicket.

The largest trove of observations on longer-term incubation comes not from scientists but artists, particularly writers. Not surprisingly, their observations on the "creative process" can be a little precious, even discouraging. "My subject enlarges itself, becomes methodized and defined, and the whole, though it be very long, stands almost complete and finished in my mind, so that I can survey it, like a fine picture or a beautiful statue, at a glance," reads a letter attributed to Mozart. That's a nice trick if you can pull it off. Most creative artists cannot, and they don't hesitate to say so. Here's the novelist Joseph Heller, for example, describing the circumstances in which valuable ideas are most likely to strike. "I have to be alone. A bus is good. Or walking the dog. Brushing my teeth was marvelous—it was especially so for *Catch-22*. Often when I am very tired, just before going to bed, while washing my face and brushing my teeth, my mind gets very clear . . . and produces a line for the next day's work, or some idea way ahead. I don't get my best ideas while actually writing."

Here's another, from the poet A. E. Housman, who would typically take a break from his work in the trough of his day to relax. "Having drunk a pint of beer at luncheon—beer is a sedative to the brain and my afternoons are the least intellectual portion of my life—I would go out for a walk of two or three hours. As I went along, thinking of nothing in particular, only looking at things around me following the progress of the seasons, there would flow into my mind, with sudden unaccountable emotion, a line or two of verse, sometimes a whole stanza at once, accompanied, not preceded, by a vague notion of the poem which they were destined to form part of." Housman was careful to add that it was *not* as if the entire poem wrote itself. There were gaps to be filled, he said, gaps "that had to be taken in hand and completed by the mind, which was apt to be a matter of trouble and anxiety, involving trial and disappointment, and sometimes ending in failure."

Okay, so I cherry-picked these quotes. But I cherry-picked them for a reason: because they articulate so clearly an experience that thousands of creative types have described less precisely since the dawn of introspection. Heller and Housman deliver a clear blueprint. Creative leaps often come during downtime that follows a period of immersion in a story or topic, and they often come piecemeal, not in any particular order, and in varying size and importance. The creative leap can be a large, organizing idea, or a small, incremental step, like finding a verse, recasting a line, perhaps changing a single word. This is true not just for writers but for designers, architects, composers, mechanics—anyone trying to find a workaround, or to turn a flaw into a flourish. For me, new thoughts seem to float to the surface only when fully cooked, one or two at a time, like dumplings in a simmering pot.

Am I putting myself in the same category as Housman and Heller? I am. I'm putting you there, too, whether you're trying to break the chokehold of a 2.5 GPA or you're sitting on a full-ride offer from Oxford. Mentally, our creative experiences are more similar than they are different.*

---

* I'll leave it to others to explain Mozart.

This longer-term, cumulative process is distinct enough from the short-term incubation we described in the last chapter that it warrants another name. Let's call it *percolation*. Let's take it as given that it exists, and that it's a highly individual experience. We can't study percolation in any rigorous way, and even if we could—("Group A, put down your pen and go take a walk in park; Group B, go have a pint of ale")—there's no telling whether what works for Heller or Housman is right for anyone else. What we can do is mine psychological science for an explanation of how percolation must work. We can then use *that* to fashion a strategy for creative projects. And creative is the key word here. By our definition, percolation is for building something that was not there before, whether it's a term paper, a robot, an orchestral piece, or some other labyrinthine project.

To deconstruct how that building process unfolds, we'll venture into a branch of science known as social psychology, which seeks to elucidate the dynamics of motivation and goal formation, among other things. Unlike learning scientists, who can test their theories directly (with students, trying to learn), social psychologists depend on simulations of social contexts. Their evidence, then, is more indirect, and we must keep that in mind as we consider their findings. But that evidence, when pieced together, tells a valuable story.

• • •

Berlin in the 1920s was the cultural capital of the West, a convergence of artistic, political, and scientific ideas. The Golden Twenties, the restless period between the wars, saw the rise of German Expressionism, the Bauhaus school of design, and the theater of Bertolt Brecht. Politics was a topic of intense debate. In Moscow, a revolutionary named Vladimir Lenin had formed a confederation of states under a new political philosophy, Marxism; dire economic circumstances across Germany were giving rise to calls for major reforms.

The world of science was tilting on its axis, too. New ideas were coming quickly, and they were not small ones. An Austrian neurologist named Sigmund Freud had invented a method of guided free association, called psychoanalysis, which appeared to open a window on the human soul. A young physicist in Berlin named Albert Einstein—then director of the Kaiser Wilhelm Institute for Physics—had published his theories of relativity, forever redefining the relationship between space, time, and gravity. Physicists like Max Born and Werner Heisenberg were defining a new method (called quantum mechanics) to understand the basic properties of matter. Anything seemed possible, and one of the young scientists riding this intellectual updraft was a thirty-seven-year-old psychologist at the University of Berlin named Kurt Lewin. Lewin was a star in the emerging field of social psychology, who among other things was working on a theory of behavior, based on how elements of personality—diffidence, say, or aggressive tendencies—played out in different social situations.

Lewin was a charismatic, open-minded man who attracted a loyal following of younger students, whom he often met, after hours, at a café near campus. It was a less formal setting than his office, a place to brainstorm over coffee or beer, and one afternoon he noticed something curious. Lewin was meeting with a student of his, Bluma Zeigarnik, a young Lithuanian in search of a research project. On that afternoon one of the two—accounts vary—noticed something about the café's waiters: They never wrote down orders. They kept them in their head, adding items mentally— . . . another espresso . . . a cup of tea . . . a slice of kuchen . . . —until the bill was paid.

Yet once the bill was paid—if, *after* paying, you questioned what was on the tab—they'd have forgotten the entire order. No recollection at all. It was as if, once that order was settled, the waiter's mind checked off the box and moved on, dropping the entire experience from memory. Lewin and Zeigarnik both knew that this wasn't a matter of orders falling out of what scientists call short-term memory, the thirty seconds or so during which we can hold, say, a phone number in mind. The waiters could remember orders for a half hour, sometimes longer.

What was going on here mentally?

Lewin and Zeigarnik came up with a hypothesis: Perhaps unfinished jobs or goals linger in memory longer than finished ones. If nothing else, Zeigarnik now had her research project. She put the question more specifically: What's the difference in memory between an interrupted activity and an uninterrupted one?

She recruited 164 students, teachers, and children to take part in an experiment and told them they'd be given a series of assignments "to complete as rapidly and correctly as possible." The assignments came one at a time and consisted of tasks like making a box out of a sheet of cardboard, sculpting a dog out of clay, or solving a word puzzle. Most of the subjects could complete them in three to five minutes—when allowed to, that is. Zeigarnik periodically interrupted their work, stopping them in the middle of an assignment and giving them another one to work on instead. The interruptions were random, and without explanation.

At the end—after eighteen to twenty-two assignments, some interrupted and left unfinished and some not—Zeigarnik asked the test subjects to write down as many of those assignments as they could remember. Those lists told the story: On average, participants remembered 90 percent more of the interrupted and unfinished assignments than the ones they'd completed. Not only that, the interrupted and unfinished jobs were at the top of their lists—the first ones they wrote down. The completed ones, if remembered at all, came at the end. "So far as amount of time is concerned, the advantage *should* lie with completed tasks, since a subject who completed a task naturally spent a longer time with it than one who did not," Zeigarnik wrote.

Was it possible, she wondered, that the "shock" of being interrupted makes an experience more memorable?

Zeigarnik performed another version of the study on a new group of participants. This time every assignment the subjects worked on was interrupted. Some of the assignments were completed, after a short break; others were not. The results, however, were nearly identical in one characteristic to the first experiment: People remembered about 90 percent more of the small jobs they *hadn't* finished. Running still more trials, Zeigarnik found that she could maximize the effect of interruption on memory by stopping people at the moment when they were most engrossed in their work. Interestingly, being interrupted at the "worst" time seemed to extend memory the longest. "As everyone knows," Zeigarnik wrote, "it is far more disturbing to be interrupted just before finishing a letter than when one has only begun."

Once people become absorbed in an assignment, they feel an urge to finish, and that urge builds as the job moves closer to completion. "The desire to complete the task may at first have been only a quasi-need," she concluded, "but later, through losing oneself in the task, a genuine need arises."

In 1931, soon after publishing her work on interruption, Zeigarnik moved to Moscow with her husband, Albert, who had taken a position at the Soviet Ministry of Foreign Trade. She secured a job at the prestigious Institute of Higher Nervous Activity. Their good fortune didn't last, however. In 1940, Albert was arrested on charges of spying for Germany and sent to a prison camp in Lubyanka, leaving Bluma in Moscow to manage a job and two young children. She continued to work as a psychologist, gradually cut off ties with Western colleagues to avoid any taint of suspicion, and died in 1988, leaving behind virtually no trace of her research. (A relative, A. V. Zeigarnik, believes she destroyed her papers.)

Yet the implications of her work survived, and then some. The Zeigarnik effect, as it's now known, became a foundational contribution to the study of goals and goal formation.

When we think about goals, we tend to think in terms of dreams.

Restoring a classic car. Living abroad. Starting a business. Writing a novel. Running a marathon. Being a better dad. Finding a stable relationship. For psychologists, however, a goal isn't nearly so grand. A goal is anything we want to possess or achieve and haven't yet, whether it's short-term or long-term, getting a Ph.D. or getting dressed. According to that definition, our heads are full of goals every waking minute, and they're all competing for our attention. Should we walk the dog, or make coffee first? Help Junior pack for camp, or catch up on some work? Go to the gym, or practice Spanish?

Zeigarnik's studies on interruption revealed a couple of the mind's intrinsic biases, or built-in instincts, when it comes to goals. The first is that the act of starting work on an assignment often gives that job the psychological weight of a goal, even if it's meaningless. (The people in her studies were doing things like sculpting a dog from a lump of clay, for heaven's sake; they got nothing out of it but the satisfaction of finishing.) The second is that interrupting yourself when absorbed in an assignment extends its life in memory and—according to her experiments—pushes it to the top of your mental to-do list.

Most interruptions are annoying—especially if it's a busybody neighbor, or the cat needing to be let out, or a telemarketer calling when you're in the middle of an important work assignment. But deliberate *self*-interruption is something else altogether. It's what Dickens did so well in his novels, with cliff-hanger endings for each chapter. Or what TV writers do when closing out one season and priming the audience for the next. The final episode ends with a scream, footsteps in a dark corridor, a relationship unexpectedly soured or kindled.

This kind of interruption creates suspense and, according to the Zeigarnik effect, pushes the unfinished episode, chapter, or project to the top of our minds, leaving us to wonder what comes next. Which is exactly where we want it to be if we're working on something long-term and demanding.

The first element of percolation, then, is that supposed enemy of learning—interruption.

• • •

The Bisaldrop Dubbel Zoute is a Dutch black licorice drop the size of a plug nickel. Bisaldrops are an acquired taste, slightly sweet and very salty, and best served with a cool glass of water. For our purposes, the important thing to know is that Bisals make you thirsty—and fast—which is why a group of scientists in the Netherlands used them in a 2001 experiment to measure the effect of goals on perception. The group, led by the psychologist Henk Aarts at Leiden University, began their trial the way so many scientists do: by lying. Researchers often attempt to disguise a study's true purpose so participants don't just play along or deliberately undermine the results. In this case, Aarts recruited eighty-four undergraduates for what he described as a study of, get this, "how well people can detect letters with their tongue under different taste conditions."

The students were divided into two groups. One group got three Bisaldrops, each branded with a letter. They had a minute to eat each candy and try to name the letter printed on it. The other group—the control group—received no candy at all; they were given instructions to trace three simple figures on paper, a form of busywork that had nothing to do with the study's aim. Afterward, the experimenter led the participants, one at a time, into a room he described as his office, to fill out a one-minute questionnaire on unrelated topics ("What is your favorite activity to relax?" and the like). The questions had nothing to do with the aim of the study, either. The room itself did. It looked like your standard academic office: a small space with a chair and desk, papers, books, pencils, a stack of folders, and a computer. Scattered about were several drink-related items, too—a water bottle, a glass, cups, an empty soda can. After finishing the questionnaire, each participant sat in that office, by him- or herself, for four minutes.

The experimenter then returned and brought the person back to the lab room for a surprise quiz. Each participant was given four minutes to write down as many objects in the office as he or she could remember. By this time, the participants must have been wondering what on earth this had to do with detecting letters with their tongues—let alone science—but they did as they were told. Some recalled only one item, and others a half dozen. Nothing surprising there; some participants were likely daydreaming for those four minutes and others scanning the bookshelves. It was *what* they wrote down that the psychologists were interested in, and that's where a significant difference became clear: The group that had been given the Bisaldrops remembered twice as many drink-related items as the control group. They were thirsty, and that influenced what they noticed in the office and remembered later, even if they weren't aware *why* they recalled those things.

The experiment was a clever demonstration of a fairly straightforward principle of social psychology: Having a goal foremost in mind (in this case, a drink), tunes our perceptions to fulfilling it. And that tuning determines, to some extent, where we look and what we notice. "The results suggest that basic needs and motives cause a heightened perceptual readiness to register environmental cues that are instrumental to satisfying those needs," the authors concluded. "It can foster the reduction of thirst by helping us to detect a can of Coke or a cool glass of beer that would go unnoticed under other circumstances."

On the surface, this is common sense, right? Of *course* we look for a drinking fountain when we're thirsty, or a snack machine when hungry. Keep in mind, though, that the thirsty students in this study were more likely than the others to notice not just bottles of water or cans of soda but *anything* in the room that was drink-related—a cup, a saucer, a bottle cap. Whether they were aware of it or not, their thirst activated a mental network that was scavenging the landscape for anything linked to liquid.

In dozens of studies going back decades, psychologists have shown that this principle of tuned perception applies not only to elemental needs like thirst, but to any goal we hold foremost in mind. This is a familiar experience, too. As soon as we decide to buy a certain brand of handbag or model of smartphone or style of jeans, we begin seeing that product far more often than we had before, in stores, at the mall, walking down the street. I remember the first time this phenomenon occurred to me. I was eleven years old, and I'd just bought my first pair of Converse All-Stars, which were standard issue, way back when, for boys my age. But I didn't want the usual colors, white or black; no, the ones I wanted were green. Bright kelly green. I remember bringing them home and putting them on and going out into the world, and suddenly feeling like, hey, wait a minute: Those sneakers were *everywhere*. I must have counted a half dozen pairs of green ones the first day I wore them. Not only that, I started to notice other, more exotic colors, as well as different styles and laces. Within weeks, I had a detailed mental map of a particular subculture: preteen Converse wearers in 1971 suburban Chicago, a subtle, intricate universe that was previously invisible to me. And I did this without "studying" at all—at least, not in the usual sense.

What does this have to do with finishing a research paper on, say, the Emancipation Proclamation? Everything, actually. Academic pursuits are goals, too, and they can tune our perceptions in the same way that a powerful thirst or a new pair of sneakers can. When we're in the middle of that paper, for example, we're far more attuned to race references all around us. A story about race riots or affirmative action in the media. An offhand comment by a friend. A review of a Lincoln biography in the newspaper. Even the way people of different races arrange themselves at a bar, or on a subway car. "Once a goal becomes activated, it trumps all others and begins to drive our perceptions, our thoughts, our attitudes," as John Bargh, a psychologist at Yale University, told me.

So the question is: How, then, do we most effectively activate that goal?

By interrupting work on it at an important and difficult moment—propelling the assignment, via the Zeigarnik effect, to the top of our mind.

This heightened awareness doesn't always deliver the big "breakthrough" or some golden, clarifying idea for our paper, of course. That's fine. If it provides a detail here or there, a sentence for the introduction, or a simple transition idea, it's free money and it earns interest, incrementally sharpening our acuity so we can recognize bigger ideas—the flashes of clarifying insight—that creative people lust after. As the French microbiologist Louis Pasteur famously put it, "Chance favors the prepared mind." Seeing that quote always made me think, Okay, but how does one prepare for chance? I have a better idea now, thanks to social psychology. I'd put it differently than Pasteur, if less poetically: *Chance feeds the tuned mind.*

My favorite articulation of how this happens comes from the novelist and short story writer Eudora Welty. In a 1972 interview, Welty was asked where her dialogue comes from. "Once you're into a story," she replied, "everything seems to apply—what you hear on the city bus is exactly what your character would say on the page you were writing. Wherever you go, you meet part of your story. I guess you are tuned in for it, and the right things are sort of magnetized—if you can think of your ears as magnets."

What's left unsaid here is that those overheard comments on the bus not only animate a character, they help move the story. The information we pick up isn't merely dumped into a mental ledger of overheard conversation. It also causes a ripple in our thinking about the story, our research paper, our design project, or our big presentation. When working on that paper about the Emancipation Proclamation, we're not only tuned into racial dynamics on the subway car, we're also more aware of our reactions to what we're noticing. This is not an obvious or trivial point. Remember, there's an incredible cacophony of competing thoughts running through our minds at any given time. What we "hear" depends on the demands, distractions, or anxieties of the moment. I am proposing that, in this example, we're better able to hear our internal dialogue about race above that chatter, and that *that* conversation, too, provides fodder for our work.

Can I prove this? No. I don't know how anyone could. But that doesn't mean no one's tried—and made an invisible process visible.

· · ·

Let's return to the classroom, then.

When I was in high school or college, trying to write an essay or research paper, I was forever looking for someone else's thinking to rely on. I would hunt for some article written by an expert that was as similar as possible to the assignment. This perfect "model" essay rarely existed, or I never found it, so I'd end up stringing together quotes and ideas from the articles and books I had looked through. If someone else said it, I figured it must be insightful. In my defense, this isn't all bad. When looking into the emergence of Christianity in ancient Rome, we *should* know who the experts are and what they think. The problem is that, when we're embarking on a research project—especially when we're younger—we don't necessarily know how to identify those intellectual landmarks. Often, we don't even know they exist. Through high school and much of college, I remember longing for someone to tell me how to proceed, sinking into a passive, tentative frame of mind, a fear of embarrassment trumping any real curiosity or conviction. The result was that I rarely consulted the wisdom of the one thinker I had easy access to: myself. I was so busy looking for better, smarter opinions that I had trouble writing—or thinking—with any confidence.

In 1992, a doctoral student in Illinois noticed the same tentative, deferential quality in her students' work. Ronda Leathers Dively, then finishing her degree in English at Illinois State University, was teaching a group of sophomores and juniors how to write for publication in an academic journal, using authoritative sources to make a cogent argument. By the end of the course, however, she was discouraged. She'd asked her students to write six essays of three to five pages, each focusing on a different social, political, or cultural controversy. Hoping for sharply argued, well-informed pieces, Dively instead received what she described as "cut-and-paste summaries of published scholars' work." Most alarming, the work was no better at the end of the semester than at the beginning. That was her fault, not theirs. She was failing them.

Dively decided that the curriculum she followed was preventing percolation (or incubation, as she calls it) from happening. For each essay, the students had only about two weeks to get up to speed on difficult, nuanced topics like waste disposal, the effects of day care on children, and drug legalization. The course, in other words, allowed for no time to meditate on the topics, no real downtime at all.

So Dively decided to throw out the program. She would conduct an experiment of sorts. It would be neither controlled, nor in any way rigorous by scientific standards; this was an undergraduate writing course, not a cognitive psychology lab. Nonetheless, it was a course she could rethink from top to bottom, and she did. The next semester she taught, she scrapped the six-essay structure, the ADHD-like jumping from one topic to another. The course would demand the same amount of writing, but in a very different format. Her students would write one essay, on a single topic, due at the end of the semester. But in the course of their research, they'd have five "prewriting" assignments—all on the experience of doing the research itself. One piece would describe an interview with an expert. Another piece would define a key term and its place in the larger debate (say, landfill dumping in solid waste disposal). A third piece would be a response to a controversial school of thought on their topic. Dively also required them to keep journals along the way, tracking their personal reactions to the sources they were using. Did the articles make sense? Did they agree with the main points? Was this expert or that one consistent in his or her opinions?

The purpose of these steps—the prewriting and the journal entries—was to force students to carry around their topic for the entire semester, and to think about it frequently, if not continually: to percolate, in our terminology. Dively was aware that their final essays would not necessarily be more incisive or readable than her previous class's. More time doesn't always add up to more authoritative writing, and sometimes means sinking deeper into indecision. In this case, however, her students showed her something extra. The biggest improvement, she wrote, was that they took on "an expert persona, an authoritative presence capable of contributing to the scholarly exchange."

At the end of the semester she surveyed her students, asking about the new format. "As time goes by and I find more research, much of the information becomes embedded in me," said one. "Now, I even question certain things which the author claims to be true. I realize I do not have to agree with everything in a professional journal." Another said, "I had a more complete understanding of the material I was dealing with because I was able to ask more questions of myself" in the journal. One student openly scoffed at an article "written for a beginner in environmental health in this somewhat prestigious journal. I would only recommend the reading of this article to someone with almost no knowledge of the subject."

In other words, her students were no longer looking to borrow someone else's opinion. They were working to discover their own.

Again, there's nothing particularly "scientific" about this evidence. It's one teacher's observations of one class. But what Dively did, in effect, was slow down the tape—and in the process reveal how a normally invisible and usually semi- or subconscious process plays out.

She made percolation visible.

Dively's findings might seem anecdotal if they didn't dovetail so well with the more rigorous work of experimental social psychologists. In effect, her preassignments were truncated "steps," a form of self-interruption that kept the final paper foremost in mind, à la Zeigarnik. Having that goal (the paper) continually active—unfinished—sensitized the students' minds consciously and subconsciously to relevant information all around them, like the thirsty participants in Henk Aarts's study. Those are the first two elements of percolation: interruption, and the tuned, scavenging mind that follows. The journal entries provided the third element, conscious reflection. Remember, Dively had the students make regular entries on what they *thought* about the sources they used, the journal articles and interviews. Their thinking evolved, entry by entry, as they accumulated more knowledge.

Assembled into a coherent whole, this research—from Zeigarnik, Aarts, Dively, and other social psychologists who've spent the past decades studying goal fulfillment—takes some of the mystery out of the "creative process." No angel or muse is whispering to anyone here. Percolation is a matter of vigilance, of finding ways to tune the mind so that it collects a mix of external perceptions and internal thoughts that are relevant to the project at hand. We can't know in advance what those perceptions and thoughts will look like—and we don't have to. Like the thirsty students in Aarts's study, the information flows in.

If more fully formed ideas (as opposed to perceptions) seem to arrive "out of the blue," it only means that that mixing happened outside of direct conscious awareness. Among scientists, there's a debate about whether percolation is largely conscious or subconscious, and the answer has interesting theoretical implications. Yet for our purposes, it's beside the point. Me, I tend to agree with the writer Stephen King, who describes percolation as the marinating of ideas "in that place that's not quite the conscious but not quite the subconscious." Either way, we take what we can get, when we get it.

What does this mean for a learning strategy? It suggests that we should start work on large projects as soon as possible and stop when we get stuck, with the confidence that we are initiating percolation, not quitting. My tendency as a student was always to procrastinate on big research papers and take care of the smaller stuff first. Do the easy reading. Clean the kitchen. Check some things off the to-do list. Then, once I finally sat down to face the big beast, I'd push myself frantically toward the finish line and despair if I didn't make it.

Wrong.

Quitting before I'm ahead doesn't put the project to sleep; it keeps it awake. That's Phase 1, and it initiates Phase 2, the period of gathering string, of casual data collecting. Phase 3 is listening to what I *think* about all those incoming bits and pieces. Percolation depends on all three elements, and in that order.

Over the years, I've found that starting in on a labor-intensive project before doing the smaller stuff has an added bonus. Psychologically speaking, it shrinks the job. The project doesn't continue to grow each day. I've already broken the skin and, as a result, the job becomes more manageable; it's easier to sit down and resume working. And even if I can't "get my head around" some concept after a few hours of work (doing integrals in calculus comes to mind), I know that taking a break is only a first step. As one of my favorite professors used to say, "The definition of a mathematician is a person who carries around the concept in their head for long enough that, one day, they sit down and realize that it's familiar."

I see percolation as a means of using procrastination in my favor. When I'm engrossed in a complex assignment, I try to do a little each day, and if I get some momentum in one session, I ride it for a while—and then stop, in the middle of some section, when I'm stalled. I return and complete it the next workday.

Admittedly, we have focused largely on one kind of creating in this chapter—writing—but that's because writers talk about it endlessly and because, in a critical sense, writing about something *is* discovering what you think about it. Yet anyone who becomes a productive artist, builder, designer, or scientist engages in similar psychological processes to refine and finish their work and often have a hard time turning them off. They allow percolation to happen instinctively, because they've discovered through experience that a tuned mind usually delivers the goods, or at least some of the goods. (Remember the poet A. E. Housman's quote, that there are gaps to be filled, gaps "that had to be taken in hand and completed by the mind." You get pieces.) Knowing just that will help you move through complex creative projects with much more confidence—and much less despair.

Chapter Eight

Being Mixed Up

Interleaving as an Aid to Comprehension

A t a certain age—nine, ten, eleven, we were all there once—most of us are capable of the kind of blind devotion it takes to master some single, obscure skill that we've decided is central to our identity. Maybe it's drawing a horse, or copying a guitar solo, or dribbling a basketball behind our back. Maybe it's an ollie, that elementary skateboarding move, a kind of standing jump where the feet never leave the board. We don't need a manual to tell us what to do, we just do it. Repeatedly. Head-down, nose-to-the-grindstone, just like we've been told. A belief in repetition is in the cultural water supply, in every how-to-succeed manual and handbook, every sports and business autobiography. There's a reason that coaches, music instructors, and math teachers often run their students through drills, followed by more drills: Perform one hundred A-minor scales (or free throws, or wedge shots) in an afternoon and you will see progress. Do another two hundred and you'll see more still.

Our faith in repetition never leaves us, not entirely. I sometimes think—if only I could channel my childlike devotion today when trying to learn something new. I'd channel it into the piano, or genetics, or mechanics. I'd practice like a machine, one skill at a time, until each one was automatic, driven deep into the marrow. Play Elgar, save some lives, fix the car when it broke down. At some level, I sort of believe it could still happen, given enough time. Some psychologists and writers have even tried to quantify that time. The path to exceptional performance, they argue, is through practice: ten thousand hours of it, to be exact. The gist of that rule is hard to resist, even if the number itself is arbitrary, because we read it in terms of *repetition*, as well as quantity. As the common exhortation goes: *Don't practice until you get it right. Practice until you can't get it wrong.*

Then I remember. I remember what happened in my own life when I did put in the time.

I was Mr. Repetition as a kid. As a student, as a music student, as an athlete. I was the one who did three hundred ollies in an afternoon, never quite getting it right. There I was, scraping up the driveway, only to look up and see some kid who didn't have anywhere near my determination roll by, popping clean jumps without even thinking about it. Same for the behind-the-back dribble, the guitar solo, the inside-skate stop in hockey. I wanted it so bad, I'd throw myself into practicing but somehow never got *good*—while other kids who weren't putting in nearly the same amount of dedicated time picked up the skills without seeming to sweat the details. Were they just . . . *naturals*? Did they have private teachers? Secret handshakes? I had no idea. I blamed my own lack of native gifts and kept looking for something that would come easily. What I never did was stop to ask whether my approach to practice was, in fact, the right one.

Nor did anyone else, at least not back in the early 1970s. At that time, scientists thought about practice in the same way we all did: the more, the better. To put it in precise terms, psychologists argued that any variation in the practice schedule that makes the target skill—whether in skating, algebra, or grammar—more immediate, more frequent, and more accurate improves learning. Brute-force repetition does that, and everyone who truly masters a skill has done at least some of it, usually lots. That's the part they tend to remember later on, too—the repetition—and not other innovations or alterations they might have incorporated along the way.

One of the first hints that there might be another way came in a 1978 experiment by a pair of researchers at the University of Ottawa. Robert Kerr and Bernard Booth were trained in kinetics, the study of human movement. Kineticists often work closely with trainers and coaches, and they're interested in the factors that contribute to athletic ability, injury recovery, and endurance. In this case, Kerr and Booth wanted to know how two distinct kinds of practice affected a simple, if somewhat obscure, skill: beanbag tossing. (It was an inspired choice, as it turned out; it's a skill that most of us have tried, at a kid's birthday party or some amusement park game, but that no one works on at home.) They recruited thirty-six eight-year-olds who were enrolled in a twelve-week Saturday morning PE course at a local gym and split them into two groups. The researchers ran both groups through a warm-up session of target practice to get the kids used to the game—and an awkward game it was, too. The children were asked to toss small golf-ball-sized beanbags from a kneeling position at bull's-eyes on the floor. But they did so while wearing a harness that held a screen blocking their eyes. They took each shot blindly, removed the screen to see where it landed—*then* took the next shot.

On an initial trial, the two groups scored equally well, displaying no discernible difference in skill level.

Then they began regular practice sessions. Each child had six practice sessions, taking twenty-four shots every time. One group practiced on one target, a bull's-eye that was just three feet away. The other group practiced on two targets, one that was two feet away and another that was four feet away, alternating their shots. That was the only difference.

At the end of the twelve-week course, the researchers gave the

children a final test on performance—but only on the three-foot target. This seems unfair. One group was practicing on the three-foot
target the whole time, and the other not at all. The group that practiced at three feet should have had a clear advantage. Yet it didn't
turn out that way. The kids in the mixed-target group won this competition, and handily. Their average distance away from the (three-
foot) target was much smaller than their peers on the final test. What
was going on? Kerr and Booth ran the same experiment again in
twelve-year-olds, just to make sure the finding held up. It did. Not
only that, but the result was even more dramatic in the older kids.
Was it luck? Did the better groups have a few ringers? Not at all, reported Kerr and Booth. "A varied practice schedule may facilitate
the initial formation of motor schema," they wrote, the variation
working to "enhance movement awareness." In other words: Varied
practice is more effective than the focused kind, because it forces us
to internalize general rules of motor adjustment that apply to *any*
hittable target.

A big idea—if true.

It might have been a fluke, given the strangeness of the task: blind
beanbag tossing. Not that it mattered at the time, in part because no
one was paying attention. The beanbag experiment was as obscure
as they come. (So much so that it disappeared entirely from the website of the journal in which it originally appeared, *Perceptual and Motor
Skills;* it took editors weeks to find it when I asked.) Yet even if the
study had made the nightly news, it's not likely to have changed
many minds, certainly not among the academics studying memory.
Kinetics and cognitive psychology are worlds apart in culture and in
status. One is closer to brain science, the other to gym class. A beanbag study with a bunch of eight-year-olds and twelve-year-olds
wasn't about to alter centuries of assumptions about how the brain
acquires new skills. At least not right away.

. . .

Psychologists who study learning tend to fall into one of two camps: the motor/movement, or the verbal/academic. The former focuses on how the brain sees, hears, feels, develops reflexes, and acquires more advanced physical abilities, like playing sports or an instrument. The latter investigates conceptual learning of various kinds: language, abstract ideas, and problem solving. Each camp has its own vocabulary, its own experimental paradigms, its own set of theories. In college, they are often taught separately, in different courses: "Motor and Perceptual Skills" and "Cognition and Memory."

This distinction is not an arbitrary one. Before we go any further, let's revisit, briefly, the story of Henry Molaison, the Hartford man whose 1953 surgery for epilepsy severely damaged his ability to form new memories. After the surgery, Molaison's brain could not hold on to any describable memories, such as names, faces, facts, and personal experiences. The surgeon had removed the hippocampus from both hemispheres of his brain; without those, Molaison could not move short-term memories into long-term storage. He could, however, form new motor memories. In one of the experiments described in chapter 1, Molaison learned to trace a star while watching his drawing hand in a mirror. He became more and more adept at this skill over time, even though he had no memory of ever practicing it.

A major implication of the Molaison studies was that the brain must have at least two biological systems for handling memory. One, for declarative memories, is dependent on a functioning hippocampus. The other, for motor memories, is based in different brain organs; no hippocampus required. The two systems are biologically distinct, so it stood to reason that they're functionally distinct, too, in how they develop, strengthen, and fade. Picking up Spanish is not the same as picking up Spanish guitar, and so psychology has a separate tradition to characterize each.

In the early 1990s, a pair of colleagues at UCLA decided to try something radical: They would combine the two traditions—motor and verbal—into a single graduate seminar, which they called "Principles of Motor and Verbal Learning." The two researchers—Richard A. Schmidt, a motor-learning specialist, and the ever-present Robert Bjork, a verbal-learning expert—thought students would gain a better understanding of the main distinctions between their respective fields and how each type of learning is best taught. "Dick and I just assumed we'd lay out what the differences were between motor and verbal, nothing more than that," Bjork told me. "But as we got deeper into it, the whole project changed course."

An odd signal echoed down through the literature, they saw. For starters, they stumbled upon the neglected beanbag study, and took its conclusions at face value, as valid. They then searched the literature to see if they could find other studies in which mixed or interrupted practice sessions led to better performance over time than focused ones. If the beanbag result was solid, and Kerr and Booth were correct in arguing that it revealed a general principle of learning, then it should show up in other experiments comparing different practice techniques.

And so it did, in papers by researchers who weren't familiar with Kerr and Booth's work at all. In 1986, for instance, researchers at Louisiana State University tested how well thirty young women learned three common badminton serves. The short serve, the long, and the drive each has a distinct trajectory and takes some practice to hit well. To make a short serve, the player has to hit the shuttlecock just over the net (no more than fifty centimeters, or a foot and a half) so that it lands in the front third of the opposing court. A long serve passes at least two and half meters (about eight feet) above the net and lands in the back third of the opposite court. A drive splits the difference and darts downward to the midline on the other side. The researchers—Sinah Goode and Richard Magill—judged the serves by two criteria: where they landed and where they passed over the net. They split the women into three groups of ten, each of which practiced according to the same schedule, for three days a week over three weeks, thirty-six serves at a time. The sessions themselves were different, however. Group A performed *blocked* practice, rehearsing only one type of serve per session: doing thirty-six short ones on one day, for instance, thirty-six long ones the next session, and thirty-six drives the next. Group B performed *serial* practice, trying the serves in a given order—short, then long, then drive—repeatedly. Group C practiced randomly, trying any serve they wanted but no more than two of the same ones in a row.

By the end of the three weeks, each participant had practiced each serve the same number of times, give or take a few for those in the random group.

Goode and Magill wanted not only to compare the relative effectiveness of each type of practice schedule. They also wanted to measure how well the participants' skills *transferred* to a new condition. Transfer is what learning is all about, really. It's the ability to extract the essence of a skill or a formula or word problem and apply it in another context, to another problem that may not look the same, at least superficially. If you've truly mastered a skill, you "carry it with you," so to speak. Goode and Magill measured transfer in a subtle, clever way. On their final test of skill, they made one small adjustment: The participants served from the left side of the court, even though they'd practiced only on the right. During the test, the examiner called out one skill after another: "Hit me a drive . . . Okay, now a short serve . . . Now give me a long one." Each participant hit each serve the same number of times on the final test—six—though never two of the same kind in a row. Goode and Magill then rated each serve, according to its arc and placement, on a scale from 0 to 24.

The winner? Team Random, by a long shot. It scored an average of 18, followed by the serial group, at 14. The blocked practicers, who'd focused on one serve at a time, did the worst, with an average of 12—and this despite having appeared, for most of the three weeks, to be improving the most. They were leading the pack going into Week 3, but come game time, they collapsed.

The authors weren't entirely sure what caused such a dramatic reversal. Yet they had a hunch. Interfering with concentrated or re-petitive practice forces people to make continual adjustments, they reasoned, building a general dexterity that, in turn, sharpens each specific skill. Which, by the way, is exactly what the beanbag study concluded. But Goode and Magill then took it one step further. All that adjusting during a mixed-practice session, they wrote, also en-hances transfer. Not only is each skill sharper; it's performed well regardless of context, whether indoors or out, from the right side of the court or the left. "The general goal of practice is to transfer to a game," the pair concluded. "A game situation varies from event to event, making random testing the best condition to appraise the ef-fectiveness of practice."

Schmidt and Bjork knew that this experiment, like the beanbag toss, proved nothing on its own; it was just one study. But there was a scattering of still others—of keyboard ability, of videogame skills, of precise arm movements—and they all had one thing in common: Whenever researchers scrambled practice sessions, in one form or another, people improved more over time than if their practice was focused and uninterrupted.

One way to think about this is in terms of practice versus perfor-mance. During practice we have a measure of control. We can block out or avoid distractions, we can slow down if needed, and most important, we decide which skill or move or formula we want to re-hearse *before* actually doing it. We're in charge. Performance is an-other story. Growing up, all of us knew kids who were exceptional in practice but only mediocre come game time. And vice versa, kids who looked awkward in drills and then came alive when it mattered, during competition, or performing in front of an audience. You can practice the step-over soccer move a thousand times in your front yard, but doing it at full speed with two opposing players running at you is much harder. It's no longer a single move anymore, practiced in isolation, but one step in an ever-changing, fast-paced dance.

The incorporation of these random demands is what made Kerr and Booth's observation plausible, and Schmidt and Bjork knew well enough that the principle wasn't only applicable to physical skills. Digging out verbal memories on a dime requires a mental—if not physical—suppleness that doesn't develop in repetitive practice as fast as it could. In one previous experiment, Bjork and T. K. Landauer of Bell Laboratories had students try to memorize a list of fifty names. Some of the names were presented for study and then tested several times in succession; other names were presented once and tested—but the test came *after* the study session was interrupted (the students were given other items to study during the interruption). In other words, each student studied one set of names in an unperturbed session and the other set in an interrupted one. Yet thirty minutes later, on subsequent tests, they recalled about 10 percent more of the names they'd studied on the interrupted schedule. Focused, un-harried practice held them back.

"It has generally been understood that any variation in practice that makes the information more immediate, more accurate, more frequent, or more useful will contribute to learning," Schmidt and Bjork wrote. "Recent evidence, however, suggests that this generalization must be qualified."

"Qualified" was a polite way to say "reconsidered" and possibly abandoned altogether.

It's not that repetitive practice is *bad*. We all need a certain amount of it to become familiar with any new skill or material. But repetition creates a powerful illusion. Skills improve quickly and then plateau. By contrast, varied practice produces a slower *apparent* rate of improvement in each single practice session but a greater accumulation of skill and learning over time. In the long term, repeated practice on one skill slows us down.

Psychologists had been familiar with many of these findings, as isolated results, for years. But it was Schmidt and Bjork's paper, "New

Conceptualizations of Practice," published in 1992, that arranged this constellation of disparate pieces into a general principle that can be applied to all practice—motor and verbal, academic as well as athletic. Their joint class turned out not to be devoted to contrasts, after all, but to identifying key similarities. "We are struck by the common features that underlie these counterintuitive phenomena in such a wide range of skill-learning situations," they concluded. "At the most superficial level, it appears that systematically altering practice so as to encourage additional, or at least different, information processing activities can degrade performance during practice, but can at the same time have the effect of generating greater performance capabilities."

Which activities are those? We've already discussed one example, in chapter 4: the spacing effect. Breaking up study time is a form of interference, and it deepens learning without the learner investing more overall time or effort. Another example, explored in chapter 3, is context change. Mixing up study locations, taking the books outside or to a coffee shop, boosts retention. Each of these techniques scrambles focused practice, also causing some degree of forgetting between sessions. In their Forget to Learn theory, Robert and Elizabeth Bjork called any technique that causes forgetting a "desirable difficulty," in that it forces the brain to work harder to dig up a memory or skill—and that added work intensifies subsequent retrieval and storage strength (learning).

But there's another technique, and it goes right back to the long-lost beanbag study. Remember, the kids who did best on the final test hadn't practiced on the three-foot target at all. They weren't continually aiming at the same target, like their peers, doing a hundred A-minor scales in a row. Nor were they spacing their practice, or changing rooms, or being interrupted by some psychologist in a lab coat. They were simply alternating targets. It was a small variation, only a couple of feet, but that alteration represents a large idea, and one that has become the focus of intense study at all levels of education.

· · ·

Let's leave the beanbags and badminton behind for now and talk about something that's more likely to impress friends, strangers, and potential mates: art. I'm not talking about creating art, I'm talking about appreciating it. One of the first steps in passing oneself off as an urbane figure (so I'm told) is having some idea who actually created the painting you're staring at. Remarking on Manet's use of light while standing in front of a Matisse can blow your cover quickly—and force a stinging retreat to the information desk for some instructional headphones.

Yet learning to identify an artist's individual touch, especially one who has experimented across genres and is not among history's celebrities, a van Gogh or a Picasso or an O'Keeffe, is not so easy. The challenge is to somehow feel the presence of the artist in the painting, and there's no simple recipe for doing so. What's the difference between a Vermeer, a de Heem, and a van Everdingen, for example? I couldn't pick any one of these Dutch masters out of a lineup, never mind identify the creative signatures that separate one from the others. "The different subjects chosen by Vermeer and de Heem and van der Heyden and van Everdingen are at once different ways of depicting life in 17th-Century Holland and different ways of expressing its domestic quality," wrote the American philosopher Nelson Goodman in one of his essays on artistic style. "Sometimes features of what is exemplified, such as color organizations, are ways of exemplifying other features, such as spatial patterns."

Got all that? Me neither.

Goodman famously argued that the more elusive and cryptic an artist's style, the more rewarding it was for the viewer: "An obvious style, easily identified by some superficial quirk, is properly decried as

a mere mannerism. A complex and subtle style, like a trenchant metaphor, resists reduction to a literal formula." And there's the rub. Art
appreciation is a world removed from biology, playing music, German 101, and the epic poets. There are no word pairs or chemical
bonds to study, no arpeggios or verses or other basic facts, no obvious
verbal or motor "tasks" to measure. The ability contains an element
of witchcraft, frankly, and learning scientists had traditionally left the
study of artistic styles to the likes of academics like Goodman.

That all changed in 2006, when Robert Bjork and postdoctoral
student Nate Kornell, now at Williams College, decided to test
whether a form of interrupted study affected aesthetic judgment in
addition to retention. The idea came from a story that one of Bjork's
colleagues had told him, about taking a trip to Italy with her teenage
daughter. She—the mother—was excited by the opportunity to visit
great museums, such as the Uffizi and Accademia in Florence, the
National and Borghese in Rome, as well as the vast Vatican collection, but she worried that the experience would be lost on her daughter, if not actively resisted. She told Bjork that she knew her daughter
would get so much more out of the trip if she learned to identify
Italian painters' styles—and had devised a flashcard game that
taught her to do just that.

Kornell and Bjork did essentially the same thing in their experiment. They chose a collection of paintings by twelve landscape artists, some of them familiar (Braque, Seurat), but most by artists
unfamiliar to the participants, like Marilyn Mylrea, YeiMei, and
Henri-Edmond Cross. They then had a group of seventy-two undergraduates study the paintings on a computer screen. Half of the
students studied the artists one at a time. For example: They saw one
Cross after another for three seconds each, with the name of the
painter below the image:

After six Crosses, they saw (let's say) six works by Braque, again for three seconds each with the artist's name below; then six by Yei-Mei; and so on. Kornell and Bjork called this blocked practice, because the students studied each artist's works in a set.

The other half of the participants studied the same paintings for the same amount of time (three seconds per piece), also with the artist's name below. But in their case, the paintings were *not* grouped together by artist; they were mixed up:

Both groups studied a total of six paintings from each of the twelve artists. Which group would have a better handle on the styles at the end?

Kornell and Bjork had the participants count backward from 547 by threes after studying—a distraction that acted as a palette cleanser, a way to clear short-term memory and mark a clean break between the study phase and the final test. And that test—to count as a true measure of performance—could not include any of the paintings just studied. Remember, the participants in this study were trying to learn painting *styles*, not memorize specific paintings. If you "know" Braque, you should be able to identify his touch in a painting of his you've never seen before. So Kornell and Bjork had the students view forty-eight un-studied landscapes, one at a time, and try to match each one to its creator, by clicking on one of the twelve names. The researchers weren't sure what to expect but had reason to suspect that blocked study would be better. For one thing, no one understands exactly how people distinguish artistic styles. For another, similar studies back in the 1950s, having subjects try to learn the names of abstract drawings, found no differences. People studying the figures in blocked sets did every bit as well as those studying mixed sets.

Not this time. The mixed-study group got nearly 65 percent of the artists correct, and the blocked group only 50 percent. In the world of science, that's a healthy difference, so the researchers ran another trial in a separate group of undergraduates to double-check it. Once again, each student got equal doses of blocked and mixed study: blocked for six of the artists, mixed for the other six. The result was the same: 65 percent correct for those studied in mixed sets, and 50 percent for those studied in blocks. "A common way to teach students about an artist is to show, in succession, a number of paintings by that artist," Kornell and Bjork wrote. "Counterintuitive as it may be to art history teachers—and our participants—we found that interleaving paintings by different artists was more effective than massing all of an artist's paintings together."

Interleaving. That's a cognitive science word, and it simply means mixing related but distinct material during study. Music teachers have long favored a variation on this technique, switching from scales, to theory, to pieces all in one sitting. So have coaches and athletic trainers, alternating endurance and strength exercises to ensure recovery periods for certain muscles. These philosophies are largely rooted in tradition, in a person's individual experience, or in concerns about overuse. Kornell and Bjork's painting study put interleaving on the map as a *general* principle of learning, one that could sharpen the imprint of virtually any studied material. It's far too early to call their study a landmark—that's for a better historian than I to say—but it has inspired a series of interleaving studies among amateurs and experts in a variety of fields. Piano playing. Bird-watching. Baseball hitting. Geometry.

What could account for such a big difference? Why any difference at all? Were the distinctions between styles somehow clearer when they were mixed?

In their experiment, Kornell and Bjork decided to consult the participants. In a questionnaire given after the final test, they asked the students which study method, blocked or interleaved, helped them learn best. Nearly 80 percent rated blocked study as good or better than the mixed kind. They had no sense that mixed study was helping them—and this was *after* the final test, which showed that mixing provided a significant edge.

"That may be the most astounding thing about this technique," said John Dunlosky, a psychologist at Kent State University, who has shown that interleaving accelerates our ability to distinguish between bird species. "People don't believe it, even after you show them they've done better."

This much is clear: The mixing of items, skills, or concepts during practice, over the longer term, seems to help us not only see the distinctions between them but also to achieve a clearer grasp of each one individually. The hardest part is abandoning our primal faith in repetition.

Math scores, however, don't lie.

* * *

Despite its leadership in technical innovation and discovery, the United States has long lagged in math education, usually ranking around ninth or tenth in the world—as measured by performance in eighth graders—far behind countries like South Korea and Finland. Experts and officials are perpetually debating how to close that gap, and in the late 1980s the nation's premier organization of math teachers—the National Council of Teachers of Mathematics—convened a meeting of leading educators to review and reshape how the subject was taught. It was a gargantuan job and, like so many grand-scale efforts, became bitterly contentious. The central disagreement was over teaching philosophy: Do students learn most efficiently in classes that emphasize the learning of specific problem-solving techniques, like factoring and calculating slope? Or do they benefit more from classes that focus on abstract skills, like reasoning and number sense—knowing, for example, that $2/3 + 3/5$ is greater than 1, without having to find a common denominator? The former approach is bottom-up; the latter is top-down.

This being education, the debate was quickly politicized. The top-down camp became "progressives" who wanted children to think independently rather than practice procedures by rote. (This group included many younger teachers and university professors with doctorates in education.) The bottom-up camp became "conservatives" who saw value in the old ways, in using drills as building blocks. (Its core was made up of older teachers and professors of math and engineering.) The math wars, as they were known, caused confusion among many teachers. Math education was virtually devoid of decent research at the time, so neither side had the ammunition to win the argument. The typical experiment involved academics or outside experts descending on a class or school with a novel math, history, or writing curriculum and announcing "improvements" that were hard to interpret, given that the measures (the tests) were often new themselves, and few experiments tracked the teachers' commitment to the program.

Teachers, then as now, see enough new approaches come and go over time that many become constitutionally skeptical. Plus, this clash over math was (and is) about *philosophies,* and in math of all subjects it is results that matter, not theories. "One of the things you see that's so baffling, when you're a new teacher, is that kids who do great on unit tests—the weekly, or biweekly reviews—often do terribly on cumulative exams on the same material," Doug Rohrer, who was a high school math teacher in Palo Alto, California, in the late 1980s, told me. "The kids would often blame the test or even blame me explicitly, saying I gave them trick questions." What made those questions so tricky, explained Rohrer, was that "math students must be able to *choose* a strategy—not just know how to use it—and choosing a strategy is harder when an exam covers many kinds of problems." For practical teaching issues like this one, the math wars debate was irrelevant.

Rohrer toyed with the idea of developing a different curriculum, one that rejected the idea of teaching in blocks (two weeks on proportions, say, then two weeks on graphs) and instead mixed problems from previously studied topics into daily homework to force students to learn how to choose appropriate solution strategies rather than blindly apply them. To solve a problem, you first have to identify what kind of problem it is. Rohrer was lying on his futon in his studio apartment one day, staring at the ceiling, and thought, *Okay, maybe it's time to write a textbook of mixed problems*. He soon found out that someone already had.

That someone was a retired Air Force officer turned math teacher in Oklahoma City. In the 1970s, John H. Saxon was teaching math at Rose State College and growing increasingly exasperated with the textbooks the college used. The books' approach left students fuzzy on the basics, and quick to forget what they'd just studied. So one day Saxon decided to write out some problem sets of his own, with the goal of building algebra skills differently—i.e., more incrementally—than the standard curriculum. His students improved fast, and soon he was developing entire lesson plans. Between 1980 and 1990, Saxon authored or coauthored twelve math textbooks for kindergarten through high school, plus a couple of college texts. His central innovation was a process of "mixed review." Each homework assignment included some new technique—solving simultaneous equations, for example—along with a number of problems from previous lessons, say, solving equations for x. Saxon believed that we grasp a new technique more clearly when using it alongside other, familiar ones, gradually building an understanding of more abstract concepts along the way. His books built a following, mostly among private schools, homeschoolers, and some public districts, and he soon became a lightning rod in the math debate. Saxon was a bottom-up man. He thought the reformers were dangerous and they returned the compliment.

Rohrer wasn't sure what he thought about the math wars or, for that matter, about Saxon. He does remember picking up the Saxon books and looking at the chapters. They were different, all right. The lessons, in Rohrer's view, were *not* in logical order. Yet the problems were mixed, from all sorts of different lessons—precisely the approach he thought would help his own students.

He let it drop. Rohrer was ready to walk away from math teaching altogether, and entered graduate school in experimental psychology. It was in 2002—eight years after he finished his degree—that he again began to think about learning. For one thing, he'd read the 1992 Schmidt-Bjork paper on motor and verbal learning. And he returned to the central problem he'd had while teaching high schoolers. His students didn't need to remember more. Their weakness was distinguishing between problem *types*—and choosing the appropriate strategy. Mixing problem types (he had not yet heard the term interleaving) looked like it might address just this weakness.

We've done well so far to avoid doing any real math in this book, but I think it's time to break the seal. In the past decade, Rohrer and others have shown in a variety of experiments that interleaving can improve math comprehension across the board, no matter our age. Let's take a look at one of those studies, just to show how this technique works. We'll keep it light. This is fourth grade geometry, and a little review never hurt anyone. In 2007, Rohrer and Kelli Taylor, both at the University of South Florida, recruited twenty-four fourth graders and gave each a tutorial on how to calculate the number of faces, edges, corners, and angles in a prism—given the number of base sides. The tutorial is self-explanatory and perfectly doable, even for people with math allergies. In the diagrams below, *b* is the number of base sides:

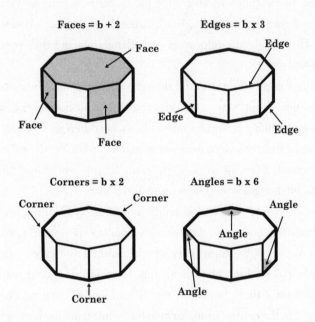

Half the children performed blocked study. They worked eight "face" problems (FFFFFFFF), then eight "edge" problems (EEEEEEEE), eight "corner" problems, and eight "angle" problems in a row, with a thirty-second break in between, all in the same day. The other half worked the same number of each type of problem, only in randomly mixed sets of eight: FCEAECFA, for example, followed by CAAEFECF. The tutorials were identical for each group, and so were the problems. The only difference was the order: sequential in one group and mixed in the other. The next day the children took a test, which included one of each type of problem. Sure enough, those in the mixed-study—interleaved—group did better, and it wasn't close: 77 to 38 percent.

One fairly obvious reason that interleaving accelerates math learning in particular is that tests themselves—the cumulative exams, that is—are mixed sets of problems. If the test is a potpourri, it helps to make homework the same. There's much more going on than that, however. Mixing problems during study forces us to identify each type of problem *and* match it to the appropriate kind of solution. We are not only discriminating between the locks to be cracked; we are connecting each lock with the right key. "The difficulty of pairing a problem with the appropriate procedure or concept is ubiquitous in mathematics," Rohrer and Taylor concluded. "For example, the notorious difficulty of word problems is due partly to the fact that few word problems explicitly indicate which procedure or concept is appropriate. The word problem, 'If a bug crawls eastward for 8 inches and then crawls northward for 15 inches, how far is it from its starting point?' requires students to infer the need for the Pythagorean theorem. However, no such inference is required if the word problem appears immediately after a block of problems that explicitly indicate the need for the Pythagorean theorem. Thus, blocked practice can largely reduce the pedagogical value of the word problem."

Rohrer puts it this way: "If the homework says 'The Quadratic Formula' at the top of the page, you just use that blindly. There's no need to ask whether it's appropriate. You know it is before doing the problem."

The evidence so far suggests that interleaving is likely applicable not just to math, but to almost any topic or skill. Badminton. History (mix concepts from related periods). Basketball (practice around the free throw line, not repeatedly from the line). Biology. Piano. Chemistry. Skateboarding. Blindfolded beanbag throwing, for heaven's sake. Certainly any material taught in a single semester, in any single course, is a ripe target for interleaving. You have to review the material anyway at some point. You have to learn to distinguish between a holy ton of terms, names, events, concepts, and formulas at exam time, or execute a fantastic number of perfect bow movements at recital. Why not practice the necessary discrimination skills incrementally, every time you sit down, rather than all at once when ramping up for a final test? As mentioned earlier, many musicians already do a version of mixed practice, splitting their sessions between, say, thirty minutes of scales, thirty minutes of reading new music, and thirty minutes of practicing familiar pieces. That's the right idea. Chopping that time into even smaller pieces, however—of fifteen minutes, or ten—can produce better results. Remember: Interleaving is not just about review but also discriminating between types of problems, moves, or concepts.

For example, I still take classes when I can in Spanish and Spanish guitar. Every time I look at a list of new vocabulary words, I take that list and combine it with a list of at least as many older words. I do more kinds of mixing with the guitar (maybe because there's more to mix than words and reading). I do one scale, two or three times, then switch to a piece I know. Then I go back and try again the portions of that just played piece—let's say it's Granados's Spanish Dance Number 5—that I messed up. Play those two times, slowly. Then I'm on to a (different) scale, followed by a few bars of a totally new piece I'm working on. Enough for one pass. I take a break and play a few riffs from the first tune I ever learned, "Stairway to Heaven" (somehow it never gets old), and after that I'm ready to dive into Spanish Classical.

That is interleaving. And it's sure to be highly individual, far more effective for some subjects or skills than for others. The important thing to know is that you're essentially surrounding the new material or new skill set with older stuff, stuff you already know but haven't revisited in a while, whether it's a Jimmy Page solo or a painting by Georges Braque.

As I read it, the science suggests that interleaving is, essentially, about preparing the brain for the unexpected. Serious climbers and hikers have a favorite phrase: *It's not an adventure until something goes wrong*. By wrong they mean *wrong* wrong. A rope snaps; the food supply flies overboard; a bear crawls into the tent. I think interleaving prepares us for a milder form of wrong. Every exam, every tournament, every match, every recital—there's always some wrinkle, some misplaced calculator or sudden headache, a glaring sun or an unexpected essay question. At bottom, interleaving is a way of building into our daily practice not only a dose of review but also an element of surprise. "The brain is exquisitely tuned to pick up incongruities, all of our work tells us that," said Michael Inzlicht, a neuroscientist at the University of Toronto. "Seeing something that's out of order or out of place wakes the brain up, in effect, and prompts the subconscious to process the information more deeply: 'Why is this here?'"

Mixed-up practice doesn't just build overall dexterity and prompt active discrimination. It helps prepare us for life's curveballs, literal and figurative.

Part Four

Tapping the Subconscious

Chapter Nine

Learning Without Thinking

Harnessing Perceptual Discrimination

What's a good eye?

You probably know someone who has one, for fashion, for photography, for antiques, for seeing a baseball. All of those skills are real, and they're special. But what are they? What's the eye doing in any one of those examples that makes it good? What's it *reading*, exactly?

Take hitting a baseball. Players with a "good eye" are those who seem to have a sixth sense for the strike zone, who are somehow able to lay off pitches that come in a little too high or low, inside or outside, and swing only at those in the zone. Players, coaches, and scientists have all broken this ability down endlessly, so we can describe some of the crucial elements. Let's begin with the basics of hitting. A major league fastball comes in at upward of 90 mph, from 60 feet, 6 inches away. The ball arrives at the plate in roughly 4/10 of a second, or 400 milliseconds. The brain needs about two thirds of that time—250 milliseconds—to make the decision whether to swing or not. In that time it needs to read the pitch: where it's going, how fast, whether it's going to sink or curve or rise as it approaches (most pitchers have a variety of pitches, all of which break across different planes). Research shows that the batter himself isn't even aware whether he's swinging or not until the ball is about 10 feet away— and by that point, it's too late to make major adjustments, other than to hold up (maybe). A batter with a good eye makes an instantaneous— and almost always accurate—read.

What's this snap judgment based on? Velocity is one variable, of course. The (trained) brain can make a rough estimate of that using the tiny change in the ball's image over that first 250 milliseconds; stereoscopic vision evolved to compute, at incredible speed, all sorts of trajectories and certainly one coming toward our body. Still, how does the eye account for the spin of the ball, which alters the trajectory of the pitch? Hitters with a good eye have trouble describing that in any detail. Some talk about seeing a red dot, signaling a breaking ball, or a grayish blur, for a fastball; they say they focus only on the little patch in their field of vision where the pitcher's hand releases the ball, which helps them judge its probable trajectory. Yet that release point can vary, too. "They may get a snapshot of the ball, plus something about the pitcher's body language," Steven Sloman, a cognitive scientist at Brown University, told me. "But we don't entirely understand it."

A batting coach can tinker with a player's swing and mechanics, but no one can tell him how to *see* pitches better. That's one reason major league baseball players get paid like major league baseball players. And it's why we think of their visual acuity more as a gift than an expertise. We tell ourselves it's all about reflexes, all in the fast-twitch fibers and brain synapses. They're "naturals." We make a clear distinction between this kind of ability and expertise of the academic kind. Expertise is a matter of learning—of accumulating knowledge, of studying and careful thinking, of creating. It's *built,* not born. The culture itself makes the same distinction, too, between gifted athletes and productive scholars. Yet this distinction is also flawed in a fundamental way. And it blinds us to an aspect of learning that even scientists don't yet entirely understand.

To flesh out this dimension and appreciate its importance, let's compare baseball stars to an equally exotic group of competitors, known more for their intellectual prowess than their ability to hit line drives: chess players. On a good day, a chess grand master can defeat the world's most advanced supercomputer, and this is no small thing. Every second, the computer can consider more than 200 million possible moves, and draw on a vast array of strategies developed by leading scientists and players. By contrast, a human player—even a grand master—considers about four move sequences per turn in any depth, playing out the likely series of parries and countermoves to follow. That's four *per turn,* not per second. Depending on the amount of time allotted for each turn, the computer might search one billion more possibilities than its human opponent. And still, the grand master often wins. How?

The answer is not obvious. In a series of studies in the 1960s, a Dutch psychologist who was also himself a chess master, Adriaan de Groot, compared masters to novices and found no differences in the number of moves considered; the depth of each search, the series of countermoves played out, mentally; or the way players thought about the pieces (for instance, seeing the rook primarily as an attacking piece in some positions, and as a defensive one in others). If anything, the masters searched *fewer* moves than the novices. But they could do one thing the novices could not: memorize a chess position after seeing the board for less than five seconds. One look, and they could reconstruct the arrangement of the pieces precisely, as if they'd taken a mental snapshot.

In a follow-up study, a pair of researchers at Carnegie Mellon University—William G. Chase and Herbert A. Simon—showed that this skill had nothing to do with the capacity of the masters' memory. Their short-term recall of things like numbers was no better than anyone else's. Yet they saw the chessboard in more meaningful chunks than the novices did.* "The superior performance of stronger players derives from the ability of those players to encode the position into larger perceptual chunks, each consisting of a familiar configuration of pieces," Chase and Simon concluded.

Grand masters have a good eye, too, just like baseball players, and they're no more able to describe it. (If they could, it would quickly be programmed into the computer, and machines would rule the game.) It's clear, though, that both ballplayers and grand masters are doing more than merely seeing or doing some rough analysis. Their eyes, and the visual systems in their brains, are extracting *the most meaningful set of clues* from a vast visual tapestry, and doing so instantaneously. I think of this ability in terms of infrared photography: You see hot spots of information, *live* information, and everything else is dark. All experts—in arts, sciences, IT, mechanics, baseball, chess, what have you—eventually develop this kind of infrared lens to some extent. Like chess and baseball prodigies, they do it through career-long experience, making mistakes, building intuition. The rest of us, however, don't have a lifetime to invest in Chemistry 101 or music class. We'll take the good eye—but need to do it on the cheap, quick and dirty.

· · ·

When I was a kid, everyone's notebooks and textbooks, every margin of every sheet of lined paper in sight, was covered with doodles:

---

* "Chunking," in psychology, is the facility to store studied items in meaningful clusters based on prior knowledge. Take the sequence of letters Y, N, B; C, B, B; C, E; F, I, F; A, C, I; A M, B; A, Y. Study those for a few minutes, then cover your eyes and try to remember as many as you can. The typical number most of us can remember is about seven. Now try it again after grouping the letters in this way: Y, NBC, BBC, FIFA, CIA, MBA, Y. You remember more, because you've stored the letters in meaningful groups.

graffiti letters, caricatures, signatures, band logos, mazes, 3-D cubes. Everyone doodled, sometimes all class long, and the most common doodle of all was the squiggle:

Those squiggles have a snowflake quality; they all look the same and yet each has its own identity when you think about it. Not that many people have. The common squiggle is less interesting than any nonsense syllable, which at least contains meaningful letters. It's virtually invisible, and in the late 1940s one young researcher recognized that quality as special. In some moment of playful or deep thinking, she decided that the humble squiggle was just the right tool to test a big idea.

Eleanor Gibson came of age as a researcher in the middle of the twentieth century, during what some call the stimulus-response, or S-R, era of psychology. Psychologists at the time were under the influence of behaviorism, which viewed learning as a pairing of a stimulus and response: the ringing of a bell before mealtime and salivation, in Ivan Pavlov's famous experiment. Their theories were rooted in work with animals, and included so-called operant conditioning, which rewarded a correct behavior (navigating a maze) with a treat (a piece of cheese) and discouraged mistakes with mild electrical shocks. This S-R conception of learning viewed the sights, sounds, and smells streaming through the senses as not particularly meaningful on their own. The brain provided that meaning by seeing connections. Most of us learn early in life, for instance, that making eye contact brings social approval, and screaming less so. We learn that when the family dog barks one way, it's registering excitement; another way, it senses danger. In the S-R world, learning was a matter of making those associations—between senses and behaviors, causes and effects.

Gibson was not a member of the S-R fraternity. After graduating from Smith College in 1931, she entered graduate studies at Yale University hoping to work under the legendary primatologist Robert Yerkes. Yerkes refused. "He wanted no women in his lab and made it extremely clear to me that I wasn't wanted there," Gibson said years later. She eventually found a place with Clark Hull, an influential behaviorist known for his work with rats in mazes, where she sharpened her grasp of experimental methods—and became convinced that there wasn't much more left to learn about conditioned reflexes. Hull and his contemporaries had done some landmark experiments, but the S-R paradigm itself limited the types of questions a researcher could ask. If you were studying only stimuli and responses, that's all you'd see. The field, Gibson believed, was completely overlooking something fundamental: discrimination. How the brain learns to detect minute differences in sights, sounds, or textures. Before linking different names to distinct people, for example, children have to be able to distinguish between the sounds of those names, between Ron and Don, Fluffy and Scruffy. That's one of the first steps we take in making sense of the world. In hindsight, this seems an obvious point. Yet it took years for her to get anyone to listen.

In 1948, her husband—himself a prominent psychologist at Smith—got an offer from Cornell University, and the couple moved to Ithaca, New York. Gibson soon got the opportunity to study learning in young children, and that's when she saw that her gut feeling about discrimination learning was correct. In some of her early studies at Cornell, she found that children between the ages of three and seven could learn to distinguish standard letters—like a "D" or a "V"—from misshapen ones, like:

These kids had no idea what the letters represented; they weren't making associations between a stimulus and response. Still, they quickly developed a knack for detecting subtle differences in the figures they studied. And it was this work that led to the now classic doodle experiment, which Gibson conducted with her husband in 1949. The Gibsons called the doodles "nonsense scribbles," and the purpose of the study was to test how quickly people could discriminate between similar ones. They brought thirty-two adults and children into their lab, one at a time, and showed each a single doodle on a flashcard:

The study had the feel of a card trick. After displaying the "target" doodle for five seconds, the experimenters slipped it into a deck of thirty-four similar flashcards. "Some of the items in the pack are exact replicas, tell me which ones," they said, and then began showing each card, one at a time, for three seconds. In fact, the deck contained four exact replicas, and thirty near-replicas:

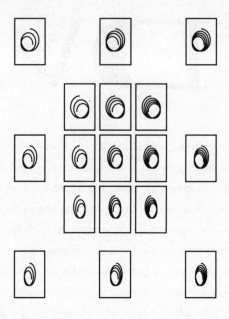

The skill the Gibsons were measuring is the same one we use to learn a new alphabet, at any age, whether Chinese characters, chemistry shorthand, or music notation. To read even a simple melody, you have to be able to distinguish an A from a B-flat on the clef. Mandarin is chicken scratch until you can discriminate between hundreds of similar figures. We've all made these distinctions expertly, most obviously when learning letters in our native tongue as young children. After that happens and we begin reading words and sentences—after we began "chunking," in the same way the chess masters do—we forget how hard it was to learn all those letters in the first place, never mind linking them to their corresponding sounds and blending them together into words and ideas.

In their doodle experiment, the Gibsons gave the participants no feedback, no "you-got-its" or "try-agains." They were interested purely in whether the eye was learning. And so it was. The adults in the experiment needed about three times through, on average, to score perfectly, identifying all four of the exact replicas without making a single error. The older children, between nine and eleven years old, needed five (to get close to perfect); the younger ones, between six and eight years old, needed seven. These people weren't making S-R associations, in the way that psychologists assumed that most learning happened. Nor were their brains—as the English philosopher John Locke famously argued in the seventeenth century—empty vessels, passively accumulating sensations. No, their brains came equipped with evolved modules to make important, subtle discriminations, and to put those differing symbols into categories.

"Let us consider the possibility of rejecting Locke's assumption altogether," the Gibsons wrote. "Perhaps all knowledge comes through the senses in an even simpler way than John Locke was able to conceive—by way of variations, shadings, and subtleties of energy."

That is, the brain doesn't solely learn to perceive by picking up on tiny differences in what it sees, hears, smells, or feels. In this experiment and a series of subsequent ones—with mice, cats, children, and adults—Gibson showed that it also *perceives to learn*. It takes the differences it has detected between similar-looking notes or letters or figures, and uses those to help decipher new, previously unseen material. Once you've got middle-C nailed on the treble clef, you use it as a benchmark for nearby notes; when you nail the A an octave higher, you use that to read its neighbors; and so on. This "discrimination learning" builds on itself, the brain hoarding the benchmarks and signatures it eventually uses to read larger and larger chunks of information.

In 1969, Eleanor Gibson published *Principles of Perceptual Learning and Development,* a book that brought together all her work and established a new branch of psychology: perceptual learning. Perceptual learning, she wrote, "is not a passive absorption, but an active process, in the sense that exploring and searching for perception itself is active. We do not just see, we look; we do not just hear, we listen. Perceptual learning is self-regulated, in the sense that modification occurs without the necessity of external reinforcement. It is stimulus oriented, with the goal of extracting and reducing the information simulation. Discovery of distinctive features and structure in the world is fundamental in the achievement of this goal."

This quote is so packed with information that we need to stop and read closely to catch it all.

Perceptual learning is active. Our eyes (or ears, or other senses) are searching for the right clues. Automatically, no external reinforcement or help required. We have to pay attention, of course, but we don't need to turn it on or tune it in. It's self-correcting—it tunes itself. The system works to find the most critical perceptual signatures and filter out the rest. Baseball players see only the flares of motion that are relevant to judging a pitch's trajectory—nothing else. The masters in Chase and Simon's chess study considered fewer moves than the novices, because they'd developed such a good eye that it instantly pared down their choices, making it easier to find the most effective parry. And these are just visual examples. Gibson's conception of perceptual learning applied to *all* the senses, hearing, smell, taste, and feel, as well as vision.

Only in the past decade or so have scientists begun to exploit Gibson's findings—for the benefit of the rest of us.

· · ·

The flying conditions above Martha's Vineyard can change on a dime. Even when clouds are sparse, a haze often settles over the island that, after nightfall, can disorient an inexperienced pilot. That's apparently what happened just after 9:40 P.M. on July 16, 1999, when John Kennedy Jr. crashed his Piper Saratoga into the ocean seven miles offshore, killing himself, his wife, and her sister. "There was no horizon and no light," said another pilot who'd flown over the island that night. "I turned left toward the Vineyard to see if it was visible but could see no lights of any kind nor any evidence of the island. I thought the island might have suffered a power failure." The official investigation into the crash found that Kennedy had fifty-five hours of experience flying at night, and that he didn't have an instrument rating at all. In pilot's language, that means he was still learning and not yet certified to fly in zero visibility, using only the plane's instrument panel as a guide.

The instruments on small aircraft traditionally include six main dials. One tracks altitude, another speed through the air. A third, the directional gyro, is like a compass; a fourth measures vertical speed (climb or descent). Two others depict a miniature airplane and show banking of the plane and its turning rate through space, respectively (newer models have five, no banking dial).

Learning to read any one of them is easy, even if you've never seen an instrument panel before. It's harder, however, to read them all in one sweep and to make the right call on what they mean collectively. Are you descending? Are you level? This is tricky for amateur pilots to do on a clear day, never mind in zero visibility. Add in communicating with the tower via radio, reading aviation charts, checking fuel levels, preparing landing gear, and other vital tasks—it's a multitasking adventure you don't want to have, not without a lot of training.

This point was not lost on Philip Kellman, a cognitive scientist at Bryn Mawr College, when he was learning to fly in the 1980s. As he moved through his training, studying for aviation tests—practicing on instrument simulators, logging air time with instructors—it struck him that flying was mostly about perception and action. Reflexes. Once in the air, his instructors could see patterns that he could not. "Coming in for landing, an instructor may say to the student, 'You're too high!'" Kellman, who's now at UCLA, told me. "The instructor is actually seeing an angle between the aircraft and the intended landing point, which is formed by the flight path and the ground. The student can't see this at all. In many perceptual situations like this one, the novice is essentially blind to patterns that the expert has come to see at a glance."

That glance took into account *all* of the instruments at once, as well as the view out the windshield. To hone that ability, it took hundreds of hours of flying time, and Kellman saw that the skill was not as straightforward as it seemed on the ground. Sometimes a dial would stick, or swing back and forth, creating a confusing picture. Were you level, as one dial indicated, or in a banking turn, like another suggested? Here's how Kellman describes the experience of learning to read all this data at once with an instructor: "While flying in the clouds, the trainee in the left seat struggles as each gauge seems to have a mind of its own. One by one, he laboriously fixates on each one. After a few seconds on one gauge, he comprehends how it has strayed and corrects, perhaps with a jerk guaranteed to set up the next fluctuation. Yawning, the instructor in the right seat looks over at the panel and sees at a glance that the student has wandered off of the assigned altitude by two hundred feet but at least has not yet turned the plane upside down."

Kellman is an expert in visual perception. This was his territory. He began to wonder if there was a quicker way for students to at least get a feel for the instrument panel before trying to do everything at once at a thousand feet. If you developed a gut instinct for the panel, then the experience in the air might not be so stressful. You'd know what the instruments were saying and could concentrate on other things, like communicating with the tower. The training shortcut Kellman developed is what he calls a perceptual learning module, or PLM. It's a computer program that gives instrument panel lessons—a videogame, basically, but with a specific purpose. The student sees a display of the six dials and has to decide quickly what those dials are saying collectively. There are seven choices: "Straight & Level," "Straight Climb," "Descending Turn," "Level Turn," "Climbing Turn," "Straight Descent," and the worrisome "Instrument Conflict," when one dial is stuck.

In a 1994 test run of the module, he and Mary K. Kaiser of the NASA Ames Research Center brought in ten beginners with zero training and four pilots with flying experience ranging from 500 to 2,500 hours. Each participant received a brief introduction to the instruments, and then the training began: nine sessions, twenty-four presentations on the same module, with short breaks in between. The participants saw, on the screen, an instrument panel, below which were the seven choices. If the participant chose the wrong answer—which novices tend to do at the beginning—the screen burped and provided the right one. The correct answer elicited a chime. Then the next screen popped up: another set of dials, with the same set of seven choices.

After one hour, even the experienced pilots had improved, becoming faster and more accurate in their reading. The novices' scores took off: After one hour, they could read the panels as well as pilots with an average of one thousand flying hours. They'd built the same reading skill, at least on ground, in 1/1,000th of the time. Kellman and Kaiser performed a similar experiment with a module designed to improve visual navigation using aviation charts—and achieved similar results. "A striking outcome of both PLMs is that naïve sub-jects after training performed as accurately and reliably *faster* than pilots before training," they wrote. "The large improvements at-tained after modest amounts of training in these aviation PLMs sug-gest that the approach has promise for accelerating the acquisition of skills in aviation and other training contexts."

Those contexts include any field of study or expertise that in-volves making distinctions. Is that a rhombus or a trapezoid? An oak tree or a maple? The Chinese symbol for "family" or "house"? A positive sloping line or a negative sloping one? Computer PLMs as Kellman and others have designed them are visual, fast-paced, and focused on classifying images (do the elevated bumps in that rash show shingles, eczema, or psoriasis?) or problems rather than solving them outright (does that graph match x—3y = 8, or x + 12 y + 32?). The modules are intended to sharpen snap judgments—perceptual skills—so that you "know" what you're looking at without having to explain why, at least not right away.

In effect, the PLMs build perceptual intuition—when they work. And they have, mostly, in several recent studies. In one, at the Uni-versity of Virginia, researchers used a perceptual learning module to train medical students studying gallbladder removal. For most of the twentieth century, doctors had removed gallbladders by making a long cut in the abdomen and performing open surgery. But since the 1980s many doctors have been doing the surgery with a laparoscope, a slender tube that can be threaded into the abdominal cavity through a small incision. The scope is equipped with a tiny camera, and the surgeon must navigate through the cavity based on the im-ages the scope transmits. All sorts of injuries can occur if the doctor misreads those images, and it usually takes hundreds of observed surgeries to master the skill. In the experiment, half the students practiced on a computer module that showed short videos from real surgeries and had to decide quickly which stage of the surgery was pictured. The other half—the control group—studied the same videos as they pleased, rewinding if they wanted. The practice session lasted about thirty minutes. On a final test, the perceptual learning group trounced their equally experienced peers, scoring four times higher.

Kellman has found that his PLMs can accelerate dermatology students' ability to identify skin lesions and rashes, which come in enormous varieties and often look indistinguishable to the untrained eye. He and Sally Krasne at UCLA Medical School have found similar results in radiology, as well as in reading ECGs. Working with other colleagues, Kellman has also achieved good results with a module that prompts chemistry students to categorize chemical bonds between molecules.

True, this is all advanced, technical stuff for people who've already done just fine in school. What about the kid watching the clock in math class, trying to figure out what on earth "slope" means or how to graph $3(x + 1) = y$?

Here, too, perceptual modules have shown great promise. At a school in Santa Monica, Kellman tested a module that works just like the instrument panel trainer, only with equations and graphs. A graph of a line pops up on the computer screen, and below it are three equations to choose from (or an equation with three choices of graphs beneath; it alternates). Again, students have to work fast: make a choice and move on; make another choice, and another, through dozens of screens. With enough training, the student begins to *feel* the right answer, "and then they can figure out why it's right afterwards, if they need to," as Joe Wise, the high school teacher working with Kellman, told me.

Scientists have a lot more work to do before they figure out how, and for which subjects, PLMs are most effective. You can play computer games all you want, but you still have to fly the plane or operate on a living human being. It's a supplement to experience, not a substitute. That's one reason perceptual learning remains a backwater in psychology and education. It's hardly a reason to ignore it, though. Perceptual learning is happening all the time, after all, and automatically—and it's now clear that it can be exploited to speed up acquisition of specific skills.

. . .

The promise of this book was to describe techniques that could help us learn more effectively without demanding more effort. The goal is to find more leisure, not less. I'm now about to break that promise, but not shatter it into little pieces.

We're going to make a slide show together.

I know, I know. But look: I once made my own flashcards in high school with old-fashioned paper and No. 2 pencils. It's just as easy to create a PLM, right here, right now, to show how it can be done, and what it can and can't do. I was determined to be as lazy as possible about this. I subcontracted the work. I hired my sixteen-year-old daughter to design the module for me, because I'm a busy professional writer, but also because, like many kids, she's digitally fluent. She's perfectly capable of making her own digital slide shows, Power-Point presentations, or videos, downloading images off the Internet. And that's what I told her to do.

I also poached the subject matter, or at least the idea. I decided to do exactly what Kornell and Bjork did in their interleaving study of painting styles described in the last chapter, with a few small changes. Those two used interleaving to teach students to distinguish individual styles among landscape artists. I changed that. My module would focus on famous artistic movements, like Impressionism. This wasn't a random choice. My motives here were selfish: I'd been embarrassed on a recent visit to the Museum of Modern Art by how little I knew of art history. I recognized a piece here and there but had zero sense of the artistic and cultural currents running through them. Van Gogh's *Starry Night* holds the eye with its swimming, blurred sky, but what did it mean for him, for his contemporaries, for the evolution of "modern" art? I sure didn't know.

Fine. I didn't have to know all that right away. I just wanted to know how to tell the difference between the pieces. I wanted a good eye. I could fill in the other stuff later.

What kind of perceptual module did I need? This took a little thinking but not much. I had my daughter choose a dozen artistic movements and download ten paintings from each. That was the raw material, 120 paintings. The movements she chose were (inhale, hold): Impressionism, Post-Impressionism, Romanticism, Expressionism, Abstract Expressionism, Abstract Impressionism, Dadaism, Constructivism, Minimalism, Suprematism, Futurism, and Fauvism. Got all that? You don't have to. The point is that there are many distinctions to make, and I couldn't make any of them. I came into the project with a thick pair of beginner's goggles on: I knew Monet and Renoir were Impressionists, and that was about it.

Kornell and Bjork had presented their landscape paintings in mixed sets, and of course that's what I had my daughter do, too. The order was random, not blocked by style. She made a PLM and rigged it just as Kellman did. A painting appears on the screen, with a choice of twelve styles below it. If I chose right, a bell rang and the check symbol flashed on the screen. If I guessed wrong, a black "X" appeared and the correct answer was highlighted.

I trained for as long as I could stand it in a single sitting: about ten minutes, maybe sixty screens. The first session was almost all guessing. As I said, I had a feel for the Impressionist pieces and nothing else. In the second ten-minute session I began to zero in on Minimalism and Futurism; baby steps. By session four I had Expressionism and Dadaism pretty well pegged. What were the distinguishing features, exactly? Couldn't say. What was the meaning of the unnatural tones in the Fauvist pieces? No idea. I wasn't stopping to find out. I was giving myself a few seconds on each slide, and moving on. This was perceptual learning, not art history.

Eventually I had to take a test on all this, and here, too, I borrowed from Kornell and Bjork. Remember, they'd tested participants at the end of their study on paintings (by the same artists) that they'd *not* studied. The idea is that, if you can spot Braque's touch, then you ought to be able to peg any Braque. That was my goal, too. I wanted

Henri Matisse, *Portrait of Madame Matisse (The Green Line)*, 1905, 2014
Succession H. Matisse/Artists Rights Society (ARS), New York.

to reach a place where I could correctly ID a Dadaist piece, even if it was one I hadn't studied in the PLM.

After a half dozen sessions, I took a test—no thinking allowed—and did well: thirty out of thirty-six correct, 80 percent. I was glancing at the paintings and hitting the button, fast. I learned nothing about art history, it's true, not one whit about the cultural contexts of the pieces, the artistic statements, the uses of color or perspective. But I'll say this: I now know a Fauvist from a Post-Impressionist painting, cold. Not bad for an hour's work.

The biggest difference between my approach and Kornell and Bjork's is that interleaving may involve more conscious deliberation. Perceptual modules tend to be faster-paced, working the visual (perceptual) systems as well as the cognitive, thinking ones. The two techniques are complementary, each one honing the other.

What I'll remember most, though, was that it was fun, from start to finish—the way learning is supposed to be. Of course, I had no exam looming, no pressure to jack up my grades, no competition to prepare for. I've given this example only to illustrate that self-administered perceptual training is possible with minimal effort. Most important, I've used it to show that PLMs are meant for a certain kind of target: discriminating or classifying things that look the same to the untrained eye but are not. To me it's absolutely worth the extra time if there's one specific perceptual knot that's giving you a migraine. The difference between sine, cosine, tangent, cotangent. Intervals and cadences in music. Between types of chemical bonds. Between financing strategies, or annual report numbers. Even between simple things, like whether the sum of two fractions (3/5 and 1/3) is greater or less than 1. Run through a bunch of examples—fast—and let the sensory areas of your brain do the rest.

This is no gimmick. In time, perceptual learning is going to transform training in many areas of study and expertise, and it's easy enough to design modules to target material you want to build an instinct for quickly. Native trees, for example, or wildflowers. Different makes of fuel injectors. Baroque composers or French wines. Remember, all the senses hone themselves, not only vision. As a parent I often wish I'd known the dinosaurs better by sight (there are way more types than you might know, and categories, too), or had a bead on fish species before aquarium visits.

The best part is, as Eleanor Gibson said, perceptual learning is automatic, and self-correcting. You're learning without thinking.

Chapter Ten

● ● ● ● ● ● ● ● ● ● ● ●

You Snooze, You Win

The Consolidating Role of Sleep

The giant rabbit hole in our lives, the dark kingdom we all visit regularly, is sleep. Sleep is a perfect mystery for most of us. We need it, we want more of it, and we long for it to be of a deeper, richer quality. On one hand, we know it can betray us on any given night. On the other, we know that there's some alchemy going on during those unconscious, dream-filled hours, some mixing of fact, fantasy, and feeling that can turn our daytime struggles to master new skills into that most precious thing—*understanding*.

You don't have to be a New Age dream therapist to believe that the brain makes connections during sleep that it doesn't while awake. Who hasn't sat upright in bed now and then at 3 A.M. and thought, *Oh, of course!*, suddenly remembering where you stashed your keys, or visualizing how to alter your golf swing, or to refinger a piece by Albéniz. Countless times I've gone to sleep in a state of self-pitying frustration—held hostage by some story I can't outflank—only to rouse myself in the middle of the night, grab the pen on my night-stand, and scribble out some thoughts that had bubbled to the surface between dreams. In the morning I wake to find a scrawl of partial sentences that, if legible, often help me write my way out.

It's not just me, either. The history of scientific discovery is salted with hints that sleep fosters profound intellectual leaps. The nineteenth-century German chemist Friedrich August Kekulé, for example, claimed that he stumbled upon the chemical structure of benzene—in which the molecule curls into a ring shape—after dreaming of snakes biting their tails. The Russian scientist Dmitri Mendeleev reportedly pulled several all-nighters, to no avail, trying to piece together what would become his famous periodic table of the elements, but it was only after nodding off, he told a colleague, that he saw "a table where all the elements fell into place." These kinds of stories always remind me of the Grimms' fairy tale "The Golden Bird," in which a young man on a mission to find a magic bird with golden feathers falls in love with a princess, whose father the king will grant her hand on one condition: that the young man dig away the hill that stops the view from his window in eight days. The only complication? This is no hill, it's a mountain, and after seven days of digging, the young man collapses in defeat. That's when his friend the fox whispers, "Lie down and go to sleep; I will work for you." And in the morning, the mountain is gone.

Sleep is the stuff of legends and fairy tales precisely because it's so unknown, a blank screen onto which we can project our anxieties and hopes. If the darkroom is locked, we can only guess at what images are being developed in there. All of which raises the question: What is the sleeping brain doing, exactly?

For that matter, why do we sleep at all?

The truth is, no one knows. Or, to be more precise, there's no single, agreed-upon scientific explanation for it. We spend fully a third of our existence unconscious, so any theory about sleep's central purpose has to be a big one. Doesn't the body need regular downtime to heal? To relieve stress? To manage moods, make muscle, restore mental clarity? Yes to all of the above. We know that sleep deprivation makes us more reckless, more emotionally fragile, less able to concentrate and possibly more vulnerable to infection. None of those amounts to an encompassing theory, though, because none explains the vast variations in sleep times and schedules. Just think of how dramatically sleep habits differ from person to person. Some people thrive on as little as three hours a night, while others feel helpless without eight; some function best awake all night and out most of the day; others need their daily nap. A truly comprehensive theory of sleep, then, would have to explain such differences. It would also need to account for the sleep-wake cycles in animals, which is breathtaking in its diversity. Female killer whales can be mobile and alert for upward of three weeks when looking after a newborn calf—nearly a month without sleep. Migrating birds fly for weeks without stopping to rest.

Two new theories have emerged that make sense of this chaos.

One is that sleep is essentially a time-management adaptation. Our body's internal clock evolved to keep us out of circulation when there's not much of a living to be made—at 3 A.M., for instance—and awake when there is. Consider the brown bat, perhaps the longest-sleeping mammal of them all. It sleeps twenty hours a day and spends the other four, at dusk, hunting mosquitoes and moths. Why only four hours at dusk? Because that's when food is plentiful. But also because, as Jerome Siegel, a neuroscientist at UCLA, says, "increased waking time would seem to be highly maladaptive for this animal, since it would expend energy and be exposed to predatory birds with better vision and better flight abilities." Siegel argues that our obsession with sleep quality and duration is, in a sense, backward. "We spend a third of our life sleeping, which seems so maladaptive—'the biggest mistake nature has made,' scientists often call it," he told me. "Another way of looking at it is that unnecessary wakefulness is a bigger mistake."

When there's hay to be made, we make it, whether the sun is shining or not. And when there's none—or too little, given the risks of being out and about—we bed down. In short: Sleeping and waking adjust themselves to the demands and risks of our life, not according to what the health manuals say.

The other theory is that sleep's primary purpose is memory consolidation. Learning. In recent years, brain scientists have published an array of findings suggesting that sleep plays a critical role in flagging and storing important memories, intellectual and physical. Also (yes) in making subtle connections—a new way to solve a tricky math problem, for example, or to play a particularly difficult sequence of notes on the viola—that were invisible during waking. Think about what we described back in chapter 1, all those streaming sensations, the sheer, insane volume of neural connections the brain has to make in the course of any given day. At some point, we have to decide which of these connections are worth holding on to, and which can be ignored. That's an easy choice sometimes, and we make it immediately: a new colleague's name; the pickup time at day care; which house on the street has the angry Dobermans. Other choices are not obvious at all. Some of the most critical perceptions we register in a day contain subtle clues—shrugs, sideways glances, suggestions, red herrings. A world of impressions swirls in our heads when we turn the lights out and, according to this theory, that's when the brain begins to sort out the meaningful from the trivial.

In the contentious field of sleep research, these two theories are typically set in opposition, one trumping the other as the primary function of our unconscious lives. In reality, they are hardly mutually exclusive. Only by putting them together, in fact, can we begin to understand how sleep aids learning—and to use that understanding to our advantage.

· · ·

The boy's brain was going haywire but he was fast asleep, out cold. His father called his name: *Armond? Armond?* No response. Was he pretending? No, it sure didn't look that way.

It was December 1951, and Eugene Aserinsky, a young graduate student at the University of Chicago, had brought his eight-year-old son, Armond, to his basement lab to perform an experiment on sleep. Aserinsky was studying for a degree in physiology and trying to build his credentials as an experimental scientist; he had little interest in sleep research as a career. He was only here pulling night duty, on orders from his academic advisor, Nathaniel Kleitman, who happened to be the father of modern sleep science. Aserinsky had been tinkering with a machine called an Offner Dynograph to track the sleeping brain. A forerunner to the EEG, the Dynograph registers electrical signals from the brain, through electrodes taped to the skull. Aserinsky was using Armond as his test subject. He'd taped a couple of electrodes to the boy's head and eyelids (to track their motion) and then tuned the machine from the next room, asking his son to look this way and that, calibrating the dials. Gradually, Armond nodded off and Aserinsky, sipping his coffee, watched as the Dynograph settled, its ink pens tracing smaller, smoother waves, as expected. But after a few hours the waves began to spike—all of them, those coming from Armond's eyelids as well as his brain—as if the boy was awake and alert. Aserinsky got up from his chair and slipped into the room where his son lay, to make sure his son was asleep and safe.

Armond? . . . Armond? No answer.

Aserinsky returned to the next room, and watched the Dynograph. Scientists at the time considered sleep a period when the brain essentially shut down, becoming a playground for the unconscious, a canvas for dreams. The Dynograph said differently. Aserinsky paced the lab—"flabbergasted," he would say later, by the frenzied wave activity—and watched as Armond's brain waves settled down again, the pens ceasing their chatter. It was late, there was no one else around. Was he seeing things? If so, then reporting the finding would be potentially embarrassing, written off as the misplaced exuberance of an inexperienced researcher. If not, his son's sleeping brain could be telling him something that no one suspected about unconsciousness.

He brought Armond back into the lab for another session weeks later, to see if his original observation was a fluke. It wasn't. At various periods during the night, Armond's brain leapt to life as if he were wide awake. Aserinsky was now confident that this pattern was no mirage. "The question was, what was triggering these eye movements?" he said years later. "What do they mean?"

He didn't have enough expertise in the field or its experimental techniques to know. He'd have to go to the top—to Kleitman—and ask whether such odd brain activity had been reported in sleep experiments before, and whether it was worth the time to follow up. Kleitman didn't hesitate. "Study more people," he told Aserinsky. "You might be on to something."

By late 1952, Aserinsky had upgraded his equipment and embarked on a study of two dozen adults. Their brain patterns looked just like Armond's: periods of slow undulations, punctuated by bursts of intense activity. The flare-ups had no precedent in the sleep research literature, so he wasn't even sure what to call them. He consulted Kleitman again, and the two of them reviewed the data. If they were going to report such an unusual finding and claim it was universal, they'd better be sure of their measurements.

Their report finally appeared in September of 1953 in the journal *Science*. The paper was all of two pages, but Aserinsky and Kleitman did not undersell the implications of their work. "The fact that these eye movements, this EEG pattern, and autonomic nervous system activity are significantly related and do not occur randomly suggests that these physiological phenomena, and probably dreaming, are very likely all manifestations of a particular level of cortical activity which is encountered normally during sleep," they concluded. "An eye movement period first appears about three hours after going to sleep, recurs two hours later, and then emerges at somewhat closer intervals a third or fourth time shortly prior to awakening." They

eventually settled on a more scientific-sounding name for the phenomenon: rapid eye movement, or REM, sleep.

"This was really the beginning of modern sleep research, though
you wouldn't have known it at the time," William Dement, then a
medical student in Kleitman's lab and now a professor of psychiatry
and sleep medicine at Stanford University, told me. "It took years for
people to realize what we had."

One reason for the delay was lingering infatuation with an old
theory. In the 1950s many brain scientists, particularly in the United
States, were still smitten with Freud's idea that dreams are wish fulfillment, played out in fantasy and symbolic imagery that's not accessible during waking. Money poured into sleep research but it was
used to investigate the *content* of dreams during REM, not the mechanics or purpose of REM per se—and to little avail. People roused
from REM described a tangle of anxieties, fantasies, and nonsense
scenes that said nothing consistent about human nature. "It was ex-
citing work to do, but in the end we weren't able to say anything
conclusive," Dement told me. Still, those dream studies and others
confirmed beyond any doubt that REM was universal and occurred
periodically through the night, alternating with other states of unconsciousness. In fact, people typically experience four or five bursts
of REM during the night—of twenty to thirty minutes in duration—as the brain swims up to the brink of consciousness before
diving back down again. By 1960, sleep scientists began to speak of
sleep as having at least two dimensions: REM and non-REM, or
NREM.

Later, using EEG recordings as well as more specific electrical
recordings from the eyes and eyelids, researchers found that NREM
has its own distinct stages as well. The definition of these stages is
arbitrary, depending mostly on the shape and frequency of the
waves. The light sleep that descends shortly after we doze off was
called Stage 1; this is when the brain's jagged waves of conscious
awareness begin to soften. In Stage 2, the waves become more regu-

lar, resembling a sine wave, or a clean set of rollers moving toward shore on a windless day. In Stages 3 and 4, the waves gradually stretch out, until they undulate gently like a swell over open ocean, a slow-wave pattern that signals the arrival of deep sleep. The brain cycles though its five sleep stages in order: from Stage 1 down to Stage 2, deeper to Stage 3, and bottoming out at Stage 4, before floating back up, through Stages 3 and 2, and then into REM. The cycle then repeats throughout the night, dropping down again to Stage 4 and back up, to REM. These four stages and REM describe what scientists call sleep architecture, which maps easily onto a graph:

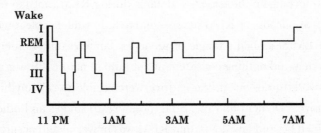

The discovery and description of this previously hidden architecture did more than banish the notion, once and for all, that our brains simply "power down" at night, becoming vessels for dreams. It also begged a question: If the brain is so active while we sleep, what's it up to, exactly? Nature doesn't waste resources on this scale. With its bursts of REM and intricate, alternating layers of wave patterns, the brain must be up to *something* during sleep. But what?

"To do science, you have to have an idea, and for years no one had one," J. Allan Hobson, a psychiatry professor at Harvard, told me. "They saw sleep as nothing but an annihilation of consciousness. Now we know different."

· · ·

One reason that palace intrigue makes for such page-turning fiction or addictive TV is what psychologists call "embedded hierarchy." The king is the king, the queen the queen, and there are layers of princes, heirs, relatives, ladies-in-waiting, meddling patriarchs, ambitious newcomers, and consigliere types, all scheming to climb to the top. Which alliances are most important? What's the power hierarchy? Who has leverage over whom? You have no idea until you see the individuals interact. And if you don't see them square off one-on-one, you play out different scenarios to see if you can judge the players' relative power. Could Grishilda have Thorian shackled and tossed in the moat if the two clashed? She is a favorite of the king's, after all. Yet Thorian might have some connections up his sleeve . . . wait, who's his mother again?

Learning scientists like embedded hierarchy problems because they model the sort of reasoning we have to do all the time, to understand work politics as well as math problems. We have to remember individual relationships, which is straight retention. We have to use those to induce logical extensions: if $A > B$ and $B > C$, then A must be $> C$. Finally, we need to incorporate those logical steps into a larger framework, to *deduce* the relationships between people or symbols that are distantly related. When successful, we build a bird's-eye view, a system to judge the relationship between any two figures in the defined universe, literary or symbolic, that's invisible to the untrained mind.

In a 2007 study, researchers at Harvard and McGill universities tested college students' ability to discern an embedded hierarchy in what looked like a simple game. The research team asked the students to study pairs of colored eggs, one pair at a time, on a computer screen. The eggs were ranked one over another. For example:

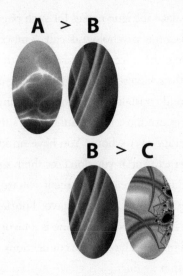

The students were split into two groups: one studied the eggs in the morning, one studied them in the evening. Both groups memorized the relative ranks of the pairs quickly and aced a test on them just afterward. But twelve hours later, the groups got another test, asking them to rank eggs they'd *not* seen directly compared. This is the "embedded" Grishilda-Thorian question, and the answer is not so obvious. If aqua trumps rainbow, does that mean it also trumps paisley? And what about coral? Does it rank third, or fourth? The students never got to see the entire ranking of all the eggs while studying, so it was hazy.

It was hazy, that is, until they slept on it.

The group that studied in the evening and took the test the next morning after a night's sleep—the "sleep group," as they were called—scored 93 percent on the most distantly related pair, i.e., the hardest question. The group that studied in the morning and took the test in the evening, without having slept—the "wake group"—scored 69 percent. A full twenty-four hours later, each student took the test yet again, and the sleep group's advantage had increased on the most distantly related pairs. That's a large difference on the hardest questions—35 percent, separating one kind of student from another—but it's not unusual in studies of sleep and learning. "We think what's happening during sleep is that you open the aperture of memory and are able to see this bigger picture," the study's senior author, Matthew Walker, told me. "There is evidence, in fact, that REM is this creative memory domain when you build different associations, combine things in different ways and so on."

In a game like this one, he and his coauthors argue, we are very good at building separate categories of associations (aqua over rainbow, paisley over coral), but the more obscure relationships *between* those categories are harder to sort out—until we sleep.

The investigation of sleep as consolidator of learning is still a work in progress. After scientists chasing Freud hit a wall in the 1960s, sleep research, like its nocturnal subjects, dropped off the deep end. The money tapered off. The window Eugene Aserinsky had opened, revealing REM sleep, seemed, for a time, to expose little more than another dark room. "You had this great excitement, basically followed by forty years of nothing; it was just horrible," Robert Stickgold, a neuroscientist at Harvard, told me. But in the past two decades, dozens of studies like Walker's have brightened the horizon, turning sleep into one of the most promising—and contentious— frontiers of learning science. The preponderance of evidence to date finds that sleep improves retention *and* comprehension of what was studied the day before, and not just for colored eggs. It works for vocabulary. Word pairs. Logical reasoning, similar to what's taught in middle school math. Even the presentation you'll be giving at work, or the exam that's coming up at school. For all of these, you need to memorize the details of important points and to develop a mental map of how they fit together. The improvements tend to be striking, between 10 and 30 percent, and scientists don't understand the dynamics of unconscious states well enough yet to explain why.

My own theory is that sleep amplifies many of the techniques we've discussed in this book. The spacing effect described in chapter 4, for instance, is especially strong with intervals of a day or two (plus sleep). Philip Ballard's "reminiscence"—that puzzling improvement in memory of "The Wreck of the Hesperus" poem described in chapter 2—crested in the first day or two. A good night's sleep could surely loosen the "fixedness" that makes it hard to see a solution to the Pencil Problem, discussed in chapter 6, right away. The brain is likely doing many of the same things with information while asleep as it does while awake—or at least performing *complementary* functions.

The story hardly ends there, however.

Scientists have begun to study the effects of interrupting particular stages of sleep, like REM, to isolate the impact those stages have on learning specific skills or topics. Remember, sleep has five dimensions that we know of: REM, and the four stages surrounding it. Our brain waves have distinct patterns in each of those periods, suggesting that different mental dynamics are at work in each one. Could it be that each stage is specialized to consolidate a specific kind of skill, whether it's a geometric proof, a writing assignment, or a tennis serve? Many scientists now suspect so, based on evidence that comes from both animals and humans. These findings have coalesced into a remarkable hypothesis, first described in 1995 by Italian scientists led by Antonio Giuditta at the University of Naples Federico II. The idea has since been fleshed out by others, mostly Robert Stickgold at Harvard and Carlyle Smith of Trent University in Peterborough, Ontario, who have contributed enough experimental heft to make this model of sleep learning a full-grown theory, the most comprehensive explanation yet for how the different stages of sleep consolidate memory.

Technically, I suppose, we should call this idea the Giuditta-Smith-Stickgold Model of Learning Consolidation. I prefer to call it, simply, the Night Shift Theory. The lights go out, and basic maintenance is done. Here's what the Night Shift Theory says happens overnight, during each stage:

Stage 1: This one is a scratch. It's impossible to deprive people of

Stage 1 light sleep, if they're going to sleep at all. Its role in consolidating memories is hard to isolate, though it's often laced with REM-like periods.

REM: These storms of neural firing appear to aid pattern recognition, as in the colored egg experiment, as well as creative problem solving and perceiving relationships that weren't apparent during the day, as in a difficult calculus problem. It likely plays the largest role, of all the stages, in aiding percolation. People still get these benefits from sleep sans REM—just not to the same degree. REM is also involved in interpreting emotionally charged memories. "We believe that it's during REM that the brain strips away the visceral feeling experienced at the time an emotional memory is formed," Matthew Walker, the Berkeley brain scientist who coauthored the colored egg study, told me, "but holds on to the actual information, the details, the where and when of what happened." That panic you felt the last time you opened a geometry exam? It's better to have that feeling "stripped"—or at least reduced—so you can recall what the panic-inducing problems actually were. Walker describes REM as "a nighttime therapy session."

Stage 2: This is the motor memory specialist. In a series of little-known studies, Carlyle Smith trained people in what he calls the "rotor task." This is a hand-eye coordination exercise in which people have to use their nonwriting hand to chase a moving spotlight across a computer screen using a joystick. It's easy enough to improve and people generally do—but not as quickly if they're deprived of Stage 2 sleep. "Stage 2 seems to be the single most critical stage for motor learning," Smith told me. "When we deprive people of Stage 2, we don't see that same level of improvement, and we believe the findings extend to all types of motor learning, whether it's music or athletics and possibly mechanical skills."

Stages 3 and 4: These two are usually lumped together in learning research as slow-wave or deep sleep. This is prime retention territory. Starve people of deep slumber, and it doesn't just dim their beauty;

they don't get the full benefit of sleep-aided recall of newly learned facts, studied vocabulary, names, dates, and formulas. "We have a lot of evidence that slow-wave is important for declarative memory consolidation, and that this doesn't happen as much in REM," Stickgold told me.

To put all this in some perspective, let's dial up the sleep architecture graph once more.

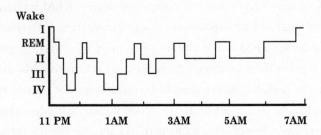

The first thing to note about this diagram is that it traces the architecture for a person who, in this case, goes to sleep at 11 P.M. and wakes up at 7 A.M. The architecture looks roughly the same for everyone, though, no matter what time he or she regularly goes to bed and wakes up. In an important sense, getting the usual doses of all five stages is the meaning of a full night's sleep. Each stage somehow complements the others' work. Where it really gets interesting is when we alter our usual sleep schedule to prepare for some performance, whether a speech, a tryout, or an exam.

Notice, for example, that the longest stretch of Stage 2 sleep is just before waking. Cut that short and you miss out on the period when your brain is consolidating a skateboarding move, a difficult piano fingering, or your jump shot. "The implication is that if you are preparing for a performance—a music recital, say—it's better to stay up late than get up early," Smith told me. "These coaches that have athletes or other performers up at five o'clock in the morning, I think that's crazy."

The same logic applies to REM. The largest dose is in the early morning, between those chunks of Stage 2. If you're prepping for a math or chemistry test, an exam that's going to strain your ability to detect patterns, better to stay up late and, if possible, hit the snooze button in the morning. Let the cock crow till he's hoarse.

Deep sleep, on the other hand, pools in the front half of a typical night's slumber, as you can see from the diagram. That's the slow wavelength you want when preparing for a test of retention, like new vocabulary, or filling in the periodic table. Arrange your studying so that you hit the sack at your regular time, get a strong dose of the deep stuff—and roll out of bed early for a quick review before dawn.

All of this is to say that if you're going to burn the candle, it helps to have some idea of which end to burn.

Here's the best part: You may not have to burn it at all.

Napping is sleep, too. In a series of experiments over the past decade, Sara Mednick of the University of California, San Diego, has found that naps of an hour to an hour and half often contain slow-wave deep sleep and REM. People who study in the morning—whether it's words or pattern recognition games, straight retention or comprehension of deeper structure—do about 30 percent better on an evening test if they've had an hour-long nap than if they haven't. "It's changed the way I work, doing these studies," Mednick told me. "It's changed the way I live. With naps of an hour to an hour and half, we've found in some experiments that you get close to the same benefits in learning consolidation that you would from a full eight-hour night's sleep."

. . .

Learning is hard. Thinking is hard. It's as exhausting, though in a different way, as physical labor and wears most of us down at a similar rate. Yes, some people can spend fourteen hours a day doing grueling mental work and then relax by solving puzzles or attending poetry readings by some Eastern European exile. Good for them.

Me, I fall more squarely in the Michael Gazzaniga camp of learning. Gazzaniga, the neuroscientist who discovered the right brain/left brain specialization we explored in chapter 1, worked long days and nights in the lab at Caltech on his landmark studies. "We had all these people at Caltech back then who became big names—Richard Feynman, Roger Sperry, Murray Gell-Mann, Sidney Coleman—but we weren't working all the time," Gazzaniga told me. "We weren't intellectuals in the sense that we were going out to see people lecturing or cultural events in the evening. That was martini time."

And we're almost there.

Let's return to Jerome Siegel's theory of sleep, the one we described at the beginning of the chapter. He argues that sleep evolved to keep us safe when the hunting and gathering was scarce or too risky. We are awake when the foraging is good, when socializing in the group is important, and asleep when there's no percentage in pursuing any of the above, when the costs are too high. Sleep occupies so much time because it's so central to immediate, day-to-day survival.

It's no stretch to say, however, that learning—in school, at work, at practice—is equally crucial to the survival game. Mastering a subject or skill may not be as urgent as avoiding some saber-toothed cat, but over a lifetime our knowledge and skills become increasingly valuable—and need to be continually updated. Learning is how we figure out what we want to do, what we're good at, how we might make a living when the time comes. That's survival, too. Yet, especially when we're young, we have a terrible time trying to sort out what's important from what's not. Life is confusing, it moves fast, we're fielding all sorts of often conflicting messages and demands from parents, teachers, friends, and rivals. There aren't enough hours in the day to think through what it all means.

That's reason enough to suspect that what the brain does at night is about more than safety. The sleep-wake cycle may have evolved primarily to help us eat and not be eaten but if that downtime can be put to good use, then evolutionary theory tells us it will. What better way to sift the day's perceptions and flag those that seem most important? A tracking skill. A pattern of movement in the bushes. An odd glance from a neighbor. A formula for calculating the volume of a cone. A new batting stance. A confounding plot in a Kafka novel. To sort all that variety, sleep might absolutely evolve distinct stages to handle different categories of learning, whether retention or comprehension, thermodynamics or Thucydides. I am not arguing that each state of sleep is specialized, that *only* REM can handle math and *only* deep sleep can help store Farsi verbs. Anyone who's pulled an all-nighter or two knows that we don't need any sleep at all to learn a pile of new material, at least temporarily. I am saying the research thus far suggests that each of sleep's five stages helps us consolidate learning in a different way.

Siegel's theory tells us that exhaustion descends when the costs of staying up outweigh its benefits. The Night Shift Theory gives us the reason why: because sleep has benefits, too—precisely for sorting through and consolidating what we've just been studying or practicing. Seen in this way, it's yin and yang. Learning crests during waking hours, giving way to sleep at the moment of diminishing returns, when prolonged wakefulness is a waste of time. Sleep, then, finishes the job.

I've always loved my sleep, but in the context of learning I assumed it was getting in the way. Not so. The latest research says exactly the opposite: that unconscious downtime clarifies memory and sharpens skills—that it's a necessary step to lock in both. In a fundamental sense, that is, sleep *is* learning.

No one is sure how the brain manages the sensory assault that is a day's input, biologically. The science of sleep is still in its infancy. Yet one of its leading theorists, Giulio Tononi of the University of Wisconsin, has found evidence that sleep brings about a large-scale weakening of the neural connections made during the previous day. Remember all those linked neural networks forming every moment we're awake? Tononi argues that the primary function of sleep is to shake off the trivial connections made during the day and "help consolidate the valuable inferences that were made." The brain is separating the signal from the noise, by letting the noise die down, biologically speaking. Active consolidation is likely going on as well. Studies in animals have found direct evidence of "crosstalk" between distinct memory-related organs (the hippocampus and the neocortex, described in chapter 1) during sleep, as if the brain is reviewing, and storing, details of the most important events of the day—and integrating the new material with the old.

I sure don't know the whole story. No one does, and maybe no one ever will. The properties of sleep that make it such an unreliable companion—often shallow, elusive when most needed, or arriving when least wanted—also make it difficult to study in a controlled way over time. It's likely that the sleep stages, arbitrarily defined by brain wave changes, may be replaced by more precise measures, like the chemical cocktails circulating during sleep states, or different types of "crosstalk." My bet, though, is that the vast promise of tweaking sleep as a means to deepen learning will tempt someone into longer-term experiments, comparing the effects of different schedules on specific topics. Those effects will likely be highly individual, like so many others described in this book. Some night owls may find early morning study sessions torturously unproductive, and some early birds get their chakras bent out of joint after 10 P.M. At least with the Night Shift Theory, we have some basis on which to experiment on our own, to adjust our sleep to our advantage where possible.

Put it this way: I no longer think of naps or knocking off early as evidence of laziness, or a waste of time, or, worst of all, a failure of will. I think of sleep as learning with my eyes closed.

Conclusion

The Foraging Brain

I began this book with the allegation that most of our instincts about learning are misplaced, incomplete, or flat wrong. That we invent learning theories out of whole cloth, that our thinking is rooted more in superstition than in science, and that we misidentify the sources of our frustration: that we get in our own way, unnecessarily, all the time. In the chapters that followed, I demonstrated as much, describing landmark experiments and some of the latest thinking about how remembering, forgetting, and learning are all closely related in ways that are neither obvious nor intuitive. I also showed how those unexpected relationships can be exploited by using specific learning techniques.

What I have *not* done is try to explain why we don't know all this already.

If learning is so critical to survival, why do we remain so ignorant about when, where, and how it happens? We do it naturally, after all. We think about how best to practice, try new approaches, ask others we think are smarter for advice. The drive to improve never really ends, either. By all rights, we should have developed pretty keen instincts about how best to approach learning. But we haven't, and the reasons why aren't at all apparent. No one that I know of has come forward with a convincing explanation, and the truth is, there may not be one.

I do have one of my own, however, and it's this: School was born yesterday. English class, Intro to Trig, study hall, soccer practice, piano lessons, social studies, art history, the Russian novel, organic chemistry, Zeno's paradoxes, jazz trumpet, Sophocles and sophomore year, Josephus and gym class, Modern Poetry and Ancient Civilizations: All of it, every last component of what we call education, is a recent invention in the larger scheme of things. Those "ancient" civilizations we studied in middle school? They're not so ancient, after all. They date from a few thousand years ago, no more. Humans have been around for at least a million, and for the vast majority of that time we've been preoccupied with food, shelter, and safety. We've been avoiding predators, ducking heavy weather, surviving by our wits, foraging. And life for foragers, as the Harvard psychologist Steven Pinker so succinctly puts it, "is a camping trip that never ends."

Our foraging past had some not so obvious consequences for learning. Think for a moment about what it meant, that lifelong camping trip. Hunting and tracking *were* your reading and writing. Mapping the local environment—its every gully, clearing, and secret garden—*was* your geometry. The science curriculum included botany, knowing which plant had edible berries and which medicinal properties; and animal behavior, knowing the hunting routines of predators, the feeding habits of prey.

Over the years you'd get an education, all right. Some of it would come from elders and peers, but most of it would be accumulated through experience. Listening. Watching. Exploring the world in ever-widening circles. *That* is how the brain grew up learning, piecemeal and on the fly, at all hours of the day, in every kind of weather.

As we foraged for food, the brain adapted to absorb—at maximum efficiency—the most valuable cues and survival lessons along the way.

It became a forager, too—for information, for strategies, for clever ways to foil other species' defenses and live off the land. That's the academy where our brains learned to learn, and it defines who we are and how we came to be human.

Humans fill what the anthropologists John Tooby and Irven De-Vore called the "cognitive niche" in evolutionary history. Species thrive at the expense of others, each developing defenses and weapons to try to dominate the niche it's in. The woodpecker evolved an extraordinary bone structure to pound holes in tough bark and feed on the insects hidden in trees. The brown bat evolved an internal sonar, called echolocation, allowing it to hunt insects at dusk. We evolved to outwit our competitors, by observing, by testing our intuitions, by devising tools, traps, fishhooks, theories, and more.

The modern institution of education, which grew out of those vestigial ways of learning, has produced generations of people with dazzling skills, skills that would look nothing less than magical to our foraging ancestors. Yet its language, customs, and schedules—dividing the day into chunks (classes, practices) and off-hours into "study time" (homework)—has come to define how we think the brain works, or should work. That definition is so well known that it's taken for granted, never questioned. We all "know" we need to be organized, to develop good, consistent study routines, to find a quiet place and avoid distractions, to focus on one skill at a time, and above all, to *concentrate* on our work. What's to question about that?

A lot, it turns out. Take "concentration," for example, that most basic educational necessity, that mental flow we're told is so precious to learning. What is concentration, exactly? We all have an idea of what it means. We know it when we see it, and we'd like more of it. Yet it's an ideal, a mirage, a word that blurs the reality of what the brain actually does while learning.

I remember bringing my younger daughter to my newspaper office one weekend a few years ago when she was twelve. I was consumed with a story I had to finish, so I parked her at an empty desk near mine and logged her into the computer. And then I strapped in at my desk and focused on finishing—focused hard. Occasionally, I looked up and was relieved to see that she was typing and seemed engrossed, too. After a couple hours of intense work, I finished the story and sent it off to my editor. At which point, I asked my daughter what she'd been up to. She showed me. She'd been keeping a moment-to-moment log of my behavior as I worked. She'd been taking field notes, like Jane Goodall observing one of her chimpanzees:

> 10:46—types
> 10:46—scratches head
> 10:47—gets papers from printer
> 10:47—turns chair around
> 10:48—turns chair back around
> 10:49—sighs
> 10:49—sips tea
> 10:50—stares at computer
> 10:51—puts on headset
> 10:51—calls person, first word is "dude"
> 10:52—hangs up
> 10:52—puts finger to face, midway between mouth and chin, thinking pose?
> 10:53—friend comes to desk, he laughs
> 10:53—scratches ear while talking

And so on, for three pages. I objected. She was razzing me, naturally, but the phone call wasn't true, was it? Did I make a call? Hadn't I been focused the whole time, locked in, hardly looking away from my screen? Hadn't I come in and cranked out my story without coming up for air? Apparently not, not even close. The truth was, she could never have invented all those entries, all that detail. I did the work, all right, and I'd had to focus on it. Except that, to an outside observer, I looked fidgety, distracted—*un*focused.

The point is not that concentration doesn't exist, or isn't important. It's that it doesn't necessarily look or feel like we've been told it does. Concentration may, in fact, include any number of breaks, diversions, and random thoughts. That's why many of the techniques described in this book might seem unusual at first, or out of step with what we're told to expect. We're still in foraging mode to a larger extent than we know. The brain has not yet adapted to "fit" the vocabulary of modern education, and the assumptions built into that vocabulary mask its true nature as a learning organ.

The fact that we can and do master modern inventions like Euclidean proofs, the intricacies of bond derivatives, and the fret board hardly means those ancient instincts are irrelevant or outmoded. On the contrary, many scientists suspect that the same neural networks that helped us find our way back to the campsite have been "repurposed" to help us find our way through the catacombs of academic and motor domains. Once central to tracking our location in physical space, those networks adjusted to the demands of education and training. We don't need them to get home anymore. We know our address. The brain's internal GPS—it long ago evolved internal communities of so-called grid cells and place cells, to spare us the death sentence of getting lost—has retuned itself. It has adapted, if not yet perfectly.

Scientists are still trying to work out how those cells help us find our way in modern-day learning. One encompassing theory is called the Meaning Maintenance Model, and the idea is this: Being lost, confused, or disoriented creates a feeling of distress. To relieve that distress, the brain kicks into high gear, trying to find or make meaning, looking for patterns, some way out of its bind—some path back to the campsite. "We have a need for structure, for things to make sense, and when they don't, we're so motivated to get rid of that feeling that our response can be generative," Travis Proulx, a psychologist at Tilburg University in the Netherlands, told me. "We begin to hunger for meaningful patterns, and that can help with certain kinds of learning."

Which kinds? We don't know for sure, not yet. In one experiment, Proulx and Steven J. Heine, a psychologist at the University of British Columbia, found that deliberately confusing college students—by having them read a nonsensical short story based on one by Franz Kafka—improved their performance by almost 30 percent on a test of hidden pattern recognition, similar to the colored egg test we discussed in Chapter 10. The improvements were subconscious; the students had no awareness they were picking up more. "Kafka starts out normally, the first couple pages make you think it's going to be a standard narrative and then it gets stranger and stranger," Proulx told me. "Psychologists don't really have a word for the feeling that he creates, but to me it goes back to the older existentialists, to a nostalgia for unity, a feeling of uncanniness. It's unnerving. You want to find your way back to meaning, and that's what we think helps you to extract these very complex patterns in this artificial grammar, and perhaps essential patterns in much more that we're asked to study."

When we describe ourselves as being "lost" in some class or subject, that sentiment can be self-fulfilling, a prelude to failure or permission to disengage entirely, to stop trying. For the living brain, however, being *lost*—literally, in some wasteland, or figuratively, in *The Waste Land*—is not the same as being helpless. On the contrary, disorientation flips the GPS settings to "hypersensitive," warming the mental circuits behind incubation, percolation, even the nocturnal insights of sleep. If the learner is motivated at all, he or she is now mentally poised to find the way home. Being lost is not necessarily the end of the line, then. Just as often, it's a beginning.

· · ·

I have been a science reporter for twenty-eight years, my entire working life, and for most of that time I had little interest in writing a nonfiction book for adults. It was too close to my day job. When you spend eight or nine hours a day sorting through studies, interviewing scientists, chasing down contrary evidence and arguments, you want to shut down the factory at the end of the day. You don't want to do more of the same; you don't want to do more at all. So I wrote fiction instead—two science-based mysteries for kids—adventures in made-up places starring made-up characters. As far from newspapering as I could get.

The science itself is what turned me around. Learning science, cognitive psychology, the study of memory—call it what you like. The more I discovered about it, the stronger the urge to do something bigger than a news story. It dawned on me that all these scientists, toiling in obscurity, were producing a body of work that was more than interesting or illuminating or groundbreaking. It was practical, and not only that, it played right into the way I had blossomed as a student all those years ago, when I let go of the reins a bit and widened the margins. I was all over the place in college. I lived in casual defiance of any good study habits and also lived—more so than I ever would have following "good" study habits—*with* the material I was trying to master. My grades were slightly better than in high school, in much harder courses. In a way, I have been experimenting with that approach ever since.

The findings from learning science have allowed me to turn my scattered nonstrategy into tactics, a game plan. These findings aren't merely surprising. They're specific and useful. Right now. Today. And the beauty is, they can be implemented without spending a whole lot more time and effort and without investing in special classes, tutors, or prep schools.

In that sense, I see this body of work as a great equalizer. After all, there's so much about learning that we can't control. Our genes. Our teachers. Where we live or go to school. We can't choose our family environment, whether Dad is a helicopter parent or helicopter pilot, whether Mom is nurturing or absent. We get what we get. If we're lucky, that means a "sensuous education" of the James family variety, complete with tutors, travel, and decades of in-depth, full-immersion learning. If we're not, then . . . not.

About the only thing we can control is *how* we learn. The science tells us that doing a little here, a little there, fitting our work into the pockets of the day is not some symptom of eroding "concentration," the cultural anxiety du jour. It's spaced study, when done as described in this book, and it results in more efficient, deeper learning, not less. The science gives us a breath of open air, the freeing sensation that we're not crazy just because we can't devote every hour to laser-focused practice. Learning is a restless exercise and that restlessness applies not only to the timing of study sessions but also to their content, i.e., the value of mixing up old and new material in a single sitting.

I've begun to incorporate learning science into a broad-based theory about how I think about life. It goes like this: Just as modern assumptions about good study habits are misleading, so, too, are our assumptions about bad habits.

Think about it for a second. Distraction, diversion, catnaps, interruptions—these aren't mere footnotes, mundane details in an otherwise purposeful life. That's your ten-year-old interrupting, or your dog, or your mom. That restless urge to jump up is hunger or thirst, the diversion a TV show that's integral to your social group. You took that catnap because you were tired, and that break because you were stuck. These are the stitches that hold together our daily existence; they represent life itself, not random deviations from it. Our study and practice time needs to orient itself around them—not the other way around.

That's not an easy idea to accept, given all we've been told. I didn't trust any of these techniques much at first, even after patting my college self on the back for doing everything (mostly) right. Self-congratulation is too easy and no basis for making life changes. It was only later, when I first began to look closely at the many dimensions of forgetting that my suspicious ebbed. I'd always assumed that forgetting was bad, a form of mental corrosion; who doesn't?

As I dug into the science, however, I had to reverse the definition entirely. Forgetting is as critical to learning as oxygen, I saw. The other adjustments followed, with trial and error. For example, I like to finish. Interrupting myself a little early *on purpose*, to take advantage of the Zeigarnik effect, does not come naturally to me. Unfortunately (or, fortunately) I have no choice. Being a reporter—not to mention a husband, dad, brother, son, and drinking partner—means having to drop larger projects, repeatedly, before having a chance to sit down and complete them. Percolation, then, is a real thing. It happens for me, all the time, and without it I could never have written this book.

Applying these and other techniques has not made me a genius. Brilliance is an idol, a meaningless projection, not a real goal. I'm continually caught short in topics I'm supposed to know well, and embarrassed by what I don't know. Yet even that experience smells less of defeat than it once did. Given the dangers of fluency, or misplaced confidence, exposed ignorance seems to me like a cushioned fall. I go down, all right, but it doesn't hurt as much as it once did. Most important, the experience acts as a reminder to check and re-check what I assume I know (to self-test).

The science of learning is not even "science" to me anymore. It's how I live. It's how I get the most out of what modest skills I've got. No more than that, and no less.

I will continue to follow the field. It's hard not to, once you see how powerful the tools can be—and how easily deployed. The techniques I've laid out here are mostly small alterations that can have large benefits, and I suspect that future research will focus on applications. Yes, scientists will surely do more basic work, perhaps discovering other, better techniques and more complete theories. The clear value of what's already there, however, begs for an investigation into how specific techniques, or *combinations*, suit specific topics. "Spaced interleaving" may be the best way to drive home math concepts, for instance. Teachers might begin to schedule their "final" exam for the first day of class, as well as the last. Late night, mixed-drill practice sessions could be the wave of the future to train musicians and athletes. Here's one prediction I'd be willing to bet money on: Perceptual learning tools will have an increasingly central role in advanced training—of surgeons and scientists, as well as pilots, radiologists, crime scene investigators, and more—and perhaps in elementary education as well.

Ultimately, though, this book is not about some golden future. The persistent, annoying, amusing, ear-scratching present is the space we want to occupy. The tools in this book are solid, they work in real time, and using them will bring you more in tune with the beautiful, if eccentric, learning machine that is your brain. Let go of what you feel you should be doing, all that repetitive, overscheduled, driven, focused ritual. Let go, and watch how the presumed *enemies* of learning—ignorance, distraction, interruption, restlessness, even quitting—can work in your favor.

Learning is, after all, what you do.

Appendix
. . . .

Eleven Essential Questions

Q: *Can "freeing the inner slacker" really be called a legitimate learning strategy?*

A: If it means guzzling wine in front of the TV, then no. But to the extent that it means appreciating learning as a restless, piecemeal, subconscious, and somewhat sneaky process that occurs all the time—not just when you're sitting at a desk, face pressed into a book—then it's the best strategy there is. And it's the only one available that doesn't require more time and effort on your part, that doesn't increase the pressure to achieve. If anything, the techniques outlined in this book take some of the pressure off.

Q: *How important is routine when it comes to learning? For example, is it important to have a dedicated study area?*

A: Not at all. Most people do better over time by varying their study or practice locations. The more environments in which you rehearse,

the sharper and more lasting the memory of that material becomes—
and less strongly linked to one "comfort zone." That is, knowledge
becomes increasingly *independent* of surroundings the more changes
you make—taking your laptop onto the porch, out to a café, on the
plane. The goal, after all, is to be able to perform well in any conditions.

Changing locations is not the only way to take advantage of the
so-called context effect on learning, however. Altering the time of
day you study also helps, as does changing how you engage the material, by reading or discussing, typing into a computer or writing by
hand, reciting in front of a mirror or studying while listening to
music: Each counts as a different learning "environment" in which
you store the material in a different way.

Q: *How does sleep affect learning?*

A: We now know that sleep has several stages, each of which
consolidates and filters information in a different way. For instance, studies show that "deep sleep," which is concentrated in
the first half of the night, is most valuable for retaining hard
facts—names, dates, formulas, concepts. If you're preparing for a
test that's heavy on retention (foreign vocabulary, names and
dates, chemical structures), it's better to hit the sack at your usual
time, get that full dose of deep sleep, and roll out of bed early
for a quick review. But the stages of sleep that help consolidate
motor skills and creative thinking—whether in math, science, or
writing—occur in the morning hours, before waking. If it's a
music recital or athletic competition you're preparing for, or a test
that demands creative thinking, you might consider staying up a
little later than usual and sleeping in. As discussed in chapter 10:
If you're going to burn the candle, it helps to know which end to
burn it on.

Q: *Is there an optimal amount of time to study or practice?*

A: More important than how long you study is how you distribute the study time you have. Breaking up study or practice time—dividing it into two or three sessions, instead of one—is far more effective than concentrating it. If you've allotted two hours to mastering a German lesson, for example, you'll remember more if you do an hour today and an hour tomorrow, or—even better—an hour the next day. That split forces you to reengage the material, dig up what you already know, and *re*-store it—an active mental step that reliably improves memory. Three sessions is better still, as long as you're giving yourself enough time to dive into the material or the skills each time. Chapter 4 explores why spacing study time is the most powerful and reliable technique scientists know of to deepen and extend memory.

Q: *Is cramming a bad idea?*

A: Not always. Cramming works fine as a last resort, a way to ramp up fast for an exam if you're behind and have no choice. It's a time-tested solution, after all. The downside is that, after the test, you won't remember a whole lot of what you "learned"—if you remember any at all. The reason is that the brain can sharpen a memory only after some forgetting has occurred. In this way, memory is like a muscle: A little "breakdown" allows it to subsequently build greater strength. Cramming, by definition, prevents this from happening.

Spaced rehearsal or study (see previous question) or self-examination (see next question) are far more effective ways to prepare. You'll remember the material longer and be able to carry it into the next course or semester easily. Studies find that people remember up to twice as much of material that they rehearsed in spaced or tested sessions than during cramming. If you must cram, do so in courses that are not central to your main area of focus.

Q: *How much does quizzing oneself, like with flashcards, help?*

A: A lot, actually. Self-testing is one of the strongest study techniques there is. Old-fashioned flashcards work fine; so does a friend, work colleague, or classmate putting you through the paces. The best self-quizzes do two things: They force you to *choose* the right answer from several possibilities; and they give you immediate feedback, right or wrong. As laid out in chapter 5, self-examination improves retention and comprehension far more than an equal amount of review time. It can take many forms as well. Reciting a passage from memory, either in front of a colleague or the mirror, is a form of testing. So is explaining it to yourself while pacing the kitchen, or to a work colleague or friend over lunch. As teachers often say, "You don't fully understand a topic until you have to teach it." Exactly right.

Q: *How much does it help to review notes from a class or lesson?*

A: The answer depends on how the reviewing is done. Verbatim copying adds very little to the depth of your learning, and the same goes for looking over highlighted text or formulas. Both exercises are fairly passive, and can cause what learning scientists call a "fluency illusion": the impression that, because something is self-evident in the moment, it will remain that way in a day, or a week. Not necessarily so. Just because you've marked something or rewritten it, digitally or on paper, doesn't mean your brain has engaged the material more deeply. Studying highlighted notes and trying to write them out—without looking—works memory harder and is a much more effective approach to review. There's an added benefit as well: It also shows you immediately what you don't know and need to circle back and review.

Q: *There's so much concern that social media and smartphones and all manner of electronic gadgets are interfering with learning—and even changing the way people think. Is this merited? Is distraction* **always bad?**

A: No. Distraction is a hazard if you need continuous focus, like when listening to a lecture. But a short study break—five, ten, twenty minutes to check in on Facebook, respond to a few emails, check sports scores—is the most effective technique learning scientists know of to help you solve a problem when you're stuck. Distracting yourself from the task at hand allows you to let go of mistaken assumptions, reexamine the clues in a new way, and come back fresh. If you're motivated to solve the problem—whether it's a proof, an integral, or a paragraph you just can't get right—your brain will continue to work on it during the break *off-line*, subconsciously, without the (fixated, unproductive) guidance you've been giving it. The evidence on this is discussed in chapter 6.

Q: *Is there any effective strategy for improving performance on longer-term creative projects?*

A: Yes. Simply put: *Start* them as early as possible, and give yourself permission to walk away. Deliberate interruption is not the same as quitting. On the contrary, stopping work on a big, complicated presentation, term paper, or composition activates the project in your mind, and you'll begin to see and hear all sorts of things in your daily life that are relevant. You'll also be more tuned into what you *think* about those random, incoming clues. This is all fodder for your project—it's interruption working in your favor—though you do need to return to the desk or drafting table before too long. The main elements in this "percolation" process are detailed in chapter 7.

Q: *What's the most common reason for bombing a test after what felt like careful preparation?*

A: The illusion that you "knew" something well just because it seemed so self-evident at the time you studied it. This is what learning scientists call "fluency," the assumption that because something is well known now it will remain that way. Fluency illusions form automatically and subconsciously. Beware study "aids" that can reinforce the illusion: highlighting or rewriting notes, working from a teacher's outline, *re*studying after you've just studied. These are mostly passive exercises, and they enrich learning not at all. Making your memory work a little harder—by self-quizzing, for example, or spacing out study time—sharpens the imprint of what you know, and exposes fluency's effects.

Q: *Is it best to practice one skill at a time until it becomes automatic, or to work on many things at once?*

A: Focusing on one skill at a time—a musical scale, free throws, the quadratic formula—leads quickly to noticeable, tangible improvement. But over time, such focused practice actually limits our development of each skill. Mixing or "interleaving" multiple skills in a practice session, by contrast, sharpens our grasp of all of them. This principle applies broadly to a range of skills, and can be incorporated into daily homework or practice—by doing a geometry proof from early in the term, for example, or playing arpeggios you learned years ago, or intermingling artistic styles in studying for an art history class. This kind of mixing not only acts as a review but also sharpens your discrimination skills, as described in Chapter 8. In a subject like math, this is enormously helpful. Mixed-problem sets—just adding one or two from earlier lessons—not only reminds you what you've learned but also trains you to *match* the problem types with the appropriate strategies.

Acknowledgments

Writing a book is one part lonely effort and two parts group therapy, and I am forever grateful to those who provided the latter. To Kris Dahl, my exuberantly effective agent, and to Andy Ward, my editor, an exacting collaborator who forced me to think through the ideas in this book more clearly and deeply—the best company anyone could have. I owe a great debt to Barbara Strauch at *The New York Times* for years of support and advice, and my colleagues at the Science Times. I thank Rick Flaste for seeing (decades ago) that behavior was a beat worth covering and for bringing me to a great newspaper that continues to cover scientific research in depth.

My work has allowed me access to the many scientists who provided the bones of this book. Among them, I am grateful to Suzanne Corkin, Michael Gazzaniga, Daniel Willingham, Philip Kellman, Steven Smith, Doug Rohrer, Matt Walker, Henry Roediger III, Harry Bahrick, Ronda Leathers Dively, the great Todd Sacktor, and especially Robert and Elizabeth Ligon Bjork, who reviewed large portions of the manuscript and helped me understand the most difficult pockets of the science. I am also in debt to the staff at Columbia University's Social Work Library and the University of Colorado's Library for Research Assistance. Any mistakes that remain in the text are all mine.

I leaned heavily on family and friends every step of the way: My parents, James and Catherine, and my sister, Rachel, who all provided big love and a place for me to hole up, pace, talk to myself, and write; my brothers, Simon and Noah; my daughters, Isabel and Flora, who helped me through tough spots; and my wife, Victoria, who provided editing and advice virtually every day. Special mention goes to my friends Mark Zaremba, who delivered the graphics, and to Tom Hicks and John Hastings, for listening to hours of arcane complaints about this project, even while splitting the bar tab.

Notes

· · · · · · · · · · · · ·

Chapter One: The Story Maker

3 **scents of daily life** For the general discussion of brain biology, I relied on two books: Eric R. Kandel, M.D., *In Search of Memory* (New York: W.W. Norton & Company, 2006); and Larry R. Squire and Eric R. Kandel, *Memory from Mind to Molecules, second edition* (Greenwood Village, CO: Roberts & Company, 2009).

3 **up its gray matter** Paul Reber, "What Is the Memory Capacity of the Human Brain?" *Scientific American*, May/June 2010.

7 **awaiting surgery** Gelbard-Sagiv, Roy Mukamel, Michal Harel, Rafael Malach, and Itzhak Fried, "Internally Generated Reactivation of Single Neurons in Human Hippocampus During Free Recall," *Science* 322, 2008, 96–100.

10 **named Henry Molaison** For my discussion of H.M., I relied on interviews with Brenda Milner and Suzanne Corkin as well as Corkin's book *Permanent Present Tense* (New York: Basic Books, 2013).

12 **drawing hand in a mirror** Squire and Kandel, *Memory from Mind to Molecules, second edition.*

16 **one hemisphere at a time** For my discussion of split-brain work, I relied on interviews with Michael Gazzaniga and the following studies: M. S. Gazzaniga, "Forty-five years of split-brain research and still going strong," *Nature Reviews Neuroscience* 6, August 2005, 653–59; M. S. Gazzaniga, J. E. Bogen, and R. W. Sperry, "Dyspraxia following division of the cerebral commissures," *Archives of Neurology*, Vol. 16, No. 6, June 1967, 606–612; M. S. Gazzaniga, J. E. Bogen, and R. W. Sperry, "Observations on visual perception after disconnexion of the cerebral hemispheres in man," *Brain*, Vol. 88, Part 2, June 1965, 221–36; M. S. Gazzaniga, J. E. Bogen, and R. W. Sperry, "Some functional effects of sectioning the cerebral commissures in man," *Proceedings of the National Academy of Sciences of the United States of America*, Vol. 48, No. 10, Oct. 1962, 1765–69.

18 **only the shovel** For this I relied on an interview with Michael Gazzaniga, for his recollection of the experiment that triggered his conclusion.

Chapter Two: The Power of Forgetting

23 **we remembered nothing** William James, *The Principles of Psychology, Volume I* (New York: Henry Holt and Company, 1890), 680.

25 **and related ideas** Robert A. Bjork and Elizabeth Ligon Bjork, "A New Theory of Disuse and an Old Theory of Stimulus Fluctuation." In A. Healy, S. Kossly, and R. Shiffrin, eds., *From Learning Processes to Cognitive Processes: Essays in Honor of William K. Estes, Volume 2* (Hillsdale, NJ: Erlbaum, 1992), 35–67.

28 **remains a mystery** David Shakow, "Hermann Ebbinghaus," *The American Journal of Psychology* 42, No. 4, Oct. 1930, 511.

30 **working-class East End** Matthew Hugh Erdelyi, *The Recovery of*

Unconscious Memories: Hypermnesia and Reminiscence (Chicago: The University of Chicago Press, 1998), 11.

31 **caused mostly confusion** Philip Boswood Ballard, *Obliviscence and Reminiscence* (Cambridge, England: Cambridge University Press, 1913).

32 **They did worse over time, on average, not better** For more on spontaneous improvements, see Erdelyi, *The Recovery of Unconscious Memories,* 44–71 , and W. Brown, "To What Extent Is Memory Measured By a Single Recall?," *Journal of Experimental Psychology* 54, 1924, 345–52.

32 **their scores plunged** J. A. McGeoch, F. McKinney, and H. N. Peters, "Studies in retroactive inhibition IX: Retroactive inhibition, reproductive inhibition and reminiscence," *Journal of Experimental Psychology* 20, 1937, 131–43.

32 **twenty-four-hour period** S. Gray, "The Influence of Methodology Upon the Measurement of Reminiscence," *Journal of Experimental Psychology* 27, 1940, 37–44.

33 **in his history of the era** Erdelyi, *The Recovery of Unconscious Memories,* 44.

33 **in other words, a phantom** C. E. Buxton, "The Status of Research in Reminiscence," *Psychological Bulletin* 40, 1943, 313–40.

34 **then at Stanford University** Matthew Hugh Erdelyi and Jeff Kleinbard, "Has Ebbinghaus Decayed with Time?: The Growth of Recall (Hypermnesia) over Days," *Journal of Experimental Psychology: Human Learning and Memory,* Vol. 4, No. 4, July 1978, 275–89.

36 **is largely their baby** Robert A. Bjork and Elizabeth Ligon Bjork, "A New Theory of Disuse and an Old Theory of Stimulus Fluctuation." In A. Healy, S. Kossly, and R. Shiffrin, eds., *From Learning Processes to Cognitive Processes: Essays in Honor of William K. Estes, Vol. 2* (Hillsdale, NJ: Erlbaum, 1992), 35–67.

Chapter Three: Breaking Good Habits

47 **guide from Baylor University** Baylor University Academic Support Programs: Keeping Focused, www.baylor.edu/support_programs.

48 **premier diving destination** For more on shipwrecks in the area, see www.divesitedirectory.co.uk/uk_scotland_oban.html.

48 **an unusual learning experiment** D. R. Godden and A. D. Baddeley, "Context-Dependent Memory in Two Natural Environments: On Land and Underwater," *British Journal of Psychology*, Vol. 66, No. 3, 1975, 325–31.

48 **two dropped out due to nausea** K. Dallett and S. G. Wilcox, "Contextual Stimuli and Proactive Inhibition," *Journal of Experimental Psychology* 78, 1968, 475–80.

49 **like some cruel school yard prank** G. Rand and S. Wapner, "Postural Status as a Factor in Memory," *Journal of Verbal Learning and Verbal Behavior* 6, 1967, 268–71.

49 **twenty feet underwater** K. Dallett and S. G. Wilcox, "Contextual Stimuli and Proactive Inhibition," *Journal of Experimental Psychology* 78, 1968, 475–80.

49 **original learning is reinstated** *Ibid.*, 330.

49 **as opposed to, say, red** S. G. Dulsky, "The Effect of a Change of Background on Recall and Relearning," *Journal of Experimental Psychology* 18, 1935, 725–40.

49 **from a neutral test proctor** E. G. Geiselman and R. A. Bjork, "Primary versus Secondary Rehearsal in Imagined Voices: Differential Effects on Recognition," *Cognitive Psychology* 12, 1980, 188–205.

50 **so-called contextual cues** Steven M. Smith, "Background Music and Context-Dependent Memory," *American Journal of Psychology*, Vol. 98, No. 4, Winter 1985, 591–603.

50 **group did the worst** *Ibid.*, 596.

54 **Memory goes** Kay Redfield Jamison, *An Unquiet Mind: A Memoir of Moods and Madness* (New York: Random House, 2009), 67.

54 **they're again manic** Herbert Weingartner, Halbert Miller, and Dennis L. Murphy, "Mood-State-Dependent Retrieval of Verbal Associations," *Journal of Abnormal Psychology* 1977, Vol. 86, No. 3, 276–84. This research was originally presented at the meeting of the American Psychological Association, New Orleans, September 1974, as "State Dependent Recall in Manic Depressive Disorders."

55 **with newly studied information** James Eric Eich, et al, "State-Dependent Accessibility of Retrieval Cues in the Retention of a Categorized List," *Journal of Verbal Learning and Verbal Behavior* 14, 1975, 408–17.

57 **the time of desired recall** *Ibid.*, 415.

59 **recommended that he go see Luria** For the discussion of Shereshevsky's memory, I relied on Alexander Luria's book on the subject, *The Mind of a Mnemonist* (New York: Basic Books, 1968).

60 **man twirling his mustache** *Ibid.*, 31.

60 **see what I've written** *Ibid.*, 70.

61 **an image of himself looking at the board** *Ibid.*, 18–19.

61 **to answer that question** Steven M. Smith, Arthur Glenberg, and Robert A. Bjork, "Environmental Context and Human Memory," *Memory & Cognition*, Vol. 6, No. 4, 1978, 342–53.

63 **has since gone digital** My discussion of Smith's recent work comes from unpublished research by Steven M. Smith that he has presented at conferences and shared with me.

64 **due position in the room** John Locke, *An Essay on Human Understanding and a Treatise on the Conduct of Understanding* (Philadelphia: Hayes & Zell Publishers, 1854), 263.

Chapter Four: Spacing Out

68 **them at a single time** Frank N. Dempster, "The Spacing Effect: A Case Study in the Failure to Apply the Results of Psychological Research," *American Psychologist*, Vol. 43, No. 8, Aug. 1988, 627–34.

68 **became known as Jost's Law** For more on Jost's Law, see Demp-

ster, 627–28. A discussion of Jost's attitude toward eugenics is included in *The Nazi Doctors: Medical Killing and the Psychology of Genocide* by Robert Jay Lifton (New York: Basic Books, 1986).

71 **the "Four Bahrick Study," as they called it—was under way** Harry P. Bahrick, Lorraine E. Bahrick, Audrey S. Bahrick, and Phyllis E. Bahrick, "Maintenance of Foreign Language Vocabulary and the Spacing Effect," *Psychological Science*, Vol. 4, No. 5, Sept. 1993, 316–21.

71 **the James Method** For my understanding of Henry James's early education, I am grateful for assistance from Greg W. Zacharias, professor of English, and director, Center for Henry James Studies, Creighton University.

72 **experience: too much** Gary Wolf, "Want to Remember Everything You'll Ever Learn? Surrender to This Algorithm," *Wired*, 16.05, http://www.wired.com/medtech/health/magazine/16-05/ff_wozniak.

73 **knowledge is still remembered** From the SuperMemo website: http://www.supermemo.net/how_supermemo_aids_learning.

74 **University of Nevada, Las Vegas, wrote** Dempster, 627.

77 **first good answer to those questions** N. J. Cepeda, E. Vul, D. Rohrer, J. T. Wixted, and H. Pashler, "Spacing effects in learning: A temporal ridgeline of optimal retention," *Psychological Science*, 19, 2008, 1095–1102. Melody Wiseheart was formerly known as Nicholas Cepeda.

77 **Pashler's group wrote** *Ibid.*, 1101.

79 **wrought into mental structure** William James, *Talks to Teachers on Psychology: And to Students on Some of Life's Ideals* (New York: Henry Holt and Company, 1899), 129.

Chapter Five: The Hidden Value of Ignorance

81 **Headmaster's table** William Manchester, *The Last Lion: Winston Spencer Churchill, Visions of Glory 1874–1932* (Boston: Little, Brown and Company, 1983), 150–51.

83　**when your memory fails** Francis Bacon (L. Jardine & M. Silverthorne, translators), *Novum Organum* (Cambridge, England: Cambridge University Press, 2000; original work published 1620).

83　**need the book once more** William James, *The Principles of Psychology* (New York: Holt, 1890).

83　**distinguished Americans** John W. Leonard, ed., *Who's Who in America, Vol. 2* (Chicago: A.N. Marquis and Company, 1901).

84　**for an experiment** Arthur I. Gates, *Recitation as a Factor in Memorizing* (New York: The Science Press, 1917).

85　**about 30 percent** Gates wrote *Ibid.*, 45.

87　**he cites it in his own** Herbert F. Spitzer, "Studies in Retention," *The Journal of Educational Psychology*, Vol. 30, No. 9, Dec. 1939, 641–56.

88　**measuring achievement of pupils** *Ibid.*, 655.

89　**testing effect, as they called it** Henry Roediger III, and Jeffrey D. Karpicke, "The Power of Testing Memory: Basic Research and Implications for Educational Practice," *Perspectives on Psychological Science*, Vol. 1, No. 3, 2006, 181–210.

90　***The Best of Myles*** Myles na Gopaleen (Flann O'Brien), *The Best of Myles* (New York: Penguin, 1983), 298–99.

91　**other on sea otters** Henry Roediger III, and Jeffrey D. Karpicke, "Test-Enhanced Learning: Taking Memory Tests Improves Long-Term Retention," *Psychological Science*, Vol. 17, No. 3, 2006, 249–55.

93　**slowing down forgetting** Roediger III and Karpicke, "The Power of Testing Memory." 181–210.

98　**remembered the material better later** Elizabeth Ligon Bjork and Nicholas C. Soderstrom, unpublished continuing research.

102　**offer a summary, a commentary** Jose Luis Borges, from the preface to *The Garden of Forking Paths* (1942), included in *Collected Fictions* (New York: Penguin, 1998).

Chapter Six: The Upside of Distraction

113 **part manifesto** Graham Wallas, *The Art of Thought* (New York: Harcourt, Brace and Company, 1926).

113 **presents itself to the mind** Henri Poincaré, *Science and Method* (London: T. Nelson, 1914), 55.

114 **hills on a sunny day** Wallas, 80.

114 **reached no result** Poincaré, 52.

115 **directly aware of it** Wallas, 137.

116 **I had only to write out the results** Poincaré, 52.

116 **than my own** Wallas, Preface.

117 **large room one at a time** Norman R. F. Maier, "Reasoning in Humans. II. The Solution of a Problem and its Appearance in Consciousness," *Journal of Comparative Psychology*, Vol. 12, No. 2, Aug. 1931, 181–94.

118 **"weight to it," one said** *Ibid.*, 188.

119 **"puzzle-picture," he wrote** *Ibid.*, 193.

119 **dominated consciousness** *Ibid.*, 187.

121 **In a series of experiments** Karl Duncker, "On Problem-Solving," *Psychological Monographs*, Vol. 58, No. 5, 1945, 1–17.

124 **Remote Associates Test, or RAT** Steven M. Smith and Steven E. Blankenship, "Incubation and the Persistence of Fixation in Problem Solving," *American Journal of Psychology*, Spring 1991, Vol. 104, No. 1, 61–87.

125 **block may wear off** *Ibid.*, 82.

127 **conservative meta-analysis** Ut Na Sio and Thomas C. Ormerod, "Does Incubation Enhance Problem Solving? A Meta-Analytic Review," *Psychological Bulletin*, Vol. 135, No. 1, 94–120.

Chapter Seven: Quitting Before You're Ahead

132 **reads a letter attributed to Mozart** Brewster Ghiselin, ed., *The Creative Process: Reflections of Invention in the Arts and Sciences* (Berkeley: University of California Press, 1985).

132 **while actually writing** Joseph Heller's description of his writing process is taken from an interview he did with George Plimpton, "The Art of Fiction No. 51," *The Paris Review*, No. 60, Winter 1974.

133 **and sometimes ending in failure** Ghiselin, *The Creative Process*, 85–91.

135 **until the bill was paid** Bluma Zeigarnik, "On Finished and Unfinished Tasks," from *A Source Book of Gestalt Psychology* (London: Kegan Paul, Trench, Trubner & Company, 1938), 300–14.

136 **as rapidly and correctly as possible** *Ibid.*, 307.

137 **a genuine need arises** *Ibid.*, 307.

137 **destroyed her papers** A. V. Zeigarnik, "Bluma Zeigarnik: A Memoir," *Gestalt Theory* 2007, Vol. 29, No. 3, 256–68.

139 **the effect of goals on perception** Henk Aarts, Ap Dijksterhuis, and Peter Vries, "On the Psychology of Drinking: Being Thirsty and Perceptually Ready," *British Journal of Psychology* 92, 2001, 631–42.

140 **under other circumstances** *Ibid.*, 188.

142 **ears as magnets** Eudora Welty's interview with Linda Kuehl appears in "The Art of Fiction No. 47," *The Paris Review*, No. 55, Fall 1972.

144 **She was failing them** Ronda Leathers Dively, *Preludes to Insight: Creativity, Incubation, and Expository Writing* (New York: Hampton Press, 2006).

145 **in a professional journal** *Ibid.*, 98.

145 **knowledge of the subject** *Ibid.*, 101.

Chapter Eight: Being Mixed Up

151 **University of Ottawa** R. Kerr and B. Booth, "Specific and Varied Practice of Motor Skill," *Perceptual and Motor Skills,* Vol. 46, No. 2, April 1978, 395–401.

152 **enhance movement awareness** *Ibid.,* 401.

154 **common badminton serves** Sinah Goode and Richard A. Magill, "Contextual Interference Effects in Learning Three Badminton Serves," *Research Quarterly for Exercise and Sport,* 1986, Vol. 57, No. 4, 308–14.

156 **appraise the effectiveness of practice** *Ibid.,* 312.

157 **a list of fifty names** T. K. Landauer and R. A. Bjork, "Optimum Rehearsal Patterns and Name Learning," In M. M. Gruneberg, P. E. Morris, and R. N. Sykes, eds., *Practical Aspects of Memory* (London: Academic Press, 1978), 625–32.

158 **published in 1992** Richard A. Schmidt and Robert A. Bjork, "New Conceptualizations of Practice: Common Principles in Three Paradigms Suggest New Concepts for Training," *Psychological Science,* Vol. 3, No. 4, July 1992, 207–17.

158 **performance capabilities** *Ibid.,* 215.

159 **such as spatial patterns** Nelson Goodman, "The Status of Style Author," *Critical Inquiry,* Vol. 1, No. 4, June 1975, 799–811.

160 **the same thing in their experiment** Nate Kornell and Robert A. Bjork, "Learning Concepts and Categories: Is Spacing the 'Enemy of Induction'?" *Psychological Science,* Vol. 19, No. 6, 2008, 585–92.

162 **all of an artist's paintings together** *Ibid.,* 590.

165 **became bitterly contentious** For more on the Math wars, see Alice Crary and Stephen Wilson, "The Faulty Logic of the 'Math Wars,'" *New York Times,* June 16, 2013; John A. Van de Walle, "Reform Mathematics vs. The Basics: Understanding the Conflict and Dealing with It," presented at the 77th Annual Meeting of the National Council of Teachers of Mathematics, April 23, 1999, and reprinted on mathematicallysane.com on April 1, 2003, at www.mathematicallysane.com/reform-mathematics-vs-the-basics/.

166 **Oklahoma City** Not much has been written about Saxon. I relied on conversations with Doug Rohrer, Department of Psychology, University of South Florida, as well as information from an obituary written by a classmate at West Point (class of 1949), published on www.westpoint.org, and biographical information provided by his publisher, Houghton Mifflin Harcourt.

168 **base sides** Kelli Taylor and Doug Rohrer, "The Effects of Interleaved Practice," *Applied Cognitive Psychology* 24, 2010, 837–48.

169 **value of the word problem** *Ibid.,* 846.

Chapter Nine: Learning Without Thinking

176 **almost always accurate—read** Dave Baldwin, "Unraveling the Batter's Brain," baseballanalysts.com, September 17, 2009; Terry Bahill and David G. Baldwin, "The Rising Fastball and Other Perceptual Illusions of Batters," *Biomedical Engineering Principles in Sports.* G. K. Hung and J .M. Pallis, eds. (New York: Kluwer Academic, 2004), 257–87; A. Terry Bahill, David Baldwin, and Jayendran Venkateswaran, "Predicting a Baseball's Path," *Scientific American,* May–June 2005, Vol. 93, No. 3, 218–25.

177 **and this is no small thing** Philip J. Kellman and Patrick Garrigan, "Perceptual Learning and Human Expertise," *Physics of Life Reviews* 6, 2009, 53–84.

178 **masters' memory** William G. Chase and Herbert A. Simon, "Perception in Chess," *Cognitive Psychology* 4, 1973, 55–81.

180 **"wasn't wanted there," Gibson said years later** Interview with Eleanor Gibson by Marion Eppler in Middlebury, VT, July 4–5, 1998, as part of Society for Research in Child Development Oral History Project; available at www.srcd.org.

181 **conducted with her husband in 1949** James J. Gibson and Eleanor J. Gibson, "Perceptual Learning: Differentiation or Enrichment?" *Psychological Review,* Vol. 62, No. 1, 1955, 32–41.

183 **subtleties of energy** *Ibid.*, 34.

184 **achievement of this goal** Eleanor J. Gibson, *Principles of Perceptual Learning and Development* (New York: Meredith Corporation, 1969), 4.

185 **instrument panel as a guide** All details about John F. Kennedy Jr.'s fatal flight are from the National Transportation Safety Board's Probable Cause Report, NTSB identification number NYC99MA178, released on July 6, 2000. It is available at www.ntsb.gov.

185 **through space, respectively** For my understanding of how pilots learn to fly and the layout of the cockpit in small private planes, I relied on information from Philip J. Kellman, professor, cognitive psychology, UCLA, and flights in his small plane between Los Angeles and San Luis Obispo, CA.

186 **or PLM** Philip J. Kellman and Mary K. Kaiser, "Perceptual Learning Modules in Flight Training," *Proceedings of the Human Factors and Ergonomic Society Annual Meeting,* 1994 38, 1183–87.

188 **other training contexts** *Ibid.*, 1187.

189 **four times higher** Stephanie Guerlain, et al, "Improving Surgical Pattern Recognition Through Repetitive Viewing of Video Clips," *IEEE Transactions on Systems, Man, and Cybernetics—Part A: Systems and Humans,* Vol. 34, No. 6, Nov. 2004, 699–707.

Chapter Ten: You Snooze, You Win

196 **snakes biting their tails** August Kekule is reported to have described his dream at the German Chemical Society meeting in 1890; the story has circulated widely since then, for instance in Robert Stickgold and Jeffrey M. Ellenbogen, "Sleep On It: How Snoozing Makes You Smarter," *Scientific American,* August/September 2008.

197 **stopping to rest** Jerome M. Siegel, "Sleep Viewed as a State of Adaptive Inactivity," *Nature Reviews Neuroscience,* Vol. 10, Oct. 2009, 747–53.

197 **better flight abilities** *Ibid.*, 751.

198 **intellectual and physical** Robert Stickgold, "Sleep-dependent Memory Consolidation," *Nature*, Vol. 437, Oct. 27, 2005, 1272–78.

199 **experiment on sleep** Chip Brown, "The Stubborn Scientist Who Unraveled a Mystery of the Night," *Smithsonian*, Oct. 2003, www. smithsonianmag.com.

200 **the journal *Science*** Eugene Aserinsky and Nathaniel Kleitman, "Regularly Occurring Periods of Eye Motility and Concomitant Phenomena, During Sleep," *Science*, Vol. 118, Sept. 4, 1953, 273–74.

203 **a simple game** Jeffrey M. Ellenbogen, Peter T. Hu, Jessica D. Payne, Debra Titone, and Matthew P. Walker, "Human Relational Memory Requires Time and Sleep," *Proceedings of the National Academy of Sciences of the United States of America*, May 1, 2007, Vol. 104, No. 18, 7723–28.

206 **Naples Federico II** A. Giuditta, M. V. Ambrosini, P. Montagnese, P. Mandile, M. Cotugno, G. Grassi Zucconi, and S. Vescia, "The sequential hypothesis of the function of sleep," *Behavioural Brain Research*, Vol. 69, 1995, 157–66.

209 **deep sleep and REM** Sara Mednick, Ken Nakayama, and Robert Stickgold, "Sleep-dependent Learning: A Nap Is as Good as a Night," *Nature Neuroscience*, Vol. 6, No. 7, 2003, 697–98.

212 **valuable inferences that were made** Giulio Tononi, Chiara Cirelli, "Sleep Function and Synaptic Homeostasis," *Sleep Medicine Reviews* 10, 2006, 49–62.

212 **integrating the new material with the old** D. Ji and M. A. Wilson, "Coordinated memory replay in the visual cortex and hippocampus during sleep," *Nature Neuroscience*, Vol. 10, No. 1, Jan. 2007, 100–107.

Conclusion: The Foraging Brain

214 **camping trip that never ends** Steven Pinker, *How the Mind Works* (New York: W.W. Norton & Company, 1997), 188.

215 **evolutionary history** J. Tooby and I. DeVore, "The Reconstruction

of Hominid Behavioral Evolution Through Strategic Modeling," from *The Evolution of Human Behavior,* Warren G. Kinzey, ed. (Albany, NY: SUNY Press, 1987), 209.

217 **academic and motor domains** *Annu Rev Neurosci.* 2008;31:69–89. doi: 10.1146/annurev.neuro.31.061307.090723. *Trends Neurosci.* 2008 Sep;31(9):469-77. doi: 10.1016/j.tins.2008.06.008. Epub Aug 5, 2008.

217 **Meaning Maintenance Model** Travis Proulx and Michael Inzlicht, "The Five 'A's of Meaning Maintenance: Finding Meaning in the Theories of Sense-Making," *Psychological Inquiry* 23, 2012, 317–35.

218 **we discussed in chapter 10** Travis Proulx and Steven J. Heine, "Connections from Kafka: Exposure to Meaning Threats Improves Implicit Learning of an Artificial Grammar," *Psychological Science,* Vol. 20, No. 9, 1125–31.

Index

Page numbers in *italics* refer to illustrations.

"mind-expanding" drugs, 55–57
Mind of a Mnemonist, The (Luria), 60
Minimalism, 191–92
minimum intervals, 72–74
mixed-drills, 149–71, 222, 228
"mixed review," 166–67
mixed-target groups, 151–56
modules, brain, 4–5, 17–19, 183
Molaison, Henry ("H.M."), 10–13, 16, 20, 153
Monroe, James, 69, 74
Montaigne, Michel de, 124
moods, xiii, 47, 53–54, 63
motor area, 10, 12–13, 14, *14,* 151–59, 207
Mozart, Wolfgang Amadeus, 50, 132, 133*n*
multiple-choice tests, 95, 97, 98–100
multiplication tables, 36, 76
Murder of Roger Ackroyd, The (Christie), 121
music notation, 182, 183
Mylrea, Marilyn, 160

naps, xii, 209, 212, 220
narration, 18–19
NASA Ames Research Center, 187–88
National Council of Teachers of
    Mathematics, 165
"naturals," 150, 175–77
navigation, 184–88, 190
negative associations, 62
neocortex, 4, *4,* 14–15, 212
networks, neural, 4–9, 18, 32, 94, 179–80,
    198, 207, 209, 211–12, 217–18
neurons, 3–8, *4, 7,* 9, 10, 14, 20, 32, 94, 198,
    206–7, 209, 210–11, 217
"New Conceptualizations of Practice"
    (Schmidt, and Bjork), 157–58, 167
New Theory of Disuse, 25
New York Times, xi
Night Shift Theory, 206–9, 211
nomads, 38–39
non-REM sleep (NREM), 201
"nonsense scribbles," 178–83
nonsense syllables, 28–29, 32, 49–50, 68,
    179
number-letter matrices, 60–61

Oban, Scotland, 47–49
Offner Dynograph, 198–200
O'Keeffe, Georgia, 159
O'Nolan, Brian, 89–91
operant conditioning, 179–80

optimal intervals, 77–79
Ormerod, Thomas C., 127–28

Pashler, Harold, 77–79
passwords, 23
Pasteur, Louis, 142
pattern recognition, xiv, 19, 31–32, 58–60,
    185–88, 209, 217–18
Pavlov, Ivan, 86, 179
Pencil Problem, 108–10, 111, 115, 120, 126,
    129–30, 131, 206
pendulum experiment, 122, 124
Penfield, Wilder, 11
Perceptual and Motor Skills, 152
perceptual discrimination, 142–46, 159–63,
    170–71, 175–94, 222
perceptual intuition, 188–89
perceptual learning modules (PLMs),
    186–94
percolation, 107–30, 131–48, 207, 218, 221,
    227
period table of the elements, 196
personality, ix–x, 15–16, 57, 134–35
perspective shifting, 62–63
physics, 53, 135
Piano Concerto Number 24 in C Minor
    (Mozart), 50
Picasso, Pablo, 159
Pinker, Steven, 214
pitches, baseball, 175–77, 184
placebos, 55–57
place cells, 217
Plato, 112
poetry, 29–34, 88, 132–33, 205–6
Poincaré, Henri, 113, 115–16
Portrait of Madame Matisse (Matisse), *192*
positive associations, 62
Post-Impressionism, 193
pretesting, xii, 94–103
prewriting assignments, 144–46
Principles of Perceptual Learning and Development
    (Gibson), 183–84
prism exercise, 167–68
problem sets, 166–67, 228
prodigies, 59–61, 178
proofs, 52–53, 58, 114, 131
protracted problems, 132
Proulx, Travis, 217–18
Psalm 23, 84
psychiatry, 54